Retrato en la Biblioteca Nacional de Caracas
Santiago de Chile, 1850

ANTHOLOGY OF ANDRÉS BELLO

Compiled by
PEDRO GRASES

With a Foreword by
RAFAEL CALDERA

Translated by
BARBARA D. HUNTLEY and PILAR LIRIA

General Secretariat
Organization of American States
Washington, D.C.
1981

Ambassador Henricus Heidweiller
Chairman of the Permanent Council

Ambassador Alejandro Orfila
Secretary General of the Organization
of American States

Ambassador Valerie T. McComie
Assistant Secretary General of the
Organization of American States

Dr. Jorge L. Zelaya Coronado
Executive Secretary for Education,
Science, and Culture

Dr. Roberto Etchepareborda
Acting Director of the Department
of Cultural Affairs

This *Anthology* is part of the diverse commemorative activities programmed by the Organization of American States in homage to Andrés Bello, on occasion of the bicentennial of his birth —1781 - November 29 - 1981—[C.P. RES. 336 (467/81)].

This publication was originated by a proposal of the Centro Venezolano-Americano, of Caracas, Venezuela, under the presidency of Mrs. Romelia de Schwede. That proposal received the approval of doctor Eduardo González Reyes, then Executive Secretary for Education, Science, and Culture.

The translation of this *Anthology* was done by Barbara D. Huntley and Pilar Liria, and the Department of Cultural Affairs was responsible for its publication.

Contents

I. POETRY

II. PROSE

FOREWORD

A true friendship, such as the one the peoples of this hemisphere must have for one another in order to save their future, means there must be better and broader mutual understanding. The truth is that we have little knowledge of one another. What reaches public opinion in each country about its neighbors in the Americas is the part that is superficial, shocking, and often unfavorable.

Ignorance in the south about the north and in the north about the south is especially prevalent. The knowledge Latin Americans have about the people of the United States is generally what we get through the mass media or from the advertising of the multinationals. People in the United States know still less about the people of Latin America, and what they do know is undoubtedly worse. We have often complained that in their coverage of Latin America the mass media make room only for coups d'etat, violence, natural disasters, and, once in a while, areas of folklore susceptible to trite interpretation. Some progress has undeniably been made in recent years but much still remains to be done.

A proper understanding of ourselves as a people must begin by looking at what the protagonists of our independence did and what projection their ideas had. The United States celebrated its bicentennial not too long ago. Latin America is also getting ready to observe a 200th anniversary, that of the birth of the figures most influential in forging our nationalities. One of them was Andrés Bello, who was born in Caracas on November 29, 1781, and died in Santiago, Chile, on October 15, 1865.

Unquestionably our broadest and most profound scholar, Bello has been called "the teacher of America," "the foremost man of letters in America," the "man who saved the integrity of Castilian in America," the "artistic liberator of Latin America." He is also recognized as the founder of Latin American international law, the man who developed the civil code of Hispanic America, and many other achievements ranging across the vast number of areas cultivated by his mind. Bello is the author of the pages collected in this anthology.

Bello was born in Caracas in the late 18th century, twenty-nine years before the South American independence movement was well under way. His background and education, therefore, reflected the conflicting traditions and concerns prevailing in the final years of colonial society. The Spanish colonization has been the object of much controversy, a black legend depicting it as the denial of all culture, all law, all sense of progress; a golden legend magnifying and sublimating it to the point of minimizing its weaknesses and faults.

An objective judgment, which appears to be gaining ground generally, declares that the Spanish colonization was a civilizing enterprise of vast proportions that successfully transmitted values developed in the protracted reconquest and unification of the Peninsula that ended in the very year of the discovery of America; that founded cities, towns, universities, and hospitals. That strived to organize a legal system, a government of magistrates and judges incredibly strong in dealing with the royal power of the conquistadors, considering the distance from the formal center of authority from which the entire hemisphere was governed. Serious errors, many abuses and undeniable crimes were committed during this process. On the other hand, the Spanish conquistador was what he was with all his virtues and faults and could do no more than transmit his own culture and his own character, which indeed we Latin Americans have been proud of on many occasions and in many ways.

Andrés Bello was one of the men who realized that the independence movement was not just an uprising of the people against unacceptable laws and tyrannical governments but more specifically, the exercise of the rigth of self-government, claimed and won at the cost of bloody sacrifice by the Hispanic American nations, which had achieved a degree of maturity entitling them to claim what rightfully belonged to them.

The readers of this book will doubtless acquire a broad knowledge, not just a mere idea, of what Andrés Bello was and signified, which I hope may be transmitted generally to the major English-speaking areas of the Western Hemisphere. We will strive to the utmost, in conjunction with the Organization of American States and other cultural institutions, to do this on as broad a scale as possible during the bicentennial of Bello's birth.

It is worth recalling that this same Andrés Bello whose writings we have here began his intellectual life in the small and sheltered city of Caracas, the capital of the Captaincy General of Venezuela. It was there that he studied in the university with brilliant results, took part in its cultural life, held a high post in the Captaincy General (perhaps the highest a native Venezuelan could aspire to), learned Latin to perfection, and mastered French and English. By the time he left for London as a member of the first diplomatic mission to the United Kingdom headed by Simón Bolívar, he was already an inspired poet, a talented historian, an impeccable translator and philosopher, philologist, jurist, to name but a few of his achievements.

Andrés Bello left for London in 1810. Circumstances kept him there, in what he thought would be a short-lived absence, for nineteen years. While in London, apart from starting a family (he married in 1815, became a widower in 1821, remarried in 1824 and left England with eight children; in Chile he would have five more), he worked in diplomatic functions first for the Junta of Caracas and later for the Republics of Chile and of Gran Colombia founded by Bolivar. His status as a diplomat alternated with that of political refugee in the years when the Spanish royalist forces ruled in his native land.

During the nineteen years in London, Bello studied, wrote, worked, and was an avid enthusiast of all facets of British cultural life. Among his accomplishments were the <u>Biblioteca</u> <u>Americana</u> and

<u>Repertorio</u> <u>Americano</u>, two journals he founded with Juan García del Río and other Spanish American emigres. In them he published his <u>Allocution to Poetry</u>, a composition regarded as the "Spanish American literary declaration of independence," and the <u>Georgic of the Tropics</u>, perhaps his finest poetic work (both compositions are part of a major unfinished poem entitled <u>América</u>).

Bello was prevented from returning to Caracas or any other destination in Gran Colombia. He also failed, as an intermediate objective for an eventual return to Venezuela, in his attempts to be sent to the United States. Instead, he was assigned other missions in Europe. He decided, however, to accept an invitation from the government of Chile and went there.

The work he did during the thirty six years he lived in Chile was so immense that its mere enunciation would overwhelm an unseasoned observer. Arriving in Chile as the Deputy Minister of Finance, he later became Deputy Minister of Foreign Affairs and leader of that country's foreign policy. He was the first rector of the University of Chile, the successor to the old University of San Felipe of the time of the colony. As rector, he directed the entire educational process in the country. In a painstaking task that took him thirty years, he drafted Chile's Civil Code, a successful synthesis of tradition and revolution, of old Hispanic and Roman law and the new legal principles spread by the French Revolution which in turn were heavily influenced by the unrest in Latin America.

He wrote a <u>Spanish Grammar for Use in America</u> for the purpose of salvaging the unity of the language from threatened desintegration. According to Amado Alonso, this grammar is still considered the best there is in the Spanish language and one of the best in the world. His <u>Principles of Civil Law</u>, later known as <u>Principles of International Law</u>, is regarded as the starting point for the conception and teaching of international law in Latin America. He received Chilean citizenship without renouncing his own and was for many years a member of the Chilean Senate where his achievements were significant. He is considered one of those directly reponsible for the administrative organization of the Chilean government. He was the soul of <u>El Araucano</u>, a newspaper that published not only national and foreign news and interpreted major events, but also covered the most important happenings icascience, literature and the theater. In short, and still leaving much to be said, Bello was a true Renaissance man.

The edition of Bello's complete works now numbers over twenty volumes and after three decades in which we have been working on it in Caracas, is still unfinished. Preparation of a Bello anthology was therefore no easy task even though several hundred pages were already available and the man making the selection was Pedro Grases, who has a full and detailed knowledge of Bello.

The <u>Anthology</u> naturally starts with Andrés Bello the poet, the founder of Latin American poetry. The selection includes both original works and translations representing the three phases of his life in Caracas, London and Santiago. The <u>Anthology</u> indicates his major works in the field of grammar, philology and criticism. It devotes a few pages to a brief presentation of the principal aspects of Bello as a jurist, educator, philosopher, historian and journalist. These pages, however, can only be a modest introduction or stimulus for the reader to delve more deeply into those facets of

Bello's thought that most attract him. All that fits in an anthology like this of his Castilian grammar, for example, or his studies on the Poem of the Cid are the prologue; of the Civil Code of Chile, the introduction; of the Principles of International Law or the Philosophy of Understanding, also the prologue and introduction. We are grateful for the inclusion of at least one complete work which in my opinion is one of Bello's best, the address he gave at the opening of the University of Chile on September 17, 1843.

It was an inspired moment when the Venezuelan-American Center of Caracas and the Organization of American States decided to open a wedge in the English-speaking world with this first Bello anthology. In 1977, the English version of my biography of Andrés Bello was published in London by Allen and Unwin. Strange as it may seem, that was the first biography published in English, despite the fact that Bello had a great deal to do with British culture. On two occasions married natives of the British Isles in England, and reflected in his thinking the powerful influence English-speaking culture had on him. Oscar Sambrano Urdaneta's chronology will be helpful in understanding the life of Andrés Bello.

Universities in the United States, other English-speaking countries in America and Europe, and faculties of literature and Latin American culture are paying increasing attention to the thought and work of Andrés Bello. We bellistas in the hemisphere hope this book will be an effective contribution to a knowledge of Bello and provide not just a better idea of what he was and thought but also stimulate other intellectuals to study this true prototype (in the best sense of the word) of Latin American man more deeply.

We are grateful to both organizations and assure the readers of this volume that they will not be disappointed in their desire to learn more about Bello. The time spent in reading and studying this book will be more than compensated by a better acquaintance with the people south of the Río Grande and a stronger current of sympathy and understanding leading to friendly relations that are more just and more stable.

Rafael Caldera

X

PROLOGUE

Spain's domination of the American hemisphere has begotten an impressive number, indeed a genuine library, of studies and interpretations on the conquest and colonization. Passion and prejudice have perhaps triumphed in most authors and confused the clarity and balance of their judgments on Spain's deeds in the vast reaches of the New World. Praise and vilification go hand in hand from the era of the discovery itself, when a major, still unresolved controversy broke out on the right of conquest, the actions of the colonizers, and the benefit or harm caused by the exploits of Spain in the territory stretching from Alaska to the southern tip of Argentina.

The historical-critical conclusions reached by historians and interpreters of the Spanish presence in America, have always been clouded by over-interference of subjective criteria. A lack of studies focused on each region deprived scholars of sound arguments for or against Spain's action in the hemisphere. The fact that most studies were made from Europe, thus inferring a priori assumptions with respect to the events on which historical accounts were being attempted, also influenced the clarity and accuracy of American historiography.

Liberation from Spain, an event which took place almost simultaneously throughout Spanish America during the first third of the nineteenth century, made a shift in perspective and the writing of history in the countries of the hemisphere themselves necessary. Even so, a rather long period elapsed before writers were able to approach history with the deliberation demanded of a scientific work. Most nineteenth century historians wrote under the pressure of too recent events, very close to the violence of war. The Hispanic trait of vehemence weighed for decades on the minds of Creole historians, and their otherwise noteworthy books lacked the objectivity for fair, impartial and sound conclusions.

Revisionism in national historiography began in America in the late 1800's and early 1900's. The undue praise and unjust condemnation that had given birth to earlier legend--black or golden--have gradually given way in this century to the more serene, more suitable criteria required of history. Silvio Zavala, a prominent Mexican writer, has examined this issue and turned the three centuries of Spanish colonial history in America into a model for modern historiography.

Monographs on hundreds of subjects (history, organization, institutions, people, education, culture, arts) have formed the background for interpretative works on the meaning of Spain's conquest and colonization in its vast empire that are fairer, better documented and more conclusive and accurate. Such works take into account both common traits and differences, as stated by Silvio Zavala, whose own starting point is the principle that each part of what was one thought to be a uniform empire was actually quite diverse in nature, whereas the liberation movement launched in the final decades of the eighteenth century developed in a simultaneous, similar manner everywhere.

The major outcome of a balanced assessment of Spanish colonial times in America, has been a reappraisal of the cultural contribution developed in the midst of the former viceroyalties and captaincy generals. There may still be controversy about cause and effect in the Creole world prior to the independence movements. But if the drive towards independence in each future republic presupposed the will and determination of its protagonists plus a robust character based on a sound education, this clearly came about because the colonies possessed schools and a cultural level in their society that fostered and promoted a consensus individually and collectively, that enabled the Creole peoples to pursue that goal.

Bello, therefore, rejected José Victorino Lastarria's assertion when he said: "We are very hesitant to agree that the people of Chile (or of any other Spanish American country for that matter) were so profoundly debased, reduced to such total subjection, so deprived of any social virtue, as Mr. Lastarria assumes. The revolution in Spanish America contradicts his assertions. A profoundly debased, totally subjected people deprived of any virtuous sentiments has never been able to perform the great deeds that inspired the campaigns waged by the patriots, the heroic acts of denial, the hardships of all kinds by means of which Chile and other parts of America won their political freedom. Anyone who observes the history of our struggle with Spain with a discerning eye will have no trouble seeing that what made us prevail was precisely the Iberian element."[1]/

The independence of Spain's former colonies is indeed looked upon today as a considerable contribution to contemporary Western civilization.

The area of the hemisphere that now constitutes the Republic of Venezuela is a special case. During the sixteenth and seventeenth centuries it was one of the least dazzling possessions in the far-flung Spanish empire, in stark contrast to the Pacific slopes where major cultural centers developed, undoubtedly because they were founded on ancient indigenous civilizations of great splendor (Mayas, Aztecs, Incas, and others), whereas the Atlantic and Caribbean had nowhere near the level of development of those societies in pre-Columbian times. But in the late eighteenth century a community flourished there whose members numbered the foremost names in the epic of liberation. One need only mention Miranda, Bello and Bolívar, the leaders of a people who would spare no effort to win the right to proclaim national independence. These are not isolated names. So much excellence presupposes many able people behind the scenes.

Andrés Bello is a good example of what I mean. Born in Caracas on November 29, 1781, he received his early schooling in his native city and remained there until 1810, when he left for London on a diplomatic mission, accredited to the British government. Heading the mission was the future liberator, Simón Bolívar. Bello used his nineteen years in England to finish his studies and discover a world of learning, yet when he left Venezuela he clearly possessed an excellent grounding in the humanities, confirmed by the writings known from the Caracas period. His poems of that time, and particularly his prose Summary of the History of Venezuela attest to the high level of education he had gained in the semi-rural city of Caracas, the headquartes of the Captaincy General of Venezuela.

Bello's major works were written in the second phase of his life and in Chile from 1829 until his death in 1865. There he concluded his admirable, voluminous writings and his work as an educator, and cast his personality over the entire Spanish-speaking world. His teachings are alive today in his literary creations and publications, and in his definitive influence on higher education. His task as a writer was a manifold one in keeping with the times when newly formed nations, compelled to tackle the demands of republican government, needed appropriate institutions and citizens learned in every discipline.

It was in this sense that Bello construed his role. From the moment he arrived in Santiago, he set aside scholarly pursuits and dedicated himself to the task of educating the Chileans. His prodigious ability enabled him to work at a variety of endeavors ranging from critic, historian, codifier, philologist, philosopher, lawmaker, craftsman of public administration, journalist, educator and president of the reformed University of Chile, while never abandoning his work as a poet.

In an assessment of Spanish-American culture today, Bello stands out as the man who fashioned the foundations of the humanistic culture that guides the actions of the Spanish-speaking hemisphere in the contemporary world. Indeed, many of Bello's ideas are valid now and will still be in the future. His life is a continuing model for men of all times of method, discipline, and the spirit of moderation. The impressive variety of themes he dealt with detracted nothing from the profound treatment they received in each of his works.

I have attempted in this Anthology to present a small sample--which I hope will suffice--of Bello's different themes. As a general principle, I should warn the reader that in order to understand Bello the humanist, each piece must be viewed as part of an interdependent whole. Each of his works represents one pre-eminent aim, that of the educator. Failure to keep this absolute in mind will result in a distorted understanding and interpretation of the humanistic effect of the life of Andrés Bello.

Pedro Grases

1. Critical note by Bello to Investigaciones sobre la influencia de la conquista y del sistema colonial de los españoles en Chile, by J. V. Lastarria, 1844.

CHRONOLOGY OF ANDRÉS BELLO

By Oscar Sambrano Urdaneta

1781   November 29. Birth in Caracas. His parents, Bartolomé Bello and Ana Antonia López. He was the eldest of eight children. His grandfather, Juan Pedro López, was the most important Venezuelan painter in the eighteenth century.

1787   Probable date when his elementary education began at a school run by Ramón Vanlosten.

1788   Probable date when he began to attend the Convent of the Merced, located opposite the house where he was born. Later he would begin studying Latin and grammar at the same school under the direction of Friar Cristóbal de Quesada, one of his most important teachers. He became an earnest reader in the library of the Convent, a habit that lasted all his life.

1792   When he was eleven years old, he was already a devoted reader of Pedro Calderón de la Barca, and shortly after of Don Quijote de la Mancha.

1797   January. Enrolled in the Royal Pontifical University of Caracas, where he graduated as a bachiller on June 14, 1800. He planned to study law and medicine but had to interrupt his studies probably for economic reasons. Between 1797 and 1800 he gave private classes to young people of his own age. One of his students at that time was Simón Bolívar, the future liberator.

1800   Bello's earliest poetic productions date from this period.

1802   November 6. Entered the Captaincy General of Venezuela as a Second Official. About this time he began studying English with the help of a grammar alone. For practice, he translated John Locke's Essay on Human Understanding.

1807   Publishes his Castilian version of the fifth book of the Aeneid from Latin, and his translation from French of Zulima, a tragedy by Voltaire of which no Spanish translation existed earlier.
        October 11. Appointment as Commissar of War, which was regarded as a purely honorary title rarely conferred on a Creole by the Spanish Government.

1808   October 24. Circulation of the first issue of the <u>Gaceta de Caracas</u>, the first newspaper printed in Venezuela, of which he was appointed editor. Bello was, therefore, Venezuela's first journalist.

1809   In about this year he wrote his <u>Resumen de la historia de Venezuela</u> for the <u>Calendario manual y guía universal de forasteros para el año de 1810</u>. This summary of the history of Venezuela was the first book printed there. In about this same period he was planning the publication of a magazine, <u>El Lucero</u>, of which only the prospectus was actually printed. His <u>Análisis ideológico de los tiempos de la conjugación castellana</u> must also date from this year, as well as his translation of Condillac's <u>Art of Writing</u>, unpublished until 1824. He was promoted to the rank of Senior Official of the Captaincy General.

1810   June 10. On this date he sailed from La Guaira, the port of Caracas, for England accompanied by Simón Bolívar and Luis López Méndez. The three were emissaries of the Junta of Caracas to the British Government in the expectation of a war with Spain.
    July 10. Bello and his companions arrived in England. Their first lodgings were in the home of general Francisco de Miranda, in whose library Bello began to study Greek. He would remain in England until 1829.

1814   May. His marriage to Maria Ana Boyland, an English woman. Three children would be born of their marriage.

1815   Bello took steps this year to return to America but the bloody struggle for independence taking place in virtually all of Hispanic America posed problems or prevented realization of his plans.

1816   In need of assistance to support himself and his family, he was granted an allowance by the British Government. His friends arranged for him to give private classes. Among his students were the children of Mr. Hamilton, who was then the Indian Secretary of State. Through other friends he was placed in charge of correcting the style of the translation of the Bible into Spanish or "decyphering" the almost illegible manuscripts of Jeremia Bentham, the master of the English Utilitarian School. During this year he began using the library of the British Museum where he undertook many varied investigations, the most important of which was his study of the <u>Poem of the Cid</u>.

1821   Death of his wife, who was 27 years old. About this time he began working on the <u>Orlando enamorado</u>, an extensive Italian poem written by Bojardo and rewritten by Berni. Bello added original introductions to some of the cantos. He withheld permission for publication of his translation until 1862.

1822   June 1. Appointed Interim Secretary of the Chilean Legation in the United Kingdom, a post he would hold until April 1824.

1823   The first issue of the journal <u>Biblioteca Americana</u> or <u>Miscelánea de Literatura, Artes y Ciencias</u> circulated, with Bello as one of its major promoters. His great heroic poem,

"Alocución a la Poesía," was published in this magazine and was part of a major composition entitled América which he had been working on and left unfinished. The early proposals by Bello and Juan García del Río also were published in this magazine for radical reform of Castilian spelling for the purpose of furthering the learning of reading and writing in Spanish America.

1824   Marriage to Isabel Antonia Dunn, an English woman who survived him. Thirteen children were born of this second marriage.

1825   February 7. Took office as the Secretary of the Legation of Gran Colombia in the Court of London.

1826   October 1. The circulation of the first issue of the journal Repertorio Americano, in which Bello published his other major silva "La Agricultura de la Zona Tórrida," also a part of the unfinished poem entitled América.

1827   April. Appointed Chargé d'Affaires of the Legation of Gran Colombia in London.

1828   September 15. The Consul General of Chile in London notifies Bello of the decision by the President of Chile to finance his trip to that country with his family, and to offer him a job consistent with his qualifications and experience.

1829   February 14. Bello and his family sail for Chile.
        June 25. Arrival in Valparaíso on board the English brigantine Grecian. His second wife, Isabel Antonia Dunn, and his children Francisco and Carlos Bello Boyland as well as Juan, Andrés, Ricardo, Ana and Miguel Bello Dunn accompany him.
        July 13. Appointed Deputy Vice Minister of the Ministry of Finance by the President of the Republic of Chile. His actual position however on his arrival in Chile was that of Consultant and Secretary in the Ministry of Foreign Relations.

1830   February 1. Appointed Director of Santiago School, founded in 1829. While there, he taught Castilian, Literature and World Law, and thus continued in Chile an activity begun in Caracas and pursued as well in London.
        September 17. Appointed Director of the Foreign News and Arts and Sciences Section of the newspaper El Araucano. On this and other Chilean newspapers, Bello performed an important task both in the area of criticism, and in the dissemination and promotion of the nascent artistic spirit in Chile.

1832   Circulation of the first work published by Bello in Chile, entitled Principios del derecho de gentes (International Law).
        February 10. On this date the students tutored by Bello in his home took examinations in Natural Law and Roman Law. This means he probably began teaching classes the year before. As of 1834, he added Latin, Castilian Grammar, Literature and Roman and Spanish Law. After 1840, he

included philosophy in his private classes. Presumably he stopped giving private classes following the organization of the University of Chile in 1843. But this decade of instruction meant the country received the support of a brilliant generation of young students who would continue the work of their teacher.

1833   November. Began publishing a series of articles in which he undertook a campaign that he would continue the rest of his life in order to improve usage in Castilian. The articles were entitled "Advertencias sobre el uso de la lengua castellana, dirigidas a los padres de familia, profesores de los colegios y maestros de escuela."

1834   June 30. Appointed Vice Minister of the Department of Foreign Relations, a post he would hold until October 25, 1852.

1835   Published his work on orthology and metrics entitled Principios de la ortología y métrica de la lengua castellana. Two later editions revised by the author came out in 1850 and 1859.

1836   November 17. Andrés Bello received the degree of bachelor of law from the President of the University of San Felipe, Juan Francisco Meneses. Although he could easily have obtained a degree as a lawyer, he did not do so. On the other hand, the interest he demonstrated since the time he was in London in studying legislation, qualified him to undertake the reform of the judicial system in Chile.

1837   Elected to the Senate. Re-elected in 1846 and 1855. He was a Senator until his death.

1839   Translated and adapted for the stage Alexander Dumas' work Therese.

1840   August 10. One of the persons selected by the Senate to codify the civil laws. On October 26, 1852, he submitted a draft Civil Code which was reviewed by a commission and passed on December 14, 1855.

1841   Publication in Valparaíso of his Análisis ideológica de los tiempos de la conjugación castellana, the first version of which was written in Caracas.

February 5, June 3. Publication of articles in El Araucano explaining his literary ideas (a synthesis of romanticism and classicism). He was a partisan of complete literary freedom.

July. Anonymous publication of his poem "El incendio de la Compañía." From this date on, he published his poetic output with greater regularity.

July 26. Bello, José Gabriel Palma, and José Miguel de la Barra appointed to examine the bill for the creation of the University of Chile, which Bello himself had written probably the year before. Recommended to the Congress on July 4, 1842, it was approved with slight amendment on November 19, 1842.

1842   May 12. Bello published in El Mercurio an article entitled
        "Ejercicios populares de lengua castellana," in defense of
        Pedro Fernández Garfias.
        May 22. Domingo Faustino Sarmiento responds with an
        article, also published in El Mercurio, in which he calls
        Andrés Bello's emphasis on the teaching of grammar and
        correct usage of Castilian as useless and even harmful.
        June 18. Publication of the poem "Los fantasmas" (imitation
        of "Les orientales," by Victor Hugo).
        July 20. Publishes the poem "A Olimpio," an imitation of
        Victor Hugo. Between 1842 and 1843, Bello published five
        more imitations of Victor Hugo.

1843   July 21. Appointed President of the recently created
        University of Chile, which replaced the former University of
        San Felipe, dissolved by governmental decree in 1839. Bello
        was the founder of the new university and its first
        president. He was re-elected president in 1848, 1853, 1858
        and 1863, always winning virtually all the votes of the
        faculty.
        July 19. Published the poem entitled "Los Duendes"
        (imitation of Victor Hugo).
        September 17. Official opening of the University of Chile
        at which Bello gave the inaugural address containing his
        university doctrine.
        October 1. Publishes "La oración por todos" (imitation de
        Victor Hugo).
        In this year and the next he published ten essays on
        philosophy in the Chilean review El Crepúsculo which would
        be joined with other materials to make up his work Filosofía
        del Entendimiento, published posthumously.

1844   January 1. Publication of "Moisés salvado de las aguas"
        (imitation of Victor Hugo).
        April 23. Passage of the Rules of Procedure governing the
        work of the Council of the University, doubtless inspired by
        Andrés Bello, who would be responsible for the organization
        and administration of education in Chile.
        In about this year and the next, Bello began work on an
        extensive unpublished, unfinished poem entitled "El
        proscrito."

1845   Description of his ideas on the reform of spelling, which he
        had been sustaining since 1823, published in El Araucano.
        Some of them had been implemented in Chile with certain
        changes.
        April 15. Submitted for consideration by the School of
        Humanities a method of accenting Spanish.
        June 13. Death of Francisco Bello Boyland, perhaps the most
        beloved of his children.

1846   Publication of his translation of the Biography of Lord
        Byron by Villamain.
        July 26. Publication of the second version of "La Cometa,"
        a fable whose first version was published in 1833.
        Composed his humorist poetic satire entitled "La moda,"
        published posthumously in 1882.

1847   Publication of his famous Gramática de la lengua castellana destinada al uso de los americanos. During his lifetime five editions of this grammar of Castilian for use in America would be published, in each one of which Bello introduced many important innovations.
September 14. In a letter, the Archbishop of Santiago criticized Bello's criteria as a theatrical censor, expressing the opinion that the works chosen by Bello scandalized even people with the most liberal views.
November 22. Approval of the regulations for university education inspired by Bello.

1848   January 1. Publication of the poem "A Peñalolén," a country home in the vicinity of Santiago where Bello used to spend some time. Publication of his Cosmografía o descripción del universo conforme a los últimos descubrimientos. In this book, Bello said, "I have set forth to make as complete an explanation of the universe, according to the present status of astronomy, as its limited length will allow me."
January 29. Passage of a law inspired by Bello which ordered adoption of the metric system in Chile.
September. Publication in the El Araucano of his draft law on the rights of authors and translators.

1849   Began translation of the work by Plautus, Rudens, which he left unpublished when he died. It was published for the first time in Caracas in 1952.
June 10. Publication of the "Diálogo entre la amable Isidora y un poeta del siglo pasado," a poem composed in about 1846.
July 17. Publication of an epigram entitled "El tabaco."
October 28. Publication of the poem "Al Biobío."

1850   Publication of the first two parts, on ancient literature of the East and ancient literature of Greece, of a course on literary history.
June 19. Publication of a little over half of the first act of Sardanapalus, which Bello regarded as one of Lord Byron's finest tragedies. This translation by Bello has rather personal adaptations of the original text.

1851   May 9. Death of Ana Bello Dunn, Bello's eldest daughter.
November 20. Unanimous election of Bello as an honorary member of the Real Academia Española. On February 28, 1861, when the category of corresponding members was created, the Academy placed Bello in this new category.

1853   On behalf of the University Council, of which he was the presiding officer, Bello announced a prize for the best book on the influence which universal elementary education would have on society.

1857   Lost the use of his legs and was compelled to use a wheelchair. He spent his time seated at a desk reading, writing and dictating.

1858   Death in Caracas of Bello's mother.
August 21. Publication of the fable, an imitation of Florian, entitled "La ardilla, el dogo y el zorro."

1860   Expresses his appreciation to Manuel Ancizar for his offer
         to help collect books in Colombia for the Hispano-American
         Library that Bello planned to found in Santiago. In the same
         month, Bello asked Juan María Gutiérrez to handle the
         acquisition of books in Buenos Aires for the same purpose.
         September 4. In a letter to the Ministry of Education on
         this date, Bello says, "Because of repeated illnesses I have
         been bedridden for three months and unable to attend
         meetings of the Board and the University Schools... I have
         felt I should submit... my resignation as President." (The
         resignation was not accepted.)
         September 12. Death in New York at 36 years of age of Juan
         Bello Dunn, Chargé d'Affairs of Chile in the United States.
         November 24. Passage of the Organic Law on Elementary
         Education in Chile, drafted by the School of Humanities
         under the chairmanship of Bello.

1861   Publication of the fables "El hombre, el caballo y el toro"
         and "Las ovejas," as well as a translation of Psalm 10
         entitled "Miserere."
         June 27. Andrés Bello, President of the University,
         submitted draft regulations for the National Library to the
         minister of Education. He was the author of the draft,
         which had been reviewed by the University Council.

1863   June 5. Submitted his resignation as President of the
         University: "It is becoming increasingly difficult and
         painful for me to take part in the Council's deliberations
         because of the respiratory problems you have no doubt
         noticed on many occasions and which will probably become
         greater each day."
         June 18. Letter to Manuel Bretón de los Herreros, Secretary
         of the Real Academia Española, describing the results of his
         research on the Poem of the Cid.

1864   Appointment, which he declined for reasons of health, to
         resolve a controversy between Ecuador and the United States.
         March 1. In a letter to Manuel Ancizar, Bello commented on
         the origin of the slander spread against him in Caracas
         which accused him of denouncing the rebellion that was to
         break out on April 1, 1810: "As to the aforementioned
         charge, I far from blame the historian José Manuel Restrepo,
         who had no doubt seen it in several works, including one by
         Torrenta. But all of them, I believe, were based on an
         account by Dr. José Domingo Díaz, a physician in Caracas
         whose services to the Government of Spain were awarded with
         appointment to high office in Puerto Rico. In justice to
         him, I believe that not even he himself thought to slander
         me because the rumor circulated in Caracas itself. It is
         likely that after all is said and done it will become a part
         of history and I resign myself to this without the least
         feeling."

1865   October 15. Death in Santiago, Chile, at 7:45 a.m., after a
         45-day illness with bronchitis and typhoid fever.

INTRODUCTION

The selection of Bello's poetry given in this Anthology is a brief sampling of the extensive work in verse written by him throughout his lifetime, beginning in his youth (I would say in his adolescence) and lasting until the eve of his death at eighty-four. This was a matter of constant dedication for Bello, who was a genuinely inspired poet irresistibly tempted to express his emotions in verse as much for his own pleasure as to communicate the products of the finest literary creations to the men of his time.

Hence, this limited sampling ranges over the entire poetic biography of Andrés Bello, from his little ballad The Anauco, one of his earliest poetic endeavors when he was still a student in Caracas before his twentieth year, to his most accomplished poems, written in his years of spiritual plenitude in London and Santiago. There he composed works such as his sylvae and the Burning of the Jesuit Temple, and re-worked poems of others and made them his own, such as The Prayer for All or the octaves of the prologue to several cantos of the Orlando innamorato, a genuine "prodigy" to quote a critic as demanding as Edoardo Crema.

Bello reached his peak as an original poet while in London, where he turned out his Allocution to Poetry and the Georgic of the Tropics, which he tells us were parts of an unfinished poem entitled América. The gradual development and breadth of this work are evident in his draft poems, found in the second volume of the Caracas edition of the Complete Works, which has an excellent prologue by Pedro Pablo Barnola.

The Spanish-speaking hemisphere understood the message contained in these works and proclaimed Bello the prince of American poets and draftsman of the cultural independence of that part of the New World.

Indeed, Bello's efforts to accommodate a handful of foreign poets and works (Byron, Delille, Bojardo, Berni, Victor Hugo, the Lay of the Nibelungs) or clasical poets (Virgil, Horace, Plautus, the Bible) to Castilian forms are not to be deplored. We have chosen a few fragments from each to give an idea of this important part of Bello's poetry.

Most critical attention has perhaps focused on Bello's poetry, an indication of the significance accorded everywhere to the civilizing influence of his work. In an anthology such as this, it is difficult to recommend a bibliography which is brief and precise yet adequate enough for a reader to use as a basic reference. Such an effort must inevitably be incomplete and perhaps not quite fair. With this handicap in mind, I shall mention a few basic studies and refer the reader to the notes to the texts for additional materials.1/

The earliest studies on Bello as a poet are found in the critical notes of Miguel Luis and Gregorio Víctor Amunátegui, who were responsible for the first compilation of his complete works in Santiago and for making the Chilean national will to honor the memory of Bello a reality. Next should be mentioned the efforts in Venezuela of Juan Vicente González 2/, Arístides Rojas 3/, and Víctor Antonio Zerpa 4/, who worked virtually at the same time that Miguel Antonio Caro 5/, in Colombia, and Marcelino Menéndez Pelayo 6/, in Spain, were providing substantial interpretations of Bello's poetry. These masters are still the basis for criticism and for the key to understanding Bello as a poet in the New World.

In more recent times, mention should be made of the following students of Bello's poetry: Edoardo Crema 7/, Alone (Hernán Díaz Arrieta) 8/, Julio Planchart 9/, Fernando Paz Castillo 10/, René L.F. Durand 11/, Juan Carlos Ghiano 12/. Among the newer generations in Venezuela are Luis Beltrán Guerrero 13/, Jose Ramón Medina 14/, Oscar Sambrano Urdaneta 15/, Augusto Germán Orihuela 16/, Mario Torrealba Lossi 17/, Emir Rodríguez Monegal 18/, Luibo Cardoza 19/, to mention just a few of the legion of contemporary bellistas.

NOTES

1. For still more information, see the bibliography of Agustín Millares Carlo, published in Mexico, Maracaibo, and Madrid, which is listed in the relevant section of this anthology.

2. Juan Vicente González, Historia del poder civil en Colombia y Venezuela. Proyecto. El Heraldo, No 1, Caracas, 1859. Mesenianas, compiled by Manuel Segundo Sánchez and Luis Correa. Prologue by Luis Correa. Caracas, 1932.

3. Arístides Rojas, "El poeta virgiliano", Estudios Históricos, II, Caracas, 1927, 1-135.

4. Víctor Antonio Zerpa, Prologue to Andrés Bello. Poesías, Curazao, 1888.

5. Miguel Antonio Caro, Prologue to Poesías de Andrés Bello, Madrid 1882.

6. Marcelino Menéndez Pelayo, Antología de poetas hispanoamericanos, Madrid, 1893, Vol. II, pp. CXVII-CLVIII.

7. Edoardo Crema, Andrés Bello, a través del romanticismo. Caracas, 1956; Trayectoria religiosa de Andrés Bello, Caracas, 1956, 259 pp.

8.   Alone (Hernán Díaz Arrieta). Historia personal de la literatura chilena, Santiago, Chile, 1954, pp. 145-151.

9.   Julio Planchart, "Lo clásico y lo romántico: Andrés Bello y Pérez Bonalde," Tendencia de la lírica venezolana a fines del siglo XIX, Caracas, 1940, pp. 13-23.

10.   Fernando Paz Castillo, "El primer clásico americano," Cultura Venezolana, Caracas, 1929, No. 98, pp. 225-232

11.   René L. F. Durand, La poesía de Andrés Bello, Dakar, 1960, 173 pp.

12.   Juan Carlos Ghiano, Las silvas americanas de Bello, Buenos Aires, 1967.

13.   Luis Beltrán Guerrero, Bello, fundamento de nuestra tradición clásica, Caracas, 1942; Perpetua heredad, Caracas, 1965.

14.   José Ramón Medina, Los homenajes del tiempo, Caracas, 1971, 361 pp.

15.   Oscar Sambrano Urdaneta, Letras venezolanas, Trujillo, 1959, 137 pp.

16.   Augusto Germán Orihuela, "El sentimiento venezolanista en la poesía de Andrés Bello," Cultura Universitaria, No. 94-95, Caracas, January-June 1967, pp. 46-50.

17.   Mario Torrealba Lossi, "Las Silvas de Andrés Bello," Acotaciones literarias venezolanas, Caracas, 1954, pp. 7-14; "Temática de la libertad en Bello," Temas literarios hispanoamericanos, Caracas, 1960, pp. 43-65.

18.   Emir Rodríguez Monegal, El otro Andrés Bello, Caracas, 1969. 476 pp.

19.   Lubio Cardozo, La poesía de Andrés Bello, Mérida, 1977, 33 pp.

II. PROSE

In order to give at least a slight and necessarily incomplete idea of Bello's work in prose, I thought it best to select a few significant pieces that would highlight the widespread themes covered by the humanist in his manifold task as educator of the new Spanish-speaking republics in the hemisphere. I am aware of how complex the web of Bello's writings is and therefore how arbitrary any attempt to reduce the colorful texture of interests he developed during his lifetime into a few categories must be. An anthologist makes his selection, however, aware that with the inevitable defect of any summarization, it will provide only a sampling and should encourage the reader to study more deeply the work of a man whose civilizing influence was exerted over such a broad spectrum of intellectual endeavors. With these limitations in mind, I believe my system of classifying Bello's work is not the worst that could be used.

I have divided this introduction to Bello's prose work into the following sections: a) Language; b) History and Literary Criticism; c) Law; d) Higher Education; e) Philosophy, and f) Journalism.

Other, also substantive parts of his work that could not be dealt with properly have been left out (Bello the legislator, parliamentarian, craftsman of public administration, the man himself). Nevertheless, I believe this Anthology will at least be useful as an initiation to a fuller reading of the subjects sampled herein and of those sections of his work not adequately represented.

Bello considered the common language of all the newly independent Spanish American nations as a providential instrument for the cultural life and fraternal relationship of the countries in the New World. On his own initiative he devoted much time during his youth to studying and perfecting the language. Before he left Caracas in 1810 when he was not yet 29 years old, Bello had already written his famous Ideological Analysis of the Tenses of Spanish Conjugations; he had worked on and arranged L'art d'ecrire by Condillac, and had done a paper on the consecutive particles que porque and pues. The only one still preserved was the Ideological Analysis, published at its author's expense by the house of Manuel Rivadeneyra in Valparaíso, in 1841.

During his years in London (1810-1829), Bello continued his studies of the language and expanded his field of interest into research into the earliest Castilian literary compositions and the relationship of Castilian with Latin and Greek.

His study on the Poem of the Cid belongs to this epoch and was done for the purpose of preparing an edition that would correct the errors found in the text of Tomás Antonio Sánchez. Bello's writings durings his stay in London on a variety of topics dealing with medieval European literature are admirable. One reproduced in this Anthology is a study on the use of assonant rhyme, regarded by experts as a valuable forerunner of contemporary criticism and scholarship.

His deep knowledge of the language and his mastery of the bibliography on philology--studies of Spanish language and literature--provided a firm foundation for his own works, which would make him the best American linguist of the nineteenth century. Four representative writings have been selected: 1) The Simplification and Standardization of Spelling; 2) Orthology and Metrics of Castilian; 3) his Grammar and 4) The Poem of the Cid.

In the notes to the texts included in this Anthology, I mention other studies that may be recommended. For any one who wants to broaden his study of Bello as the foremost linguist of the Spanish language, additional useful studies are those by Rodolfo Oroz 1/, Guillermo Rojas Carrasco 2/, Marco Fidel Suárez 3/, Baltasar Isaza Calderón 4/, Juan Bautista Selva 5/, Luis Juan Picardo 6/, Angel Rosenblat 7/, Carlos Clavería 8/, and Aurelio Espinosa Pólit 9/.

History and literary criticism are equally difficult to separate in Bello's own work and in the bibliography of studies and monographs that set out to interpret his role in steering the course of Spanish American culture. The two are closely related in Bello's thought, writings and ideas as an educator and, therefore, the bibliography necessarily includes monographs that interpret his humanistic effort as a whole. Some deal with specific aspects reflected in their titles, but most are comprehensive approaches to the importance of Bello as a humanist. The following authors are useful for consultations: Luis Correa 10/, Rufino Blanco Fombona 11/, Augusto Mijares 12/, Mariano Picón Salas 13/, Arturo Uslar Pietri 14/. The necessarily concise nature of these notes prevents me from listing others.

Useful studies have been made of Bello's legal works, some of which are mentioned in the notes to the text selected for the Anthology. In addition, other references are: Gumersindo de Azcárate 15/, Pedro Lira Urquieta 16/, Carlos Stuardo Ortiz and Sergio Villalobos R. 17/, Libros de la Semana de Bello 18/, Fernando Chumaceiro Chiarelli 19/, Hessel E. Intema 20/, Guillermo Feliú Cruz 21/, Ricardo Donoso 22/.

To conclude these bibliographic references, brief mention is made for the general reader of the major bibliographical works on Bello, as well as a few useful books on a particular aspect of his life.

The voluminous bibliography on Bello constitutes a tradition in hispanic culture. From it, I have selected a few significant milestones for a comprehensive understanding and interpretation of Bello's personality. The earliest bibliographic studies were made in Chile and Venezuela, the two countries where he lived the longest. In Caracas, the years of his youth until he was 29 years old, where his rigorous intellectual formation took place; and the 36-year period in Chile from 1829 until his death in 1865, which represent his productive teaching years, and outpouring of the fruits of his apprenticeship in Caracas and the experience, meditation, and study of his nineteen years of residence in London.

The foundation for the biography of Bello was laid by the brothers Miguel Luis and Gregorio Víctor Amunátegui Aldunate 23/, by Juan Vicente González 24/, and Arístides Rojas 25/, in Caracas. To them must be added a pleiad of nineteenth century writers, including José Victorino Lastarria 26/, and Ana Prats Bello 27/, whose personal reminiscences complement references to Bello's days in Santiago.

Authors of more recent times whose biographic works represent another historiographic approach are: Antonio Balbín de Unquera 28/, Eugenio Orrego Vicuña 29/, Rafael Caldera 30/, Pedro Lira Urquieta 31/, Lucy Pérez Luciani de Castillo 32/, José Antonio Escalona 33/, and Manuel Salvat 34/. Although not strictly biographic, the work by Sergio Fernández Larraín 35/, should be mentioned for its documentary value.

Pedro Grases

1. Rodolfo Oroz, "Bello filólogo," _Atenea_, CLX, No. 410, Concepción, Chile, October-December 1965, 134-151. He has other earlier works.

2. Guillermo Rojas Carrasco, _Filología chilena. Guía bibliográfica y crítica_, Santiago, 1940.

3. Marco Fidel Suárez, "Introducción a las obras filológicas de Andrés Bello," _Andrés Bello. Estudios gramaticales_, Madrid, 1885.

4. Baltazar Isaza Calderón, _La doctrina gramatical de Bello_, 2nd ed., Madrid, Real Academia Española, 1967, 309 pp.

5. Juan Bautista Selva, _Trascendencia de la gramática de Bello y el estado actual de los estudios gramaticales_, Buenos Aires, 1950, X, 245 pp.

6. Luis Juan Piccardo, _Dos momentos en la historia de la gramática española_, Montevideo, 1949, 33 pp.

7. Angel Rosenblat, _El pensamiento gramatical de Bello_, Caracas, 1961, 14 pp., and _Andrés Bello a los cien años de su muerte_, Caracas, 1966, 50 pp.

8. Carlos Clavería, _La gramática española de Rasmus Rusk_, Madrid, 1946, 22 pp.

9. Aurelio Espinosa Pólit, "Bello latinista," prologue to Vol. VIII of the _Obras completas de Bello_, Caracas, 1958.

10. Luis Correa, "Andrés Bello y su concepto de la historia," _Cultura Venezolana_, XLVIII, No. 117, Caracas, January-March 1932, 53-57.

11. Rufino Blanco Fombona, "Andrés Bello, 1781-1865," _Grandes escritores de América (siglo XIX)_, Madrid, 1919, pp. 11-75.

12. In his book _Hombres e ideas en América. Ensayos_, Caracas, 1946, Augusto Mijares has two chapters on Bello, and another chapter in his book _La interpretación pesimista de la sociología hispanoamericana_, Madrid, 1952.

13. Mariano Picón Salas, "Bello y la historia," prologue to Vol. XIX of the _Obras completas de Bello_, Caracas, 1957. Picón Salas also has other useful studies.

14. Arturo Uslar Pietri, "Los temas del pensamiento crítico de Bello," prologue to Vol. IX of the _Obras completas de Bello_, Caracas, 1956, and other works including "Bello, el desterrado," _Hombres y letras en Venezuela_, México, 1948, pp. 59-74.

15. Gumersindo de Azcárate, "Juicio sobre el Código Civil de la República de Chile," introduction to the edition of the Código Civil de la República de Chile, Madrid, 1881.

16. Pedro Lira Urquieta, Temas universitarios, Santiago, 1945.

17. Carlos Stuardo Ortiz and Sergio Villalobos R., Génesis histórica del Código Civil de Chile (1811-1955). Los codificadores, Santiago, 1956, 89 pp.

18. Minister of Education, Directorate of Culture and Fine Arts, Caracas, fourth, fifth and sixth book of the Week of Bello in Caracas. Caracas, 1955, 1956, 1957. Materials on the Civil Code on the occasion of its one hundredth anniversary.

19. Fernando Chumaceiro Chiarelli, Bello y Viso Codificadores. Estudio comparado del Código Civil y el proyecto de Julián Viso, Maracaibo, 1959, 361 pp.

20. Hessel E. Intema, prologue to Derecho Romano, Vol. XIV of the Obras completas de Bello, Caracas, 1959.

21. Guillermo Feliú Cruz, "Andrés Bello y la administración pública de Chile," prologue to Vol. XVI of the Obras completas de Bello, Caracas, 1964, and Andrés Bello y la redacción de los documentos oficiales administrativos, internacionales y legislativos de Chile, Caracas, 1957, XXVIII, 329 pp. The edition of Estudios sobre Andrés Bello, Santiago, 1966, directed by Feliú Cruz, is important.

22. Ricardo Donoso, prologue to Vol. XVII of the Obras completas de Bello. Labor en el Senado de Chile, Caracas, 1958.

23. Miguel Luis, and Gregorio Víctor Amunátegui Aldunate Biografías de americanos, Santiago, 1854, pp. 155 and 125. This was the first bibliographic essay on Bello. Later in 1882, Miguel Luis published his classical work and still fundamental Vida de don Andrés Bello, VI, 672 pp., of which a second edition was published in Santiago in 1962 with a preliminary study by Wolfgang Larrazabal and a letter-prologue by Guillermo Feliú Cruz. Miguel Luis Amunátegui published a four-volume Ensayos biográficos in 1843. Volume II is devoted to Bello and his descendents.

24. Juan Vicente González mentioned interpretative biographic traits of Bello in several of his works. He summarizes the humanist in La meseniana in 1865 when he learned of Bello's death. Many editions of this have been published.

25. Arístides Rojas devoted several studies to the personality of Bello in addition to his "Don Andrés Bello, poeta virgiliano," cited as a reference to the poetry. Particularly worth mentioning is "Recuerdos de 1810, Andrés Bello y los supuestos delatores de la revolución," dated 1876, published in La Opinión Nacional and inserted in Estudios históricos, Caracas, 1927, II, pp. 36-90.

26. José Victorino Lastarria, Recuerdos literarios, Santiago, 1878-1879, with vivid reminiscences of Bello by Lastarria, who was a student of the latter.

27. Ana Prats Bello, <u>Andrés Bello.</u> <u>Estudio biográfico</u>, <u>1781-1865</u>, Santiago, 1916, 77 pp., an evocation of the humanist by his granddaughter.

28. Antonio Balbín de Unquera, <u>Andrés Bello.</u> <u>Su época y sus obras</u>, Madrid, 1910, IX, 324 pp., a prize-winning biography in Spain.

29. Eugenio Orrego Vicuña, <u>Don Andrés Bello</u>, Santiago, 1935. This work has gone through many editions since it first appeared in the <u>Anales de la Universidad de Chile</u>, first semester 1935, pp. 5-267.

30. Rafael Caldera, <u>Andrés Bello</u>, Caracas, 1978, 6th ed., the first in 1935, Caracas. The book has been published in French (1972), Italian (1972), Portuguese (1973), and English (1977). A long fragment has been published in Russian (1972).

31. Pedro Lira Urquieta, <u>Andrés Bello</u>, México-Buenos Aires, 1948, 211 pp.

32. Lucy Pérez Luciani de Castillo, <u>Andrés Bello</u> (1781-1865), Caracas, 1952. A biography for scholars re-edited in Chile in 1965. Another edition was published in Caracas in 1973.

33. José Antonio Escalona-Escalona, <u>Bello y Maitrín</u>, Caracas, 1974.

34. Manuel Salvat Monguillot, <u>Vida de Bello</u>, Santiago, 1971, pp. 12-77.

35. Sergio Fernández Larraín, <u>Cartas a Bello en Londres, 1810-1829</u>, Santiago, 1968, 356 pp.

I. POETRY

THE ANAUCO

One of Bello's first original poems, composed in
Caracas when he was a young man. Arístides Rojas
suggested it was composed in about 1800 when Bello was
19, an assertion that has been repeated but not
documented.

———————

Let cupidity
along unknown paths
quicken the ire of Thetis
and of the howling winds,
and the pines
on the amaranth-covered shores
of the hallowed Betis
admire unchastened
the Ganges fields
teeming and balm-anointed.
Thou, verdant and gentle bank
of the Anauco,
more joyous to me,
than the Idalian forests
and sweet meadows
of the placid Paphos
shalt echo with my modest songs;
and when in the dreaded boat
my shadow visits
the solitary valleys of Erebus
I may leave
the Stygian lakes
and silent shores
to wander one day
through thy shaded forests
and hidden caves.
The saddened crowds
of the nearby towns
shall evoke the spirit of my dead
with grievous laments;
and by the tomb,
strewn with funerary branches
and Indian scents,
Phillis shall cry,
"Here rests Fabio!"
A thousand times blessed!
But curs'd be thou

should old age come on thee
in foreign lands.
May thy bones be devoured
by the bloodthirsty dogs
that roam Caribdean crags;
and thy dust
find no peace
in the sighs
of a faithless mate
encircled in another man's embrace.

ECLOGLE

(Imitation of Virgil)

This composition, clearly belonging to Bello's early years in Caracas, dates from sometime between 1806 and 1808. Inspired by Virgil, its language is heavily influenced by Garcilaso de la Vega and Francisco de Figueroa. See Pedro Grases, Sobre la elaboración de una égloga juvenil de Bello, Caracas, 1947.

Thyrsis, who lived in the shade of the Tagus
loved Chloe with a most vivid fire;
but Chloe returned his tender longing
with rustic indifference.

He wandered along the beckoning shore
in search of consolation;
and poured forth his sorrow
to the distant cause of such heavy grief.

Thou, shepherdess, fleest from me
swifter than the lamb from the tiger;
thou fearest me more than the bird a vulture
or the sheep a hungry wolf.
Thou esteemest not a simple love,
thou hearest not my complaint.
Because of thee my rustic labors are forgotten;
the laughingstock I've become of other shepherds.

"In the end, Chloe, thine obstinate denials
shall cause my death.
My tale carved on these trees
will say that in loving thee I died.
Those who worship thee now
shall read my fate in horror;
None shall dare tell of their love;
the shepherds shall execrate thy name.

"Even the beasts yearn
for the entangled shade of the woods;
Speckled lizards hide
under the meadow grass.
Cattle graze in the field

and birds feed in the vineyard.
I alone endure the high summer sun
to follow one who deigns me not.

"Thou art heedless and scornest my love,
yet shepherdesses there are
who would have Thyrsis, should a clement god
but loose the bond of my suffering.
Shouldst I not, heartless nymph,
render my gifts to Galatea
or accept Tyrrhena's flattery
though she be dark and thou art fair?

"Too proud thou mayst be, Chloe,
of thy milk-white skin.
But, like a tender rose, color too
at the least offense can be subdued.
The faded violet is admired,
and the languid jasmine
may die on the branch
unplucked by the hand of the nymphs.

"Once stretched on the sand,
I vilified my love and thy beauty
when Tyrrhena saw me and said,
'O unjust Venus, cruel goddess,
instead of joining two souls,
thou dost divide them:
Thou, Thyrsis, endurest Chloe's scorn,
yet I adore thee, thou who despisest me.'

"Alas, I know not why such tender love
is so loathesome to thine eyes!
Any shepherd hears me jealously
as I play on my rebec.
Does not my plentiful flock
cover the pastures always?
Have I not juicy and tender fruits
in summer and winter both?

"And, unless my image
in that crystal stream deceives me,
I am not unbecoming.
Surely the conqueror of a soul so harsh
would be surpassed by my grace,
my beauty and my valor,
if, thou being the judge,
he dared compete with me.

"Come live with me, thou beauteous nymph,
Come! The dryads bestow thee
with baskets of roses
and for thee the fields abound.
For thee alone I keep
the fruit of my orchards,
for thee alone I cover the fields
with hyacinths, violets and cloves.

"Remember'st when thou yet a maid,
would come to my enclosure
and beg me for the tender apples
still covered with down.
From the ground thou couldst not
reach the red cluster
and, after failing again and again,
would implore my help.

"Then was I thy master,
yet tender of age I excelled
among other youth
as the thyme exceeds
all herbs in the meadow.
Twas then, cruel love,
that thou piercest me with the arrow
that is my torment day and night.

"O Chloe, thou knowest not how Jove chastens
cruel and ungrateful mortals;
for them a dark grotto exists
in the gloom of Avernus
where a hungry vulture with unclean beak
rips them asunder
and the living heart devoured
anguishes, its beat restored.

"Alas, my sad words of naught avail
with one who is heartless.
What delirium, what dream is this of mine?
I strove to catch the shadows, harness the wind,
follow the clouds and halt the river.
And while I try what cannot be,
my vineyards stand rotting at home,
in the wood my herds abandoned."

To what avail these entreaties
to the heavens?
I cannot burn a heart of ice
nor change my fate.
Though Chloe scorns me
another will requite my love.
The sun is dipping in the west.
Return, my flock, return to the fold.

TO THE SHIP

(Ode in imitation of Horace, O Navis, referent*)*

Generally dated 1808 although no authentic
testimony exists to this effect.

———————

What new hopes
sweep thee seaward? Turn back,
back, brave ship,
to thy native coast.

Dost thou see the remains
of the last storm
and yet would surge forth
to try fortune anew?

The course abounds
with syrtes,
whose perils will
too late be seen.

O ship! turn back now
while the gentle waves
of the sea still caress
the shells on the beach.

Soon standings mountains
shall beat the rocks,
and shipwrecked relics
Neptune's carpet be.
The fastuous pomp of the sails
as naught shall be
against the fury
of the tempest.

Of what avail against the wind,
the tyrant of the waves,
the stripes and lions 1/
on your golden stern?

What power evokes
thy name still,
once renowned
from east to west?

Another serenely poised
and arrogant prow,
that yesterday
braved these winds
Now, moss-covered,
lies on a naked shoal,
infaust memorial
to the astonished mariner.

Dost thou now hear me?
Dost thou not change course?
With new sails unfurled,
Wouldst thou, fearless, plunge into the waters?

Dost thou not see, ill-fated seafarer,
the sky clouding over
and the lightening sheared
by the roar of the thunder?

Dost thou not see white caps
swell and billow?
nor does the wind not frighten thee
as it wails in the ropes?

Come back, beloved object
of my travail,
return to the gentle beach
before the sunset.

NOTE

1. The emblem of Aragon and Castile.

TO THE VICTORY OF BAILÉN

This sonnet, believed to have been composed in 1808, had an unusual fate. Between 1820 and 1823, Tomás J. Quintero (Th. Farmer) published it in Spain; it later became a poem of eulogy to General José Antonio Páez. After Bello went to Chile, he recited the verses from memory to the Amunátegui brothers who in turn published it in 1861 in Juicio crítico de algunos poetas suramericanos. See Pedro Grases, La singular historia de un drama y un soneto de Andrés Bello, Caracas, 1943.

The proud lion bursts the fetters
with which tyranny would subject him,
and fiercely tosses
the man on his robust neck.

A foam of furor covers his lips,
and when he utters his angry roars
the tiger trembles in his den
and the whole forest echos aghast.

The lion awakes. Tremble, you traitors!
What you thought age
was but repose.
His youthful strength is unimpaired

Pursue, you faithless hunters,
the timid hare
and submissive deer.
Challenge not the king of beasts!

NOT FOR ME, OF DECLINING WINTER

These are verses from an unfinished poem found on
a sheet of paper probably written in London in about
1820, judging from the handwriting.

May brings me not bright skies and green earth
when it breaks the harsh sceptre of declining winter
With the gentle breeze comes not love
nor is the woodland filled with the song of dawn.
For one far from the nest of his homeland
and the loves of his youth,
All is winter still.

AMERICAN SYLVA

(From drafts of the poem)

Volume II of Bello's <u>Complete</u> <u>Works</u> (Caracas, 1962) gives the complete text of the drafts of his poems, a voluminous repertory of verse that had been unpublished until that time. The most extraordinary and valuable section is indeed the one devoted to the <u>Silvas</u> <u>americanas</u>, or <u>American</u> <u>Sylva</u>. This was a symbolic fragment of <u>América</u>, a poem Bello was working on that he had announced in the first issue of the <u>Repertorio</u> <u>Americano</u> (London, October 1826), when he published the <u>Georgic</u> <u>of</u> <u>the</u> <u>Tropics</u> under the general heading of <u>American</u> <u>Sylva</u>.

<u>Georgic</u> <u>of</u> <u>the</u> <u>Tropics</u> and his <u>Allocution</u> <u>to</u> <u>Poetry</u> (published earlier, see below) were part of the long unfinished poem of which the drafts now published are so illustrative of the creative process. Two fragments are given here, without the notes and variants found in the <u>Complete</u> <u>Works</u>. See the preliminary study to volume II by Pedro P. Barnola, S.J., for an understanding of the quality of this unfinished poem. Father Barnola called the second fragment the "expatriot's elegy."

First, if a dark woods you must
demolish, take care that the curved steel
fell the stout trees
and tangled underbrush in the right season,
so the sun can dry the natural juices,
their freshness and maternal nourishment gone
and the fire easily devour what once was forest
from one extreme to the other.

First, if a dark woods you must
demolish, take care that the curved steel
fell the stout trees
and tangled underbrush in the right season;
so the sun can dry the natural juices,
their freshness and maternal nourishment gone,
and the fire easily devour what once was forest
from one extreme to the other
before the first rains come.

May brings the rainy season
to Caracas, and when February early
starts stripping the bucare
of its proud foliage, in the woodsman's hand
the sickle glitters and pitilessly
drives the beasts from their lair.
The axe sounds, the distant echo
repeating the blows. And the old rain tree,
over many hurricanes triumphant,
sighs its last and reels
to the ground: The deer flees in fright,
the bird its beloved nest and untrained little ones
abandons, sorrowfully looking for another wood unknown to man.
Yet take care that the treacherous serpent
coiled and alert in the hollow trunk
of an old tree, not strike with venemous fang.
....
Once the tall forest is felled and dey,
set fire there and let it be blown
elsewhere by the wind.
Before that, though, you must ready a barrier
around what might feed the advancing fire,
for the unbridled flames will otherwise destroy
trees, fields and all that stands in their way,
with no green forest or human power to contain them...
My God, what a swirl of smoke spirals into the air
cloud upon cloud, shielding the light! As if the
rebel spirits one hurled into hell
had risen anew against the Eternal Being
and trampled the doors of their infernal prison.
Or the yawning abyss had vomited
fire-brandishing hosts who scaled
mount after mount to reach the Empireous. When the black night
spreads its mantle, the horror grows; from the Avila 1/
the forest is aflame in a thousand spots.
The far-away splendor of the fire
reverberates in streets, squares, roofs, windows,
as if the people were celebrating that night
a great feast and thousands of torches
were lighting palaces, cornices and doors.
The anxious flame, off in a hundred directions,
reaching out hungrily everywhere,
is visible from the high peak.
Alas, it heralds not joy
but impending ruin and devastation.
Wretched laborer with farm nearby
who thought your harvest safe, you will ne'er see the day
to take your crop to market.
The crowd hurries too late to ready the barriers;
the insane hydra begets new heads, the wasteland of ashes
silent witness to their passage.
Had not God at last, touched by human misery,
fettered the wind and loosed the southern rain
to quench the fire,
no end to that devastating plague could be devised

O who would lead me with you, beloved Poetry,
to the banks of the Cauca and let me inhale
the mild breath of eternal spring there forever
with its court.
O rid of wretched cares
might I with free and uncertain step
tread the shores of the Aragua,
or stretched under a young palm tree
watch your four torches,
O Southern Cross, light up the bluish dome;
you, who measure the night hours
for the wanderer
in his spacious and vagrant solitude;
or watch the luminous trail of the glow-worm
cleave the air like a starry host;
and from the distant inn the sorrowful song
of a lonely lover breaks the silence of the night.
Am I to live ever sorrowful
far from the dear and beautiful land
where my eyes first saw the light?
O, how often my soul, in brief respite
absorbed in memory, gazes on youth's lost scenes,
gone in hurried and irrevocable flight.
O mountains, O hills, O prairies,
beloved shadow of my country,
joyful banks of the Anauco,
and my soul sorrows and weeps!
I see too human shadows round me
and credulously count them one by one.
I again hear the familiar accents
of love and friendship and turn back.
What have you to say? Where are you now,
companions, friends,
witnesses of my first ravings,
and desires and mad hopes,
cheated like yours by an unfriendly fate?
In a foreign clime
I sigh in vain for the native air,
under iron chains I must suffer
or turn my hand to unused toil.
Why, o God, why, this fading sun
that here barely lights a tired world,
on the other side of the Atlantic
shines bright and pure,
or gilds the tombstone or the whitened bones
left by inhuman revenge unburied
in a wasteland or deserted beach?
Ah! Fortune inexorably drew the curtain
on the joyous drama
where you and I were players
of lighthearted ambition
and the delirium of love's young flame.
But you, dear images, break now
the silence of my solitude
as you did in other times in soft discourse
and dispel the sadness of long absence;
cross the seas, unlatch

the jail and tombs.
May Parca, moved by my cry,
for once let loose her prey.
What else, what other pleasure awaits me
than this illusory farce of memory
though merciful heaven accord me the return,
so long in coming, to my native land?
Again I will visit the ridge, the green glade,
the clear river, the pleasant brook.
But you, dear friends, I will not see.
I will not hear your merry welcome nor feel your embrace.
I'll ask the echo where my dear friends are,
my beloved, my confident, my companion?
Where are they? Where have they gone?
Gone! the echos will answer in solace.
And, alas, in my own land I shall be a stranger.

NOTE

1. Mountain nearby Caracas (A).

22

ALLOCUTION TO POETRY

(Fragment of a poem entitled América)

A selection of 226 verses is given from the total of 832 in this work, which was first published in the Biblioteca Americana, London, 1823 (the first major journal Bello had in the British capital), vol. I, pp. 3-16; vol. II, section 1 (the only one published), pp. 1-12. Its full title was "Allocution to Poetry, in praise of the nations and people of America who have distinguised themselves in the war of independence. (Fragments of an unpublished poem entitled América)." Subsequent publications derive therefrom. This poem is regarded as the manifesto of Spanish American literary independence.

———————

Divine Poetry,
you who dwell in solitude
and wrap your songs
in the silence of the shaded forest;
you who lived in the green grotto,
the mountain echos your company.
Time it is to abandon Europe,
no lover of your native rusticity,
and turn your fancy to the great setting
unveiled by the New World.

There too heaven reveres the laurel
with which you crown excellence;
there too the blooming field,
the entangled forest, the twisting river
give colors galore to your brush;
and Zephyr gently stirs the roses;
stars gleaming bright
adorn the chariot of night;
and the king of the sky rises
between nacre-lined clouds
and a sweet little bill
warbles unlearned songs of love.

What care you, O rustic nimph,
for the pomp of royal palaces?
Will you too go with the cortesan crowd

to render the torpid incense of flattery?
You were not thus in your noblest days
when in man's infancy,
teacher of nations and kings,
you proclaimed the world's first laws.

Be not detained, O goddess,
by this region of wretchedness and light
where your ambitious rival Philosophy,
submitting virtue to discretion,
has usurped your sceptre;
where the crowned hydra threatens
to bring back the night of crime and barbary
to man enslaved by thought;
where freedom is vain delirium,
faith servility, greatness pomp,
culture corruption.
Take down from the withered oak
your sweet golden lyre where once
you sang to spellbound men
of meadows and flowers, the whisper
of dense wood, the peaceful
murmuring of the brook
the allure of nature's innocence.
And opening your restless wings
cross over the vast Atlantic
to another sky, another world,
another people, where the earth
is still in primitive array,
unsubdued by man,
and America, young bride of the Sun,
last daughter of the ancient Ocean,
breeds in her fertile breast
the wealth of every clime.

What dwelling awaits you? what peak,
what comely meadow, what replenished forest
shall be your home? What beach
shall first feel the tread
of your golden sandle? Where the river
that saw the heroes of Albion humbled,
where the blue pendons of Buenos Aires
now flutter, and proudly
bears the tribute of a hundred currents
down to the astounded sea? Or where the double crest
of the Avila 1/ breaks through the clouds
and the city of Losada 2/ is reborn?
Or shall the valleys of Chile blessed,
with their suave fruits and golden harvests,
where the innocence and candor
and hospitality of the Old World
blend with patriotism and valor,
smile upon you more, O Muse?
Or the city shown the errant Aztecs 3/
by the eagle in the nopal,
with its soil of measureless ores
that almost sated Europe's greed?
The queen of the southern ocean
whose daughter's grace was Nature's dowry,
provides a haven under her mild sky

24

untouched by wind or rain.
Or will your home be the heights of Quito,
perched between white peaks,
listening to the roar of tempests at its feet,
with its clear air propitious
to your celestial inspiration?
Yet listen as the churning Bogotá
thunders its way
between walls of groomed rock,
and, wrapped in a cloud of rainbow mist,
boldly leaps towards the valleys
of the Magdalena.
Where memories of early days
await your lyre;
when Cundinamarca in sweet idleness
and native innocence gave easy sustenance
to her dwellers,
the first offspring of her generous breast,
before the curved plough broke the soil
or foreign vessel touched the distant shores.
Ambition had not yet stirred
the atrocious iron;
still undegenerate men
sought refuge in dark-roofed
forests and caves;
the land still had no master,
fields no fences, towns no wall.
Freedom flourished without law;
peace, contentment, joy abounded;
when a jealous Huitaca 4/,
goddess of the waters,
deluged the valley with the swollen
torrents of the Bogotá.
Some took refuge in the hills;
others were swallowed in the voracious abyss.
You shall chant the wrath of Nenqueteba,
child of the Sun,
at the havoc of his almost extinct race;
who parted the mountain with his sceptre
to make a channel for the waves;
and the once vast lake of the Bogotá,
whose dominion reached from peak to peak,
scorned its prison and
pounding on its narrow banks
with mighty fury plunged through the gap.
You shall sing of Nenqueteba, the pious,
who gave laws, art, and religion
to the new nations,
after turning the naughty nymph
into the light of the night
and the silver moon first ploughed the Olympus.

Go extol the equatorial wonders;
sing of the sky made joyous
by the chorus of the stars,
where at once the dragon of the north
with its golden tail
encircles the north star,
and the dove of Arauco
dips its wings in the southern seas.

Grind your richest colors
and take your finest brushes
to portray the climes
preserved in pristine vigor
with which the omnipotent voice
swelled the earth freshly created
from the abyss of chaos
and covered it with vegetation and life.
Eternal forest, who dare name or number
the multitude that peoples your labyrinths
proudly boastful of their many forms
and heights and dress?
Silk-cotton trees, acacias, myrtles
intertwined, reeds, vines, grasses;
branches striving to reach the light
and the sun, in endless struggle;
the ground can ill contain so many roots.

O could you but take me, cherished Poetry,
to the shores of the Cauca
and let me inhale the gentle breath
of the eternal spring air
in its kingdom there!
O could I but carefree wander
along the shores of the Aragua
or, haply stretched under a palm tree on the plain,
watch in the heavens your four stars,
O Southern Cross, that measure the nocturnal hours
of the errant traveler
through the night's vast solitude.
Or see the trail of the firefly
cutting the gloam,
or hear from the far-off hostel
the sounds of the yaraví! 5/

There will come a time
when an American Virgil
inspired by you, O Goddess,
will sing of the crops and cattle
of a land tamed by man
and the fruits of a region
beloved of Phoebus;
where cane bears sweet honey,
and the tuna bright carmine,
where cotton waves its snowy head,
and pineapple ripens its ambrosia;

the palm tree bears its varied abundance,
the naseberry its sweet buds,
the avocado its butter, the indigo brings forth its dye,
the banana tree droops under its sweet burden,
coffee concentrates the aroma of its white blossoms,
and the cacao jells its beans in purple urns.
....
Yet, alas, would you rather chant the terror
of a merciless war, and depict hosts
hurrying to destruction, bent on filling the land
with mourning, to the beat of drums
that make every mother cow and tremble?
O if only you offered, land of mine,

less themes for songs of war!
What cities, what fields have not been deluged
with the blood of your sons and Spain's?
What wasteland has not fed human members
to the condor? What rustic homes
were spared the fury of civil strife?
But love of country worked no such
wonders in Rome or Sparta
or Numancia.
Nor does any page of history give deeds
more glorious for your song, O Muse.
What province or man will earn your tribute
in your first hymn of praise?

NOTES

1. Mountain near Caracas (A).

2. The founder of Caracas (A).

3. Mexico, founded by the Aztecs, a native people of America (A).

4. Huitaca, wife of Nenqueteba or Bochica, lawmaker of the
    muiscas. Humboldt, Vues por cordilleres, I (A).

5. Yaraví, melancholy music native to Peru and the Plains of
    Colombia (A).

GEORGIC OF THE TROPICS

When Bello published the Georgic of the Tropics in the Repertorio Americano (London, October 1826, pp. 7-18), he gave it a title indicating it was the first part of the American Sylva, a grandiose plan which he explained in a note as follows: "These verses are part of the fragments printed in the Biblioteca Americana under the title América. The author intended to merge them all into a single poem; persuaded that this is impossible, he will publish them in their original form with some additions and corrections. Only two or three verses of those fragments will be found in this first part." (See note to the American Sylva regarding the drafts of the unfinished poem).

The numerous subsequent editions of the Georgic of the Tropics are based on the 1826 edition. Of all Bello's poetry, this is probably the work that has been most re-edited.

———————

Hail, fertile region,
thou who embracest the farflung course
of thy loving sun, and conceivest
through its caressing light
every being in every clime.
Thou weavest the summer wreath
of golden wheat and offerest the grape
to the seething vat;
thy glorious fields lack no shade
of purple, red or yellow; from them
the wind inhales a thousand aromas.
Countless herds graze
in thy pastures, from the plain
reaching to the horizon
up to the mountain heights
covered with inaccesible snow.

Thou bringest forth the graceful sugarcane
with its concentrated molasses
for which the world now scorns the honeycomb.
In coral urns thou jellest the beans
that overflow the frothing cups of chocolate;
bright carmine shimmers on thy prickly pear trees,
disdainful 'twere of the purple of Tyre.

And the generous flow of thine indigo
emulates the light of the sapphire.
The wine that spills from a wounded century plant 1/
for the children of the Anahuac is thine;
and thine the tobacco leaf
whose spirals of playful smoke
comfort the tedium of idle hours.
Thou adornest with jasmine flowers
the shrub of Sheba 2/
and givest it the aroma
that will temper the insane fever
of drunken revelry.
For thy children the noble palm 3/
nourishes its varied wealth,
and the pineapple ripens its ambrosia,
the cassava its white bread,4/
the potato its blond tubers;
and the golden roses and snowy fleece of cotton
stir in the gentle breeze.

For thee the passion plant 5/
in bowers of pristine greenness
displays sweet buds and striped flowers
hanging from its runners.
For thee the cornstalk, arrogant chief
of the cereal tribe, swells its seed;
and for thee the banana tree 6/
droops under its sweet burden;
the banana tree, superior
to them all, a gift lavished by Providence
on the fortunate people of the tropics.
It yields its fruit
unhelped by human hand,
owing no debt
to man's pruning or his plough;
a little effort suffices, wrought
from a weary slave's hand;   .
quick to grow, as soon as it dies
its own ready seedlings assume its place.
O, if only as with thy gifted land,
fertile region, surpassing all others,
nature had turned its care
to thine indolent dwellers!
O, if only they would place
the true happiness beckoning them
from the simple peasant's threshold
above the empty pomp,
the delusive luster,
the pestilent idleness of the city!
What dismal illusion
makes the masters
of such varied and plentiful soil
forsake their lands to the care
of mercenary hands,
to imprison themselves
among the blind mob
of wretched cities
where peevish ambition fans
the flames of civil rivalry

or indolence devitalizes patriotism;
where comfort harries custom
and evil in a powerful league
contends with the artlessness of youth?
There no manly exercise
toughens the young to hardship;
instead their health is consumed
in the embrace of perfidious beauty
who sells her favours on the block;
enflaming illicit love
in an innocent heart
is thought a pastime,
or dawn finds men drunk
at a gamester's table.
Meanwhile, the consort succumbs
to the seductive words of an eager lover;
the tender virgin is raised
in the maternal school
of flirtation and dissipation
so that sin is goaded
before desire by example.
Is this how we would mold
the heroic and intrepid spirits
that found and sustain nations?
Could the debauchery of drunken feasts
or the choruses of lewd dances
produce a hardy, sober youth,
the pride and hope of its homeland?
Could a man who slept as an infant
to the murmur of lascivious lullabies,
who curls his hair, perfumes
and decks himself out
with effeminate care,
who spends his days in lazy indolence
or criminal lust, master
with steady pulse the reins of the law;
remain serene in the midst
of a doubtful combat; or
withstand the haughty spirit
of an arrogant leader?
Rome in its conquests dealt not
thus with peace and war;
but entrusted the reins of government
to a robust hand
tanned by the sun and hardened by the plough.
Under a humble peasant roof
Rome raised its sons
to subject a hostile world to Latin valor.

O happy dwellers, born in a land of beauty
where Nature flagrantly
displayed its plenty
as if to lure and win you!
Break this harsh spell
that walls you in a prisoner.
The common man who works at a craft,
the merchant, necessary for comfort
and claiming it in turn,
those who yearn after the temptation
of high place and pompous honor,

the parasitic flock of sycophants:
let them live in that infested chaos;
Yours is the open land. Rejoice therein!
Are you lovers of freedom? Go seek it there,
not where the magnates live
protected by their armed satellites;
not where justice is chained
to the triumphal chariot of universal lady Fashion;
not where the foolish crowd worships fortune
and the nobleman, a commoner's applause.
Or are you lovers of virtue?
Then the best teacher in life
is solitude and quiet
where the soul, judge of itself,
examines its own works.
Seek you lasting joy
and happiness--as much as man is allowed
to have in this earthly life--
where tears merge with laughter
and every rose has a thorn?
Go find joy in a peasant's life,
in the gift of peace unspoiled
by rancor or envy;
the restful sleep of night made ready
by work, fresh air and contentment;
and seek the relish of simple vittles
unsoured by wasteful gluttony;
and the safe haven
of your paternal hearth,
host to health and gladness.
Go inhale the mountain air
that restores lost strength
to a weary body, that stems
the approach of an irksome old age,
and tinges with pink the face of youth.
Is perchance the flame of love
tempered by modesty weaker there?
or beauty untouched
by false adornment
less appealing?
Or is the heart indifferent
to innocent words
that express true feeling
and match promises with intentions?
No need to rehearse before a mirror
laughter, step or gesture.
An honest face flushed with modesty and health
needs not the glow of carmine.
The sidelong gaze of a timid lad
loses not its way to the soul.
Would you expect hymeneal ties
arranged, at the behest
of a tyrant of love,
by an alien hand for fame and fortune
to be more enduring than a marriage
bound by common taste and age,
free choice and mutual ardor?
There are duties too to be done there;
close, close the deep wounds of war

Put the rich soil, rough now and wild,
under a new yoke of human care
and let it pay its tribute.
From clogged-up pond and mill
let the waters find again their course,
axes fell and fire consume
the forest; open up long lanes
in its dark, barren splendor.
Let the valleys shelter
the thirsty came;
let the apple and pear
grow in the mountain coolness,
forgetting the sky of their mother Spain.
Let coffe trees
adorn the slopes; on river banks
the maternal shade of the bucare 7/
protect the young cacao; let flowers and vegetables
toss their heads in glee.
Are all these dreams sheer folly?
O agriculture, wetnurse of the people,
in docile heeding of thy voice
the servile swarm sets forth with curved scythes.
I watch as they invade the thicket
of the gloomy forest; I hear their voices,
the confusing murmur, the ringing
of the iron,
the far echo redoubling the blows.
The ancient ceibo, long wearying
its army of woodsmen,
buffeted by a hundred axes, quivers,
snaps at last and renders its broad crown.
The wild beast fled; the bird left its beloved nest,
left its untrained little ones,
sorrowfully looking for another wood
unknown to man.
What see I now? A tall torrent
of crackling flames rushes and spreads
over the arid ruins
of the prostrate forest.
The fire roars afar
and the smoke rises in black whirlwinds
piling cloud upon cloud.
Dead trunks and ashes alone
are all that remain of what was
a woodland once fresh and green;
a monument to mortal happiness,
a plaything of the wind.
Yet the savage tangle
of dense and wild growth
is soon replaced by fruitful plantations
in proud patterns of tidy design.
Branch reaches out to branch,
and stealing the sunlight from the stout shoots
the first flowers grow.
Beautiful to behold, uplifting hope,
hope that laughs and mops the forehead
of the weary laborer.
Hope that paints in bright colors in the distance
the best of fruits, the fullest of harvests.
Hope that takes the tribute from the fields

in overflowing baskets and billowed skirts.
Hope that under the weight of a generous return
accruing to the planter
makes vast warehouses creak.
Dear God! Let not this sweat be in vain.
May Thou be moved to greater pity and compassion
by the peasants of the equatorial region,
now reviving from the despair
of such great anxiety, turmoil and care,
so many years of cruel devastation
and military outrage,
who now implore greater mercy than in the past.
May their rustic yet sincere devotion
find grace in Thine eyes;
may they not weep over the unrealized dream,
the false vision of a smiling future that lightens
today's sorrow;
may no unseasonal rain damage,
nor gnawing insects devour,
nor the fury of the wind
snatch away their delicate seedlings;
may no parching thirst of drought
exhaust the maternal sap of their trees.
And, finally, my prayer I raise to Thee,
arbiter of supreme destiny,
that the men of America, rid of
the foreign yoke, may look towards heaven
and with Thy blessing, their freedom take root and thrive:
war be cast to the deepest confines of hell
and fear of the razing sword
not keep the husbandman from his toil
that feeds families and nations.
May souls be free of anxiety
and the ploughshare free of rust.
We have atoned enough
for the barbarous conquest
of our luckless forefathers.
What stubbled wilderness exists
as far as the eye can see where once
were fields of crops, where once were cities!
Who can count the frightful sum
of dead, banished,
tortured, motherless?
The ghosts of Atahualpa and Montezuma
slumber gorged with Iberian blood.
From the footstool of Thy throne
made by the angels who reverently covered
their faces with their wings
before the light of Thine image
(should man in his wretchedness
be worthy of Thy gaze),
send us Thine angel,
the angel of peace, to make the ruthless Spaniard
renounce past tyranny
and abide by the law of freedom
Thou gavest man as a sacred trust,
and to make him stretch out his unarmed hand
(so stained with blood) to his injured brother.

And should innate meekness sleep,
make it stir in the American breast.
A young heart scornful of
the joys of ignorance,
eager for power and glory,
embraces noble perils.
May such a heart esteem
but vituperation and affront
a prize not awarded by the homeland,
find freedom sweeter than empire
and the olive branch more beautiful than the laurel.
May a warrior, laying aside his uniform,
become a citizen;
the garland of victory
be hung on the altar of the homeland
and merit alone be worthy of glory.
Then shalt thou see the longed-for day,
native land, when peace shall triumph,
peace in whose sight the world is filled
with serenity an joy;
man shall return to his labor,
ships raise their anchor and
entrust themselves to gentle breezes,
shops swarm, plantations hum
and sickles be wanting for the harvest.
O young nations who raise over
a stunned Western world
a head garlanded with tender laurels;
honor the fields, honor the simple life
of the peasant and his frugal plainness.
So shall freedom have its dwelling place
among you forever,
ambition a rein and the law a temple.
And men shall take heart
on the steep and arduous path of immortality,
by citing your example,
which shall be emulated
by your heirs;
and adding new names
to those now acclaimed
fame shall cry out,
"Sons are these, sons
of those who conquered the peaks
of the Andes;
of those who in Boyaca,
Maipo, Junin,
and in the glorious campaign of Apurima
humbled the lion of Spain."

NOTES

1. The maguey or pita (Lat., Agave americana) which yields a
    fermented juice called pulque (A).

2. Coffee is native to Arabia. The kind most valued in commerce
    still comes from that part of Yemen over which the Queen of
    Sheba reigned, the area known today as Mocha (A).

3. No family of vegetables can compete with the palms in the variety of products useful to man: bread, milk, wine, oil, fruit, getable, wax, firewood, rope, clothing, etc. (A).

4. The plant from whose root cassava bread is made (namely the Jatropha manihot of Linnaeus, known generally in Spanish as yuca) should not be confused (as has been done in a dictionary of great and well-deserved authority) with the yucca of the botanists (A).

5. The name parcha, passion flower, is given in Venezuela to the Pasifloras or Pasionarias, a genus most abundant in species, all beautiful and some bearing a most delicious fruit (A).

6. The banana is a plant cultivated by the slaves on plantations or haciendas, mainly for themselves, from which they derive either directly or indirectly both their sustenance and everything else that makes life bearable. The banana tree, in proportion to the land it covers, is known to bear more abundantly than any other crop or plant and entails less work and care than all other food producers (A).

7. The cacao (Lat., Theobroma cacao) is usually planted in Venezuela in the shade of the large tree called the bucare.

LES JARDINS [1]

(Translation of Jacques Delille. Fragment)

While in London, Bello translated from the French 536 verses of <u>Les</u> <u>Jardins</u> by Jacques Delille (1738-1813). They were first published in <u>Repertorio</u> <u>Americano</u>, IV, London, in August 1827. We reproduce 196 verses here.

Le doux printemps revient et ranime à-la-fois
Les oiseaux, les zéphyrs, et les fleurs, et ma voix.
Pour quel sujet nouveau dois-je monter ma lyre?
Ah! lorsque d'un long deuil la terre enfin respire;
Dans les champs, dans les bois, sur les monts d'alentour,
Quand tout rit de bonheur, d'espérance et d'amour;
Qu'un autre ouvre aux grands noms les fastes de la gloire,
Sur son char foudroyant qu'il place la victoire;
Que la coupe d'Atrée ensanglante ses mains:
Flore a souri; ma voix va chanter les jardins.
Je dirai comment l'art embellit les ombrages,
L'eau, les fleurs, les gazons, et les rochers sauvages;
Des sites, des aspects sait choisir la beauté,
Donne aux scènes la vie et la variété:
Enfin l'adroit ciseau, la noble architecture,
Des chefs-d'oeuvre de l'art vont parer la nature.
   Toi donc qui, mariant la grace à la vigueur,
Sais du chant didactique animer la langueur,
O muse! si jadis, dans les vers de Lucrece,
Des austères leçons tu polis la rudesse;

Si par toi, sans flétrir le langage des dieux,
Son rival a chanté le soc laborieux;
Viens orner un sujet plus riche, plus fertile,
Dont le charme autrefois avoit tenté Virgile (1).
N'empruntons point ici d'ornement étranger;
Viens, de mes propres fleurs mon front va s'ombrage
Et, comme un rayon pur colore un beau nuage,
Des couleurs du sujet je teindrai mon langage.
   L'art innocent et doux que célébrent mes vers,
Remonte aux premiers jours de l'antique univers.
Dès que l'homme eut soumis les champs à la culture,
D'un heureux coin de terre il soigna la parure;

Et plus près de ses yeux il rangea sous ses lois
Des arbres favoris et des fleurs de son choix.
Du simple Alcinoüs le luxe encor rustique
Décoroit un verger. D'un art plus magnifique,
Babylone éleva des jardins dans les airs.
Quand Rome au monde entier eut envoyé des fers
Les vainqueurs, dans des parcs ornés para la victoire,
Alloient calmer leur foudre et reposer leur gloire.
La Sagesse autrefois habitoit les jardins,
Et d'un air plus riant instruisoit les humains.
Et quand le dieux offroient un Elysée aux sages,
Etoient-ce des palais? c'étoient de verts bocages;
C'étoient des prés fleuris, séjour des doux loisirs,
Où d'une longue paix ils goûtoient les plaisirs.
  Ouvrons donc, il est temps, ma carrière nouvelle,
PHILIPPE m'encourage, et mon sujet m'appelle.

  Pour embellir les champs simples dans leurs attraits,
Gardez-vous d'insulter la nature à grands frais.
Ce noble emploi demande un artiste qui pense,
Prodigue de génie et non pas de dépense.
Moins pompeux qu'élégant, moins décoré que beau,
Un jardin, à mes yeux, est un vaste tableau.
Soyez peintre. Les champs, leurs nuances sans nombre,
Les jets de la lumière et les masses de l'ombre,
Les heures, les saisons variant tour-à-tour
Le cercle de l'année et le cercle du jour,
Et des prés émaillés les riches broderies,
Et des riants coteaux les vertes draperies,
Les arbres, les rochers, et les eaux et les fleurs,
Ce sont là vos pinceaux, vos toiles, vos couleurs:
La nature est à vous; et votre main féconde
Dispose, pour créer, des éléments du monde.
  Mais avant de planter, avant que du terrain
Votre bêche imprudente ait entamé le sein,
Pour donner aux jardins une forme plus pure,
Observez, connoissez, imitex la nature.
N'avez-vous pas souvent, aux lieux infréquentés,
Rencontré tout-à-coup ces aspects enchantés,
Qui suspendent vos pas, dont l'image chérie
Vous jette en une douce et longue rêverie?
Saisissez, s'il se peut, leurs traits les plus frappants,
Et des champs apprenez l'art de parer les champs.
  Voyez aussi les lieux qu'un goût savant décore:
Dans ces tableaux choisis vous choisirez encore.
Dans sa pompe élégante admirez Chantilli,
De héros en héros, d'âge en âge embelli.
Beloeil, tout-à-la-fois magnifique et champêtre,
Chanteloup, fier encor de l'exil de son maître,
Nous plairont tour-à-tour. Tel que ce frais bouton
Timide avant-coureur de la belle saison,
L'aimable Tivoli d'une forme nouvelle
Fit le premier en France entrevoir le modéle.
Les Graces en riant dessinèrent Montreuil.
Maupertuis, le Désert, Rincy, Limours, Auteuil,
Que dans vos frais sentiers doucement on s'égare!
L'ombre du grand Henri chérit encor Navarre.
Semblable à son auguste et jeune déité,
Trianon joint la grace avec la majesté.
Pour elle il s'embellit, et s'embellit par elle.

Et toi, d'un prince aimable ô l'asile fidéle,
Dont le nom trop modeste est indigne de toi,
Lieu charmant! offre-lui tout ce que je lui doi,
Un fortuné loisir, une douce retraite,
Bienfaiteur de mes vers, ainsi que du poëte,
C'est lui qui, dans ce choix d'écrivains enchanteurs,
Dans ce jardin paré de poétiques fleurs,
Daigne accueillir ma muse. Ainsi du sein de l'herbe,
La violette croît auprès du lis superbe.
Compagnon inconnu de ces hommes fameux,
Ah! si ma foible voix pouvoit chanter comme eux,
Je peindrois tes jardins, le dieu qui les habite,
Les arts et l'amitié qu'il y mène à sa suite.
Beau lieu, fais son bonheur! et moi, si quelque jour,
Grace à lui, j'embellis un champêtre séjour,
De mon illustre appui j'y placerai l'image.
De mes premières fleurs je lui promets l'hommage:
Pour elle je cultive et j'enlace en festons
Le myrte et le laurier, tous deux chers aux Bourbons;
Et si l'ombre, la paix, la liberté m'inspire,
A l'auteur de ces dons je dévouerai ma lyre.

Riche de ses forêts, de ses prés, de ses eaux,
Le Germain offre encor des modéles nouveaux.
Qui ne connoît Rhinsberg qu'un lac immense arrose,
Où se plaisent les arts, où la valeur repose;
Potsdam, de la victoire héroïque séjour,
Potsdam qui, pacifique et guerrier tour-à-tour,
Par la paix et la guerre a pesé sur le monde;
Bellevue où, sans bruit, roule aujourd'hui son onde
Ce fleuve, dont l'orgueil aimoit à marier
A ses tresses de jonc des festons de laurier;
Gosow, fier de ses plans, Cassel, de ses cascades;
Et du charmant Vorlitz les fraîches promenades?
L'eau, la terre, les monts, les vallons et les bois,
Jamais d'aspects plus beaux n'ont présenté le choix.

Dans les champs des Césars, la maîtresse du monde
Offre sous mille aspects sa ruine féconde:
Par-tout entremêlés d'arbres pyramidaux,
Marbres, bronzes, palais, urnes, temples, tombeaux,
Parlent de Rome antique; et la vue abusée
Croit, au lieu d'un jardin, parcourir un musée.

L'Ibère aved orgueil dans leur luxe royal
Vante son Aranjuez, son vieil Escurial;
Toi sur-tout, Ildephonse, et tes fraîches délices.
Là ne sont point ces eaux dont les sources factices,
Se fermant tout-à-coup, par leur morne repos
Attristent le bocage, et trompent les échos:
Sans cesse résonnant dans ces jardins superbes,
D'intarissables eaux, en colonnes, en gerbes,
S'élancent, fendent l'air de leurs rapides jets,
Et des monts paternels égalent les sommets;
Lieu superbe où Philippe, avec magnificence,
Défioit son aïeul, et retraçoit la France.

Le Batave à son tour, par un art courageux:
Sut changer en jardins son sol marécageux:
Mais dans le choix des fleurs une recherche vaine,
Des bocages couvrant une insipide plaine,
Sont leur seule parure; et notre oeil attristé
Y regrette des monts la sauvage âpreté:
Mais ses riches canaux et leur rive féconde,

De ses moulins dans l'air, de ses barques sur l'onde,
Des troupeaux dans ses prés les mobiles lointains,
Ses fermes, ses hameaux, voilà ses vrais jardins.
   Des arbres résineux la robuste verdure,
Les mousses, les lichens qui bravent la froidure,
Du Russe, presque seuls, parent le long hiver;
Mais l'art subjugue tout: le feu, vainqueur de l'air,
De Flore dans ces lieux entretient la couronne,
Et Vulcain y présente un hospice à Pomone.
Par ses hardis travaux, tel le plus grand des czars
Sut chez un peuple inculte acclimater les arts.
Heureux, si des méchants l'absurde frénésie
Ne vient pas en poison changer leur ambrosie;
Et si de Pierre un jour quelque heureux successeur,
Sans craindre leur danger, sait goûter leur douceur!
   Le Chinois offre aux yeux des beautés pittoresques,
Des contrastes frappants, et quelquefois grotesques,
Ses temples, ses palais richement colorés,
Leurs murs de porcelaine, et leurs globes dorés.
   Vous dirai-je quel luxe, aux rives ottomanes,
Charme dans leurs jardins les beautés musulmanes?
Là, les arts enchanteurs prodiguent les berceaux,
Le marbre des bassins, le murmure des eaux,
Les kiosks élégants, les fleurs toujours écloses;
L'empire d'Orient est l'empire des roses.

NOTE

1.   From J. Delille, <u>Oeuvres</u> (Paris: L. G. Michaud, 1824), vol.
     VII, pages 31-27 (<u>T</u>).

THE BURNING OF THE JESUIT TEMPLE IN SANTIAGO

Elegy

Published in pamphlet form in Santiago, July 1841, by the government press, with the following comment by Miguel Luis Amunátegui when he published it later: "The old Jesuit church in Santiago burned down on the night of May 31, 1841." The poem is regarded as the earliest work of romanticism in Chile.

I

Jesuit temple
holy house of prayer,
thou who callest
the devout to worship
night and day.

What light, what radiance
burst o'er thee?
'Tis no nocturnal celebration
But a devastating flame,
a funeral pyre.

'Tis no sound of joy
that rushes through the air;1/
wails enveloped in smoke
go forth from thy tower,
sighs of agony.

N'er did a hidden spark
spread with such blind fury;
a tiny flicker first
was next a towering
vault of fire
'Tis like a swift volcano
spewing lava
and piling cloud upon cloud
of red and brown smoke
heavenward.

As a famished lion
pulls apart his careless prey,

40

so the ferocious element
rears up and roars,
and reduces thee to ashes.

Though the people come round
longing to help
the fire spreads quickly,
diffusing its terrifying light
to the farthest hill,

Awesome reflections
as far as the eye can see
tinge every street and every plaza,
threatening and fear-inspiring
though seem from afar.

A gigantic vision,
black wings flapping,
swirls overhead;
gusting, it stirs the fire
and quivers the smoke-laden torch.

Might this be the angel
once cast into hell
to whom misery is joy?
Hideous delight shines
from his darkened face.

From the roof the thread of fire
descends like burning rain
that lights and consumes
the nave and spreads
with uncontained voracity.

O Virgin Mary, ever attentive
to human prayers; detain
the course of the fire;
stretch thy sovereign mantle
over thy beloved mansion.

Over thy beauteos dwelling
where in ardent supplication
thou wast ever implored;
where a thousand devout lips
named thee their protector.

Titular archangel,2/
how canst thou allow
the offending flames?
Would their fury be vented on thine image
and thine altar turned to cinders?

Nothing placates their furor;
Destruction is everywhere,
everything aflame;
the consuming fire
respects not its God.

Thou too art devoured,
boisterous sentinel,
a vigilant tower that hour by hour
marked off a century
of time in the city.

Thou soundest nine spellbound
by the blaze that would
cause thy death;
'twas thy last stroke
and last farewell.

Who thought to lose thee
when the prophetic tolling
sealed thy fate,
or that the voice of death
was on the wings of the wind?

I seemed to hear thee say,
"Farewell, beloved land!
Heaven would no more have me
voice thy succeeding
days and hours.

"A thousand forms I saw
borne into the world
flourish at my feet
and descend into the void
from whence they came.

"I saw thee, Santiago,
in thy early youth,
a sleeping slave,
no omen in they breast
of thy future fate.

"I saw thee awaken
proud and ardent
from thy long slumber
to oppose the tyrant
with indomitable will.

"I saw the tri-color
replace the Spanish pendant;
and a plain luxuriant in fauna and flora
follow upon a wasteland,
and the citizen replace the slave.

"Farewell, Santiago! No more
shall be heard
thy faithful herald
marking thy mute steps
on the way to the tomb.

"Farewell; my ill-fated hour came
as thine will too.
All is defeated and

destroyed by time;
very empires are swallowed."

III

The downcast guardian angel
of our new-born land,
once the fire is quenched,
hovers, hand on forehead,
in the Empyrean.

The.city sleeps now,
the fire spent in the temple,
the turbolence ended;
and silent dismay reigns
about the hollow building.

A dense brightness ugly to see
adds to the dismay and horror;
a cold north wind whips up the smoke;
the blackened debris
flickers here and there.

Among the vast ruins
a sudden flame may revive,
raise its head
in a ghost-like glare
and light up the temple.

But once again it dies;
and the moon alone,
coming out from the clouds,
shines brightly
over arch and column.

In a dull stupor
the nave and chapel
receive this new radiance,
a lonely light shining
in front of the Ark of the Lord.

Except for the caw
of a nocturnal bird
in pointless search for its nest
or the languid sigh
of a taciturn buzzard,

Or a nearby watchman,
or a bell announcing
morning prayers,
or the rain falling
on the venerable ruins,

Beating on the high wall
and sacred pavements,
ill-fated field of battle
of adversary elements;
everything slumbers and is still.

With such havoc before us,
is there any ideal sentiment
to strengthen the anguished breast
or any fibre
that finds comfort in sorrow?

Is it a divine instinct
revealing our higher destiny
when the hand of fortune
crumbles and destroys
a peerless monument?

Or touches the soul
with unaccustomed power
and stirs the imagination,
Dark night, death-like quiet,
solemn melancholy?

I do not truly know
what then bears the soul away;
absorbed in an idea,
earthly ties are severed
and the mind becomes lost in reverie.

The image created
is no faded picture;
to a mind lost in thought
past becomes present
and memory life.

The old traditions
take on fresh colors,
and dead generations
break open the prisons
of their sepulchral coffers.

What strange rustling is that?
what unprecedented whispers?
Whose voice thus disturbs
the secular silence
of the sanctuary of death?

Cold bones dressed in black
rise up from their beds;
and, emaciated shadows,
descend from the niches
where they dwell.

I stand there and watch
as the repulsive procession
climbs from its abysmal retreat
and in two well-ordered rows
slowly circles round and round.

An old man leads them,3/
gray hairs visible
under his white miter.

They chant, and their song resembles
a far-off muffled murmuring.

Their lips move,
and the sighing of faint echos follows;
the moon traverses
their bodies; their feet
leave no print in the dust.

Their penetrating gaze
is not of human eyes
nor of this world;
the axes in their hands
have a death-like glare.

The sound that I hear
rustling through the air
and dying in melancholy cadence
is the doleful Miserere,
the psalm of the dead.

"Do good in thy good pleasure,
Author of all good!
build thou the walls of Jerusalem."4/

                        V

But the dawn broke
and in its light the vision
gradually subsides
until at last, like a light gas,
it evaporates in the air.

The early sun of June
rises over the great range
and races between the clouds
as if in flight
from such misfortune.

Who could imagine
that what yesterday seemed
eternal, would today be
scorched timbers, naked
walls, cold ashes?

The curious crowd
gazes with reverence and awe
(horrible, wretched object)
at the mutilated skeleton
of the once beautiful temple.

The once bright lamp is no more;
the soft incense burns no longer;
unsightly dust covers the altar.
Yet, why dwell my thoughts
on what matters least?

The Holy Tabernacle...
Cast down thy face on earth,
Jerusalem, rip the mantle;
the tears fall one by one
down thy pale cheek.

Thy Tabernacle afire, an insane fire,
O Lord; the solemn feast
that week forgotten.
Thy house demolished
and Thine altar destroyed.5/

Church, tower, chorus,
gone forever;
silenced the penitent prayer;
silenced the sonorous pealing;
silenced the eloquent pulpit.

The voice of the psalms has ceased;
mourning and chaos
blanket the empty tabernacle;
and the daughter of Zion
is but a charred corpse.

NOTES

1. The alarm sounded by the tolling of the bells of the burning church (A).

2. The name of the Jesuit church was St. Michael Archangel (A).

3. Bishop Juan Melgarejo, buried in the Jesuit cemetery (A).

4. and preceding verse. Psalm 50, v. 19: Benigne fac, Domine, in bona voluntate tua Sion, ut aedificentur muri Jerusalem (A).

5. Inspired in Chapter 2, Lamentation of Jeremiah (A).

THE PRAYER FOR ALL

(Imitation of Victor Hugo)

This poem is valued as an authentic draft by Bello, modeled on La priere pour tous by Victor Hugo (1802-1885). It was first published in El Crepúsculo, vol. I, no. 6, Santiago, October 1, 1843.

I

Go pray, my child. This is the hour
for thought and meditation;
The day's work is done and shadows
drop their veil over the world.
The tree by the road, swaying
in the evening breeze, shakes off its dust;
and the old tower glitters,
wrapped in the loose cloak of the mist.

Watch as the wheel of iridescent nacre
recedes in the west;
and the evening star lights its beacon
over the coastal hills.
The humble hut is lit, the frugal supper ready,
and the laborer's wife and children
stand in the doorway
awaiting his late return.

The stars, like diamonfs, come out singly
in the heavens;
a returning cart
complains in the distance.
All is drowned in shadow: mountain, valley,
church, hut, and farmhouse.
And the last rays of daylight
guide the traveler in the wilderness.
All nature sighs: the wind
in the trees, the bird in its nest,
the sheep with quivering bleat,
and the riverlet along its fast course;
Daylight is for evil doing and toil.
Here the serene and placid night!
Man, after his labor and care
needs rest, prayer and quiet.

The bell tolls in the tower; children
talk with winged spirits;
and their eyes lifted to heaven,
kneel and pray to the Lord.
Barefooted, hands clasped,
happy faces filled with faith,
they pray together with a single voice
for the Universal Father to grant them love.

Then they sleep,
and a joyous host of dreams,
visions no brush can capture,
waft over their cribs.
Angels kiss their tender foreheads,
and drink the breath of little red lips
as bees suck on carnations and lilies.
Like a tiny bird that hides its head
under its wing to sleep,
so infants with their simple prayers
lull their innocent minds into slumber
O sweet devotion that prays and laughs!
first sign of genuine piety!
fragance of the flower of paradise!
prelude to the celestial concert!

II

Go pray, my child.
Pray first for your mother; for the one
who gave you life, the best part
of her existence bound therein;
in her womb she sheltered your soul,
borne of a celestial flame;
of life's two parts,
she kept the bitter and gave you the sweet.
Then pray for me. I need it
more than she who was simple, tender,
good like you,
bearing her sorrow in silence.
In the unhappy times that befell us
she had compassion for many,
envy of none.
Like a shadow over glass,
so passed evil over her soul.
Impervious to the fickle turns of fate
or to troublesome cares that advance old age
--and may you be, too!
or the harmful pain of a hidden sin,
the thorn that pierces a guilty conscience,
or the restless fever that burns the soul
and tinges the face with a sickly pallor.

But I know, to my misfortune, what life is like.
I know the world and its treachery.
Someday I may tell you
how worthless are its pleasures.

And you will learn what awaits those who gamble
in wealth and power, the urn of chance,
and that the path to seeming glory
ends in wretchedness.

Innocence becomes clouded in living
and each moment some new fault
is added to the stream that leads
in rapid descent to the grave.
Temptation seduces; judgment misleads,
everyone leaves something on the
brambles of the path; the sheep
its wool, man his goodness.
Go pray for me to heaven,
my child, with these few words,
"Lord, thou who art Goodness and Might,
have mercy and pardon the man of thy creation."
And God will listen; as the alter smoke
rises to the heavens,
so prayer ascends from the innocent heart
to the throne of the eternal father.

All things thrust towards their goal: a plant
reaches out to the sunlight, a tethered fawn
seels the freedom of the mount; an exile
yearns for the land of his birth; bees
in the valley are drawn
by the aroma of new thyme;
and prayer rises on the wings of a dove
to the dwelling place of the Lord.

When you pray for me to God,
I am like the weary pilgrim
Who lays down his burden
on the side of the road and stops to rest;
for the sweet lilt of your prayer
soothes the bitterness of life,
and strips the guild and care
from my trouble-laden shoulders.
Pray for me, so that in the darkness
the flight of a merciful angel
I may see descending from heaven
to bring me the light since lost.
And pure at last as
the altar marble washed in the temple,
may my soul burn in hallowed flame,
like a censer standing before the cross.

III

Pray, my daughter, for your brothers
who grew up with you,
who suckled on the same breasts
and who lived under the same roof.
Pray not only for those
who love you.

Christ died on the cross
for the just and the wicked too.

Pray for the proud
with their haughty strut
and foolish arrogance,
naught but splendid finery;
and for the humble beggar
who endures the winebibber's
miserly brow
for the sake of his pittance alone.
Pray for the wicked
mired in sin,
who howl obscene ditties
in nocturnal debauchery;
and for the consecrated virgin
who, on her lonely bed,
does penance
reciting the psalm of the dead.

Pray for heartless men
whose bosoms never shelter
tenderness
for sorrow or affliction;
who give not food to the hungry,
clothing to the naked,
a hand to those who falter,
or pardon to the offender.

Pray for the man who rejoices
in seeinng his dagger dipped in blood
in pursuit of wealthy spoil
or cruel revenge;
and for the man who destroys
the good name of his neighbor
and spits poison
into an open wound.
Pray for those who sail
on an ocean frought with peril;
for those in chains
and their harsh jailers;
for those who live in truth
by the good book;
for those who doubt,
and for those who follow error.

Remember, finally, all men
who labor and suffer,
and those who travel
through this mortal life.
Remember too the wicked
who insult their God with blasphemy,
Prayer is infinite,
its waters never ending.

My child, pray also for those
who rest under the lifeless tombstone,
into whose depths men fall
by the thousands;
abyss where all dust
and all races mingle
as autumn leaves falling from the trees
blend with others on the forest floor.
Kneel down on the earth
where my Lola lies,
crowned with an angelic halo;
where, cold, sleep her mortal remains;
where captive souls petition prayers
to purge the relics of their earthly vessel
and restore them to their primitive state.

My child, as you sleep you smile
and strange spirits waft about
and frolic at your window;
a mischievous, happy, watchful swarm.
And once again you open your eyes
when the dawn too
opens its pink eyelids
giving earth the light it yearned for.

But those poor souls, if you knew
how they sleep! Their pillow is cold,
their bed hard; no angelic music
delights their prison.
Their heavy slumber is no rest;
no early dawn awaits their night;
an their conscience like a restless worm,
gnaws inexorably at their heart.
A single prayer or word of yours
will give momentary relief
and a warm ray from heaven
will enter their dark dwelling;
remorse will grant
its victims truce
and let in the peaceful murmur
of water, air and trees.

When you watch with secret dread
as shadows fall on the field,
the snow that covers the peak with shrouds
and the red hue of the sunset;
in the murmur of the water and the fountain
do you not hear an echoing voice
a mournful voice that says, "Child,
when you pray, will you remember me?"

It is the voice of the departed. The dead
reached by prayers are unharmed
by the fallen angel, and their tombs
are ever carpeted with flowers.
But alas! Those souls who lie forgotten

are covered with perpetual horror; strange weeds
choke their sepulchres; dreadful roots
wrap around their bowels.
I too (the day is not far)
shall dwell in darkness,
and invoke the prayer of innocence
to console my long suffering.
Sweet twould be for you to come
and implore my eternal rest
and scatter flowers on the bare stone,
a simple tribute of loving faith.

Will you, sweet child, forgive
the adverse stars that slowly dimmed
my hopes for your happiness?
You will, I know, and my memory
will bring a tear, a sigh
that will reach into the dark retreat
and make my cold dust stir.

SARDANAPALUS [1]

(Translation of Lord Byron. Fragment)

Translation of a little over half of Act I of Lord Byron's tragedy, with personal adaptations by Bello who published it in the Revista de Santiago, vol. IV, June 1850. Commenting on the poem, he said, "Sardanapalus is one of Lord Byron's finest tragedies. The character of the protagonist is an original approach, an attempt to rehabilitate this personage whom history treated too severely. For Lord Byron's Sardanapalus, pleasure was the prime object in life but he was not the soft, cowardly prince whose dissolution and effeminacy have become proverbial; in this sense, history fell victim to prejudice and injustice.

According to history, Sardanapalus fought bravely against Arbaces, the rebel leader of a formidable army, in concert with the Chaldean priests and some of the provincial governors. Sardanapalus conquered Arbaces three times, and in the third battle showed no less skill than he did courage. Arbaces, wounded, took refuge in the hills of Chaldea with the remnants of his army. The insurrection seemed to have been smothered and Sardanapalus firmly placed on the throne with the arrival of the Bactrian troops from the East to defend their king. But Belesis, the Chaldean priest behind the uprising, beguiled the Bactrian leaders and persuaded them to try their fortune a fourth time. Taken by surprise and routed, Sardanapalus did not lose heart. Under seige in Nineveh, he prepared a vigorous defense while Salamenes, the head of the remnants of his army, confronted the enemy outside its walls. The latter's defeat and death led to an uprising of the empire provinces still loyal to the ancient dynasty. Sardanapalus, reduced to the precincts of his capital, held out for three years, until a flood on the Tigris ripped a hole in the city's walls and let the beseigers in. Sardanapalus then had a pyre built, placed his royal insignia, treasures, wives and eunuchs on top, set it afire and threw himself into the flames (817 B.C.). Such was the true Sardanapalus, rehabilitated by Byron after two thousand years in the dark.

"The sample presented will give some idea of Byron's tragic style and of his superbly intelligent development of Sardanapalus and Salamenes. Myrrha, the Greek slave, in her brief appearance represents the qualities of virtually all of Byron's women (tenderness, detachment, devotion to the object of their love), but has all the traits of a daughter of Greece.

"The meter of the translation is the same as in the original. The speakers are Sardanapalus, king of Astria; Salamenes, brother of the queen; Myrrha, the Greek captive and concubine of Sardanapalus, group of women."

    Sar. Let the pavilion over the Euphrates
Be garlanded, and lit, and furnish'd forth
For an especial banquet; at the hour
Of midnight we will sup there: see nought wanting,
And bid the gallery be prepared. There is
A cooling breeze which crips the broad clear river:
We will embark anon. Fair nymphs, who deign
To share the soft hours of Sardanapalus,
We'll meet again in that the sweetest hour,
When we shall gather like the stars above us,
And you will form a heaven as bright as theirs;
Till then, let each be mistress of her time,
And thou, my own Ionian Myrrha, choose,
Wilt thou along with them or me?
    Myr.   My Lord---
    Sar. My Lord, my life! why answerest thou so
          coldly?
It is the curse of kings to be so answer'd (...)
    Myr.   The king's choice is mine.
    Sar. I pray thee say not so: my chiefest joy
Is to contribute to thine every wish.
I do not dare to breathe my own desire,
Lest it should clash with thine; for thou art still
Too prompt to sacrifice thy thoughts for others.
    Myr. I would remain: I have no happiness
Save in beholding thine; yet---
    Sar.   Yet! what YET?
Thy own sweet will shall be the only barrier
Which ever rises betwixt thee and me.
    Myr. I think the present in the wonted hour
Of council; it were better I retire.
    Sal. The Ionian slave says well: let her retire.
    Sar. Who answers? How now, brother?
    Sal.   The queen's brother,
And your most faithful vassal, royal lord.
    Sar.   As I have said, let all
       dispose their hours
Till midnight, when again we pray your presence
               (The court retiring)
            Myrrha! I thought
   thou wouldst remain.
    Myr.   Great king,
Thou didst not say so.
    Sar.   But thou lookedst it:
I know each glance of those Ionic eyes,
Which said thou wouldst not leave me
    Myr.   Sire! your brother
    Sal. His consort's brother, minion of Ionia!

How darest thou name me and not blush?
     Sar.   Not blush!
Thou hast no more eyes than heart to make her
         crimson
Like to the dying day on Caucasus,
Where sunset tints the snow with rosy shadows,
And then reproach her with thine own cold blindness
Which will not see it. What, in tears, my Myrrha?
     Sal. Let them flow on; she weeps for more than one,
And is herself the cause of bitterer tears.
     Sar. Cursed be he who caused those tears to flow!
     Sal. Curse not thyself---millions do that already.
     Sar. Thou dost forget thee: make me not remember
I am a monarch.
     Sal.   Would thou couldst!
     Myr.   My sovereign,
I pray, and thou, too, prince, permit my absence.
     Sar. Since it must be so, and this churl has check'd
Thy gentle spirit, go; but recollect
That we must forthwith meet: I had rather lose
An empire than thy presence.
     Sal.   It may be,
Thou wilt lose both, and both for ever!
     Sar.   Brother,
I cant at least command myself, who listen
To language such as this: yet urge me not
Beyond my easy nature.
     Sal.   'Tis beyond
That easy, far too easy, idle nature,
Which I would urge thee. O that I could rouse thee'
Though' twere against myself.
     Sar.   By the god Baal!
The man would make me tyrant.
     Sal.   So thou art.
Think'st thou there is no tyranny but that
Of blood and chains? The despotism of vice---
The weakness and the wickedness of luxury---
The negligence---the apathy---the evils
Of sensual sloth---produce ten thousand tyrants,
Whose delegated cruelty surpasses
The worst acts of one energetic master,
However harsh and hard in his own bearing.
The false and fond examples of thy lusts
Corrupt no less than they oppress, and sap
In the same moment all thy pageant power
And those who should sustain it; so that whether
A foreign foe invade, or civil broil
Distract within, both will alike prove fatal:
The first thy subjects have no heart to conquer;
The last they rather would assist than vanquish.
     Sar. Why, what make thee the mouth-piece of
        the people?
     Sal. forgiveness of the queen, my sister's wrongs;
A natural love unto my infant nephews;
Faith to the king, a faith he may need shortly,
In more than words; respect for Nimrod's line;
Also, another thing thou knowest not.
     Sar. What's that?
     Sal.   To thee an unknown word.

<u>Sar</u>.   Yet speak it;
I love to learn.
        <u>Sal</u>.   Virtue.
        <u>Sar</u>.   Not know the word!
Never was word yet rung so in my ears---
Worse than the rabble's shout, or splitting trumpet:
I've heard thy sister talk of nothing else.
        <u>Sar</u>. To change the irksome theme, then, hear of vice
        <u>Sar</u>. From whom?
        <u>Sal</u>. Even from the winds, if thou couldst listen
Unto the echoes of the nation's voice.
        <u>Sar</u>. Come, I'm indulgent, as thou knowest, patient,
As thou hast often proved---speak out, what moves thee?
        <u>Sal</u>. Thy peril.
        <u>Sar</u>.   Say on.
        <u>Sal</u>.   Thus, then: all the nations,
For they are many, whom thy father left
In heritage, are loud in wrath against thee.
        <u>Sar</u>. 'Gainst me! What would the slaves?
        <u>Sal</u>.   A king.
        <u>Sar</u>.   And what
Am I then?
        <u>Sal</u>.   In their eyes a nothing; but
In mine a man who might be something still.
        <u>Sar</u>. The railing drunkards! why, what would
             they have?
Have they not peace and plenty?
        <u>Sal</u>.   Of the first
More than is glorious; of the last, far less
Than the king recks of.
        <u>Sar</u>.   Whose then is the crime,
But the false satraps, who provide no better?
        <u>Sal</u>. And somewhat in the monarch who ne'er looks
Beyond his palace walls, or if he stirs
Beyond them, 'tis but to some mountain palace,
Till summer heats wear down. O glorious Baal!
Who built up this vast empire, and wert made
A god, or at the least shinest like a god
Through the long centuries of thy renown,
This, thy presumed descendant, ne'er beheld
As king the kingdoms thou didst leave as hero,
Won with thy blood, and toil, and time, and peril!
For what? to furnish impost for a revel,
Or multiplied extortions for a minion.
        <u>Sar</u>. I understand thee---thou wouldst have me go
Forth as a conqueror. By all the stars
Which the Chaldeans read---the restless slaves
Deserve that I should curse them with their wishes,
And lead them forth to glory.
        <u>Sal</u>.   Wherefore not?
Semiramis---a woman only---led
These our Assyrians to the solar shores
Of Ganges.
        <u>Sar</u>. 'Tis most true. And how return'd?
        <u>Sal</u>. Why, like a man---a hero; baffled, but
Not vanquish'd. With but twenty guards, she made
Good her retreat to Bactria
        <u>Sar</u>.   And how many
Left she behind in India to the vultures?

<u>Sal.</u> Our annals say not.

<u>Sar.</u>   Then I will say for them---
That she had better woven within her palace
Some twenty garments, than with twenty guards
Have fled to Bactria, leaving to the ravens,
And wolves, and men---the fiercer of the three,
Her myriads of fond subjects. Is this glory?
Then let me live in ignominy ever.

<u>Sal.</u> All warlike spirits have not the same fate.
Semiramis, the glorious parent of
A hundred kings, although she fail'd in India,
Brought Persia, Media, Bactria, to the realm
Which she once sway'd---and thou might'st sway.

<u>Sar.</u>   I sway them---
She but subdued them.

<u>Sal.</u>   It may be ere long
That they will need her sword more than your
          sceptre.
I would but have recall'd thee from thy dream;
Better by me awaken'd than rebellion.

<u>Sar.</u> Who should rebel? or why? what cause?
          pretext?
I am the lawful king, descended from
A race of kings who knew no predecessors.
What have I done to thee, or to the people,
That thou shouldst rail, or they rise up against me?

<u>Sal.</u> Of what thou hast done to me, I speak not

<u>Sar.</u>   But
Thou think'st that I have wrong'd the queen: is't not so?

<u>Sal.</u> Think! Thou hast wrong'd her!

<u>Sar.</u>   Patience, prince, and hear me.
She has all power and splendour of her station,
Respect, the tutelage of Assyria's heirs,
The homage and the appanage of sovereignty.
I married her as monarchs wed---for state,
And loved her as most husbands love their wives.
If she or thou supposedst I could link me
Like a Chaldean peasant to his mate,
Ye knew nor me, nor monarchs, nor mankind.

<u>Sal.</u> I pray thee, change the theme: my blood
          disdains
Complaint, and Salemenes' sister seeks not
Reluctant love even from assyria's lord!
Nor would she deign to accept divided passion
With foreign strumpets and Ionian slaves.
The queen is silent.

<u>Sar.</u>   And why not her brother?

<u>Sal.</u> I only echo thee the voice of empires,
Which he who long neglects not long will govern.

<u>Sar.</u> The ungrateful and ungracious slaves! they
          murmur
Because I have not shed their blood, nor led them
To dry into the desert's dust by myriads,
Or whiten with their bones the banks of Ganges;
Nor decimated them with savage laws,
Nor sweated them to build up pyramids,
Or Babylonian walls.

<u>Sal.</u>   Yet these are trophies
More worthy of a people and their prince

Than songs, and lutes, and feasts, and concubines,
And lavish'd treasures, and contemned virtues.

    <u>Sar</u>. Or for my trophies I have founded cities:
There's Tarsus and Anchialus, both built
In one day---what could that blood-loving beldame,
My martial grandam, chaste Semiramis,
Do more, except destroy them?

    <u>Sal</u>.   'Tis most true;
I own thy merit in those founded cities,
Built for a whim, recorded with a verse
Which shames both them and thee to coming ages.

       <u>Sar</u>. Shame me! By Baal, the cities, though well
            built,
Are not more goodly than the verse! Say what
Thou wilt 'gainst me, my mode of life or rule,
But nothing 'gainst the truth of that brief record.
Why, thoses few lines contain the history
Of all things human: hear---"Sardanapalus,
The king, and son of Anacyndaraxes,
In one day built Anchialus and Tarsus.
Eat, drink, and love; the rest's not worth a fillip.

    <u>Sal</u>. A worthy moral, and a wise inscription,
For a king to put up before his subjects!

       <u>Sar</u>. Oh, thou wouldst have me doubtless set up
            edicts---
"Obey the king---contribute to his treasure---
Recruit his phalanx---spill your blood at bidding---
Fall down and worship, or get up and toil."
Or thus---"Sardanapalus on this spot
Slew fifty thousand of his enemies.
These are their sepulchres, and this his trophy."
I leave such things to conquerors; enough
For me, if I can make my subjects feel
The weight of human misery less, and glide
Ungroaning to the tomb: I take no license
Which I deny to them. We all are men.
(....)

    <u>Sal</u>.   Alas!
The doom of Nineveh is seal'd.---Woe---woe
To the unrivall'd city!

    <u>Sar</u>.   What dost dread?

    <u>Sal</u>. Thou art guarded by thy foes: in a few
           hours
The tempest may break out which overwhelms thee,
And thine and mine; and in another day
What <u>is</u> shall be the past of Belus' race.

    <u>Sar</u>. What must we dread?

    <u>Sal</u>.   Ambitious treachery,
Which has environ'd thee with snares; but yet
There is resource: empower me with thy signet
To quell the machinations, and I lay
The heads of thy chief foes before thy feet.

    <u>Sar</u>. The heads---how many?

    <u>Sal</u>.   Must I stay to number
When even thine own's in peril? Let me go;
Give me thy signet---trust me with the rest.

    <u>Sar</u>. I will trust no man with unlimited lives.
When we take those from others, we nor know
What we have taken, nor the thing we give.

<u>Sal</u>. Wouldst thou not take their lives who seek
        for thine?
    <u>Sar</u>. That's a hard question---But I answer, Yes.
Cannot the thing be done without? Who are they
Whom thou suspectest?---Let them be arrested.
    <u>Sal</u>. I would thou wouldst not ask me; the next
        moment
Will send my answer through thy babbling troop
Of paramours, and thence fly o'er the palace,
Even to the city, and so baffle all.---
Trust me.
    <u>Sar</u>.   Thou knowest I have done so ever:
Take thou the signet.
    <u>Sal</u>.   I have one more request.---
    <u>Sar</u>. Name it.
    <u>Sal</u>. That thou this night forbear the banquet
In the pavilion over the Euphrates.
    <u>Sar</u>. Forbear the banquet! Not for all the plotters
That ever shook a kingdom! Let them come,
And do their worst: I shall not blench for them;
Nor rise the sooner; nor forbear the goblet;
Nor crown me with a single rose the less;
Nor lose one joyous hour.---I fear them not.
    <u>Sal</u>. But thou wouldst arm thee, wouldst thou not,
        if needful?
    <u>Sar</u>. If it must be so, and these rash slaves
Will not be ruled with less, I'll use the sword
Till they shall wish it turn'd into a distaff
    <u>Sal</u>. They say thy sceptre's turn'd to that already.
    <u>Sar</u>. That's false! but let them say so.
....
The populace of all the nations seize
Each calumny they can to sink their sovereigns.
    <u>Sal</u>, Thay did not speak thus of thy fathers.
    <u>Sar</u>.   No;
They dared not. They were kept to toil and combat;
And never changed their chains but for their armour
Now they have peace and pastime, and the license
To revel and to rail; it irks me not.
I would not give the smile of one fair girl
For all the popular breath that e'er divided
A name from nothing. What are the rank tongues
Of this vile herd, grown insolent with feeding,
That I should prize their noisy praise, or dread
Their noisome clamour?
    <u>Sal</u>.   Thou stopp'st
Short of the duties of a king; and therefore
They say thou art unfit to be a monarch.
    <u>Sar</u>. They lie.---Unhappily, I am unfit
To be aught save a monarch; else for me
The meanest Mede might be the king instead.
    <u>Sal</u>. There is one Mede, at least, who seeks to be so.
    <u>Sar</u>. What mean'st thou?---'tis thy secret; thou
        desirest
Few questions, and I'm not of curious nature.
Take the fit steps; and, since necessity
Requires, I sanction and support thee. Ne'er
Was man who more desired to rule in peace
The peaceful only: if they rouse me, better

They had conjured up stern Nimrod from his ashes,
"The mighty hunter." I will turn these realms
To one wide desert chase of brutes, who were,
But would no more, by their own choice, be human
What they have found me, they belie; that which
They yet may find me---shall defy their wish
To speak it worse; and let them thank themselves.
     Sal. Then thou at last canst feel?
     Sar.   Feel! who feels not
Ingratitude?

NOTE

1.   From The Works of Lord Byron.... By Thos. Moore Esquire,
London, 1847, vol. XIII, 69-85 pp., act I, scene 2. Sar.
stands for Sardanapalus; Sal., for Salamenes; Myr., for Myrrha
(T).

ORLANDO INNAMORATO

(Translation of the poem of Matteo Maria Bojardo, rewritten by Francesco Berni. Fragment)

The original introductions by Bello to the first, second, twelfth, thirteenth, and fourteenth cantos are published in this anthology. See Edoardo Crema, El prodigio del 'Orlando enamorado' by Andrés Bello, Caracas, 1971.

Bello's version and adaptation of the Italian work of Mateo Maria Bojardo (1434-1494), rewritten by Francesco Berni (1497-1535), was developed over a long period of time. He began it in London and reworked it during his years in Chile. It was first published in the Correo del Domingo, Santiago, on April 27, 1862, with an introductory note by Diego Barros Arana explaining the nature of the Italian work and Bello's translation, as follows: "Mr. Andres Bello translated a large portion of Bojardo's poem into Castilian octaves years ago, allowing himself some license which by no means harms the original. He raised the tone of its descriptions to better conform to the epic, did away with or amended some passages that were too free and placed an introduction written in entirely original octaves at the head of each canto. Apart from this, Bello has done a masterful job of preserving the general style, nature, easy flow of verse and movement of the work.

"Mr. Bello had his manuscript put away with other studies that are still unpublished and had no intention of publishing it during his lifetime. After repeated urgings by some of his friends, he has finally agreed to publish this work of his youth.

"The Orlando innamorato was translated into Castilian verse by Francisco Garrido de Villena and published twice in the sixteenth century. Mr. Bello was familiar with this very rare book only by reference and quotations from it ·by other authors, which reveal the faults of the Spanish translator. Nevertheless, the translations of some of the verses probably coincide. However, the translation whose publication we begin today has nothing to fear in a comparison with the complicated and cumbersome octaves of Garrido de

Villena. Nor do the agile introductions placed by Mr. Bello at the head of each canto admit of comparison with the work of the Spanish translator, who places on stage the Valencian knights most to his liking."

Bello's translation was later printed in a volume entitled <u>El</u> <u>Orlando</u> <u>Enamorado</u> <u>del</u> <u>Conde</u> <u>Mateo</u> <u>María</u> <u>Boyardo,</u> <u>escrito</u> <u>de</u> <u>nuevo</u> <u>por</u> <u>Berni</u> <u>traducido</u> <u>al</u> <u>castellano</u> <u>por</u> <u>don</u> <u>Andrés</u> <u>Bello</u>, Santiago (Imprenta Nacional, Calle de la Moneda, 46), October 1862, p. iii, 249, with an introduction by Diego Barros Arana.

Canto I

I sorely regret
that Rocinante's mighty horseman
failed to revive the glad era
of errant knighthood;
had he done so, iniquity
would be not triumphant,
as it is, nor human society
corrupted by greed, as it is.

For everything today is slave to gain;
where now the daring
that would brave peril and death
to perform a glorious deed?
Our once proud culture is a crust
over a pestilent ferment;
a splendid sepulchre of shining jade
without, a nest of worms within.

What became if the valiant knights
who championed maids and orphans
against treacherous rascals
in wilderness, field and royal court;
who galloped to the farthest reaches,
their sword their passport,
and a fair damsel on their mount
riding scot free behind them?

O happy age! a thousand times blessed!
Not these present times when the man
who would set out to defend justice
(the knight of the Mancha be my witness)
should know the world is his enemy
and that a jail, hospital, cage
or the Peña Pobre de Amadis 1/
will be his only prize.

A captain who shoulders a good cause
and humbly seeks a crowm in return,
who then hears a nation discontent
unhappy with its new monarch,
woe to him should he dare talk back!

Long live the King --
and the hangman's whip be readied!
Still another, a noisy damagogue,
proclaims, "Glory to holy democracy,"
and under his breath he adds,
"A post I want,
for instance, as Minister of State."

Were you alive, noble Roger,
and you, Roland, and you, Cyrongil of Thrace,
you would know how to settle accounts
with all the rascals around us.

But, though gone down to the grave,
O glorious generation of poets,
and the human race burdened with sin
is condemned to live in prose,
let your name not be forgotten,
buried under the same headstone,
but shine clear and fine forever
and our souls therein rejoice.

Canto II

The Jousts

I hear Aristarchus' stern reproof,
"Tis a strange whim to put old stories
to verse that were cherished in the past,
unloved today even by old women and children;
our ears are keener now.
Wrong it is to tell such tales
to our wise age.

"How now a princess in a glade
with a laurel tree her shade,
the bank of a stream her drawing room, and
pretected in her bed not by a lady-in-waiting
but by an outrageously ugly giant?
How now a knight
who slays four monsters in a wink
despite Cervantes and all common sense?"

For this you would rub out
everything I have written?
I say those are nun's scruples.
The best part is yet to come.
What's gone before 'tis not worth a fillip.
Set aside your high-brow ways
and go on with the tale;
things you will find there to your liking.

You will see men so big
that Goliath by comparison was a pigmy,
visit lands not to be found
though you ruin your eyes in Ptolemy,
see sphynxes and griffins

never named in Linnaeus' systema naturae,
dozens of enchanted gardens,
and other wonders galore.
"Quodcumque ostendis mibi sic."
Would I ask you, stupid, to believe it?
Tis the privilege of Parnassus to lie,
and if you don't think so, don't read me
or Ariosto ot Milton ot Tasso
or the great poets of Achilles or of Aeneas
Study instead the commentators of the law,
or take your compass and be off,
and good riddance to you!

And if you like history,
beware that despite a stiff-necked,
stern facade, its talk is illusory;
lies it markets as truths.
Worse still, history ever glorifies
the strong and disparages the weak,
protects tyrants more than peoples.
My lies at least are of another ilk.

Canto XII

Melidor and Floridana

That war is the worst plague
sent into the world by a righteous God
and that plain people are the ones who pay,
is unfortunately evident everyday.
Hundreds and thousands are swallowed up
by the insatiable harpy,
and while all its harm falls on the humble
all its benefits go to the powerful.

Since there is no greater fortune for man
than what a king can provide,
His Majesty, who thinks it his royal burden
to procure the common good,
out of sheer benevolence adds one more land
and another and another to his crown;
let him keep on
and he will make all humanity happy.

Yet another august personnage
also aspires to do the same,
to make other nations his vassals;
this one tugs at one end, that one at the other;
and he who pulls the hardest
and gets the biggest piece
is most deserving of man's applause
and the best and greatest sovereign.

But, honestly, isn't it sad
to see a world torn by inmoral ambition,
wherein strength is the only law?
When will reason resist

the allure of ill-begotten glory
and value the treasures
still to be found in a good man's soul?
Yet if it be so wrong and wicked,
so deceptive for a king
to pursue such a false end
at so much peril and harm to others,
what might be said of a man
paid the wages of an assassin
in someone else's service
who puffs up and vaunts his terrible deeds?

Must blood stream from his hand
so that a man unknown today
can get to be a duke or marshall
and wear on his chest a cross or a star
that proclaims him the tool of a tyrant;
and in exchange for that vain glory
is the people's suffering mockery and jest?

May the soldier who fights for his country
and faith earn eternal glory;
otherwise, o war, may your name
be cursed forever!
Glad I am to detain you awhile,
just the thought of you makes me tremble;
drunken with blood it seems I see you
brandishing the scythe of Death.
Grateful am I for that noble pair,
Reinaldo and Fleur-de-Lis,
whose arrival disrupted
the tragic process of merciless reaping.
I go back to the point where the knight
was offering his arm and sword
to the maiden, and Fleur-de-Lis,
wavering, gave in and accepted him at last.

Canto XIII

The Tower of Poliferno

After listening to the case of the beauteous Fleur-de-Lis
there may be some who think
she deserved her troubles
for her wayward ways,
and that if she had been more sheltered,
merely gone to mass with her duenna,
and, instead of wandering here and there,
had stayed at home spinning and sewing,

She would not be in such peril,
the prey of that semi-human monster;
nor was it wise, when you think of it,
for her to go over hill and dale
hand in hand with the knight of Montalban;
even though the thing was as clean
and natural and honest as could be,

I doubt if anyone you find will believe it.
Turpin says (and he is my witness)
that the subject is touchy,
and that he would not swear
to the honor of Fleur-de-Lis or any of her kind.
As for myself, I neither claim it nor deny it,
I just came from my village and know nothing.

Reinaldo, it is true, was a rascal,
young and handsome to boot...so much the better!
Can there be anything but tender endearments
when a man and woman are alone together?
What's probable is not always so,
nor everything in this world treachery and deceit.
Still, remember what went before.
In your school, Love, I've ever been the loser
and rarely (alas, well you know)
placed gifts on your altar.

Canto XIV

Orlando in Albrace

The Latin philosopher-poet
said that women (I translate not word for word,
for Horace himself forbids it;
and though the same thing
can be said in the same space
in plain English,
'twould be very rude
to the fair sex to do so).

He said that even before Helen,
women were the cause of many fatal wars,
in the time when man, with a long beard
and bushy hair, lived a hazardous life
in caverns and on mountain sides,
and let out his primitive
instincts with shouts and screams;
no kings, no law, no judges or sheriffs.

There were no swords or shields or coats of mail;
the joys of love were fought over
with kicks and flying fists;
our ancestors walked around naked;
but then later things changed; science
and the art of destruction advanced;
the bow, the slingshot, the spear and the sword were
invented.

The law of nations, though just,
as now, spoke a different language;
a strong man, tyrant among the weak,
in his rough and ready way
would claim he could do as he pleased
for he was bolder and hardier.

Said he, "Whoever dare oppose me
will be cut to bits and pieces."
Thus was the talk of law and reason;
a king today (with but few exceptions)
behaves not that way;
when he takes his army to the field,
he must first prove that
a righteous cause protects him.
Any man would be a fool who could not do that
in this wise nineteenth century of ours.

Nor were later heroines
the same as Aspasia and Lucretia;
thick-necked, broad-shouldered, fleshy,
feet calloused from so much walking;
and something of coarseness and folly
were thought elegant and winning ways;
and healthy, chubby tots tugged
merrily at the maternal udder.

This primitive instinct was what
made huts burn one day, an early Troy;
the river ran red with blood
and the dynasty was changed.
Another kind of men prevailed
here and there; Greek fantasy
depicted its own in living bronze;
but were they any better than those who went before?

I think a hunchback not a thing of beauty,
and that a man without a nose is no Apollo;
too, a bald head is ugly, no matter where;
I also go along with the popular idea
that two eyes are better than one,
Those are my thoughts on beauty,
As to the rest, I am not sure.

But whatever the canons of beauty
of an age may be;
whatever words are used
to praise and patronize it;
the mischievous god of love
(Solomon who said so,
is its own best proof)
always gets the best of intelligence and reason.

NOTE

1. Allusions to the Quijote and the Amadis de Gaula, a 16th century
    novel of chilvalry (T).

MISERERE

(Translation of Psalm 50)

This version from the Latin was first published
in Juicio crítico de algunos poetas sudamericanos, by
Miguel Luis and Gregorio Víctor Amunátegui Aldunate,
Santiago, 1861.

Miserere mei, Deus,
secundum magnam misericordiam tuam.
Et secundum multitudinem
miserationum tuarum, dele iniquitatem meam.
Amplius lava me ab iniquitate mea;
et a peccato meo munda me.
Quoniam iniquitatem meam ego cognosco;
et peccatum meum contra me est semper.
Tibi soli peccavi,
et malum coram te feci;
ut justificeris in sermonibus tuis,
et vincas cum judicaris.
Ecce enim in iniquitatibus conceptus sum;
et in peccatis concepit me mater mea.
Ecce enim veritatem dilexisti;
incerta et occulta sapientiae tuae manifestasti mihi.
Asperges me hyssopo, et mundabor;
lavabis me, et super nivem dealbabor.
Auditui meo dabis gaudium et laetitiam;
et exultabunt ossa humiliata.
Averte faciem tuam a peccatis meis:
et omnes iniquitates meas dele.
Cor mundum crea in me, Deus:
et spiritum rectum innova in visceribus meis.
Ne projicias me a facie tua:
et spiritum sanctum tuum ne auferas a me.
Redde mihi laetitiam salutaris tui:
et spiritu principali confirma me.
Docebo iniquos vias tuas:
et impii ad e convertentur.
Libera me de sanguinibus, Deus, Deus salutis meae;
et exultabit lingua mea justitiam tuam.
Domine, labia mea aperies;
et os meum annuntiabit laudem tuam.
Quoniam si voluisses sacrificium, dedissem utique;
holocaustis non delectaberis.
Sacrificium Deo spiritus contribulatus;

cor contritum et humiliatum, Deus, non despicies.
Benigne fac, Domine, in bona voluntate tua Sion;
ut aedificentur muri Jerusalem.
Tunc acceptabis sacrificium justitiae, oblationes, et
   holocausta;
tunc imponent super altare tuum vitulos.

RUDENS or THE ROPE [1]

(Translation of Plautus. Prologue)

Miguel Luis Amunátegui published the prologue of Bello's translation of the Rudens in his introduction to Bello's poetry, Santiago, 1883. The 119-verse prologue, read in Amunátegui's words "from among a handful of papers of all sizes written with erasures instead of letters," is all that has been published in the past. Menéndez Pelayo regretted not seeing it printed in its entirety, "What a pity no one can decipher the Rudens manuscript." (Caro, Epistolario, Bogotá, 1941, p. 255).

The date of the manuscript can be fixed fairly accurately at 1849, both because the handwriting matches other texts of that time and because some of the manuscript scraps have a date on them. One passage is written on the back of a letter written to Bello by José M. Núñez on April 19, 1849; another piece is on the back and in the empty spaces of a printed invitation to the presentation of prizes at the Minvielle School in Santiago, signed by Rafael Minvielle on April 18, 1849.

ARCTVRVS

.

Qui gentis omnis mariaque et terras mouet,
Eius sum ciuis ciuitate caelitum
Ita sum ut uidetis splendens stella candida,
Signum quod semper tempore exoritur suo.
Hic atque in caelo nomen Arcturost mihi.
Noctu sum in caelo clarus atque inter deos,
Inter mortalis ambulo clam interdius.
Et alia signa de caelo ad terram accidunt:
Quist imperator diuom atque hominum Iuppiter,
Is nos per gentis aliud alia disparat,
Qui facta hominum moresque, pietatem et fidem
Noscamus, ut quemque adiuuet opulentia.
Qui falsas litis falsis testimoniis
Petunt quique in iure abiurant pecuniam,
Eorum referimus nomina exscripta ad Iouem.

Cotidie ille scit quis hic quaerat malum.
Qui hic litem apisci postulant peiurio
Mali, res falsas qui inpetrant apud iudicem,
Iterum ille eam rem iudicatam iudicat:
Maiore multa multat quam litem auferunt.
Bonos in aliis tabulis exscriptos habet.
Atque hoc scelesti si in animum inducunt suom,
Iouem se placare posse donis, hostiis,
Et operam et sumptum perdunt. id eo fit, quia

Nihil ei acceptumst a periuris supplici
Facilius si qui pius est a dis supplicans
Quam qui scelestust inueniet ueniam sibi.
Idcirco moneo uos ego haec, qui estis boni
Quique aetatem agitis cum pietate et cum fide:
. . . .
Retinete porro, post factum ut laetemini
Nunc, huc qua causa ueni, argumentum eloquar.
      Primumdum huic esse nomen urbi Diphilus
Cyrenas uoluit illic habitat Daemones
In agro atque uilla proxuma propter mare,
Senex qui huc Athenis exul uenit, hau malus.
Neque is adeo propter malitiam patria caret,
Sed dum alios seruat, se inpediuit interim:
Rem bene paratam comitate perdidit.
Huic filiola una uirgo periit paruola:
Eam de praedone uir mercatur pessumus:
Is eam huc Cyrenas leno aduexit uirginem.
Adulescens quidam ciuis huius Atticus
Eam uidit ire e ludo fidicinio domum.
Amare occepit: ad lenonem deuenit,
Minis triginta sibi puellam destinat
Datque arrabonem et iureiurando adligat.
Is leno, ut se aequomst, flocci non fecit fidem
Neque quod iuratus adulescenti dixerat.
Ei erat quidam hospes par sui, Siculus senex
Scelestus Agrigentinus, urbis proditor:
Is illius laudare infit formam uirginis
Et aliarum itidem quae eius erant mulierculae.
Infit lenoni suadere, ut secum simul
Eat in Siciliam: ibi esse homines uoluptarios
Dicit: potesse diuitem ibi eum fieri.
Ibi esse quaestum maxumum meretricibus.
Persuadet. nauis clanculum conducitur.
Quidquid erat, noctu in nauem conportat domo
Leno: adulescenti, qui puellam ab eo emerat,
Ait sese Veneri uelle uotum soluere
---Id hic est Veneris fanum---atque adeo ad prandium
Vocauit adulescentem huc. ipse hinc ilico
Conscendit nauem atque auehit meretriculas.
Adulescenti alii narrant ut res gesta sit:
Lenonem abisse. ad portum adulescens quom uenit,
Illorum nauis longe in altum apscesserat.
Ego quoniam uideo uirginem asportarier,
Tetuli et ei auxilium et lenoni exitium simul:
Increpui hibernum et fluctus moui maritumos.
Nam Arcturus signum sum omnium unum acerrumum:
Vehemens sum exoriens, quom occido uehementior.
Nunc ambo, leno atque hospes, in saxo simul

Sedent eiecti: nauis confractast eis.
Illa autem uirgo atque altera itidem ancillula
De naui timidae desuluerunt in scapham.
Nunc eas ab saxo fluctus ad terram ferunt
Ad uillam illius, exul ubi habitat senex,
Quoius deturbauit uentus tectum et tegulas.
Sed seruos illic est eius qui egreditur foras.
Adulescens huc iam adueniet, quem uidebitis,
Qui illam mercatust de lenone uirginem.
Valete, ut hostes uostri diffidant sibi.

NOTE

1. From The Rudens of Plautus, with an English translation by
    Cleveland K. Chase, Clinton, N.Y., 1919.

THE NIBELUNGS [1]
(Translation. Fragment)

Bello translated only this fragment of the *Nibelungs*, which belongs to the first two adventures, "The Dream of Kriemhild" and "Siegfrid" (verses 97–142). There are two manuscripts of the translation, which according to the handwriting are of rather distant intervals. One is from the time Bello lived in London, prior to 1829, the other, ca. 1849, after he went to Santiago.

Bello did not finish or polish the translation, particularly from verse 97 on, which accounts for the indecision even in proper names (Jilesar vs. Giselar and Segismundo vs. Sigismundo in the Spanish version). Some of the verses are also incomplete, which breaks the rime. We have left the manuscript untouched.

(First Adventure, Kriemhild's Dream)

In stories of our fathers high marvels we are told
Of champions well approved in perils manifold.
Of feasts and merry meetings, of weeping and of wail,
And deeds of gallant daring I'll tell you in my tale.

In Burgundy there flourish'd a maid so fair to see,
That in all the world together a fairer could not be.
This maiden's name was Kriemhild; through her in dismal strife
Full many a prowest warrior thereafter lost his life. 2/

Many a fearless champion, as such well became,
Woo'd the lovely lady; she from none had blame,
Matchless was her person, matchless was her mind.
This one maiden's virtue grac'd all womankind.

Three puissant Kings her guarded with all the care they might,
Gunther and eke Gernot, each a redoubted knight,
And Giselher the youthful, a chosen champion he;
This lady was their sister, well lov'd of all the three.

73

At Worms was their proud dwelling, the Rhine fair flowing by,
There had they suit and service from haughtiest chivalry
For broad lands and lordships, and glorious was their state,
Till wretchedly they perish'd by two noble ladies' hate.
Dame Uta ws their mother, a queen both rich and sage;
Their father hight Dancrat, who the fair heritage
Left to his noble children when he his course had run;
He too by deeds of knighthood in youth had worship won.

A dream was dreamt by Kriemhild the virtuous and gay,
How a wild young falcon she train'd for many a day,
Till two fierce eagles tore it; to her there could not be
In all the world such sorrow as this perforce to see.

To her mother Uta at once the dream she told,
But she the threatening future could only thus unfold;
"The falcon that thou trainedst is sure a noble mate;
God shield him in his mercy, or thou must lose him straight."

"A mate for me? what say'st thou, dearest mother mine?
Ne'er to love, assure thee, my heart will I resign.
I'll live and die a maiden, and end as I began,
Nor (let what else befall me) will suffer woe for man."

Nay, said her anxious mother, "renounce not marriage so;
would'st thou true heartfelt pleasure taste ever here below,
Man's love alone·can give it. Thou'rt fair as eye can see,
A fitting mate God send thee, and nought will wanting be."
"No more," the maiden answer'd, "no more, dear mother, say;
From many a woman's fortune this truth is clear as day,
That falsely smiling Pleasure with Pain requites us ever,
I from both will keep me, and thus will sorrow never."

So in her lofty virtues, fancy-free and gay,
Liv'd the noble maiden many a happy day,
Nor one more than another found favour in her sight;
Still at the last she wedded a far-renowned knight.

He was the self-same falcon she in her dream had seen,
Foretold by her wise mother. What vengeance took the queen
On her nearest kinsmen who him to death had done!
That single death atoning died many a mother's son.

(Second Adventure. Of Siegfried)

In Netherland then flourish'd a prince of lofty kind
(Whose father hight Siegmund, his mother Siegelind)
In a sumptuous castle down by the Rhine's fair side;
Men did call it Xanten; 't was famous far and wide.

I tell you of this warrior, how fair he was to see;
From shame and dishonour liv'd he ever free.
Forthwith fierce and famous wax'd the mighty man.
Ah! what height of worship in this world he wan!
Siegfried men did call him, that same champion good;
Many a kingdom sought he in his manly mood,
And through strength of body in many a land rode he.
Ah! what men of valour he found in Burgundy!

74

Before this noble champion grew up to man's estate,
His hand had mighty wonders achiev'd in war's debate,
Whereof the voice of rumour will ever sing and say,
Though much must pass in silence in this our later day.

In his freshest season, in his youthful days,
One might full many a marvel tell in Siegfried's praise,
What lofty honours grac'd and how fair his fame,
How he charm'd to love him many a noble dame.

As did well befit, him, he was bred with care,
And his own lofty nature gave him virtues rare,
From him his father's country grace and honour drew,
To see him prov'd in all things so noble and so true.

He now, grown up to youthhead, at court his duty paid;
The people saw him gladly; many a wife and many a maid
Wish'd he would often thither, and bide for ever there;
They view'd him all with favour, whereof he well was ware.

The child by his fond parents was deck'd with weeds of pride,
And but with guards about him they seldom let him ride,
Untrain'd was he by sages, who what was honour knew,
So might he win full lightly broad lands and liegemen too.

Now had he strength and stature that weapons well he bore;
Whatever thereto needed, he had of it full store.
He began fair ladies to his love to woo,
And they inclin'd to Siegfried with faith and honour true.

Then had his father Siegmund all his liegemen tell,
With his dear friends to revel it would please him well.
Where other kings were dwelling the tidings took their course.

NOTES

1. From The Fall of the Nibelungers, an English verse translation
   by William Nanson Lettsom, London, 1850. There is no record of
   the source translation for Bello's own rendition into Spanish.
   He himself knew no German and presumably worked from either and
   English or French version.
   Bello may well have been familiar with an English translation of
   parts of the Nibelungs which appeared in Weber and Jamieson's
   Illustrations of Northern Antiquity, Edinburgh, 1814. This was
   the only one published in English during his London years. It
   is probably safe to conjecture that he knew of Carlyle's
   translation of some of the strophes, published in the
   Westminister Review in 1831, later included in Critical and
   Miscellaneous Writings, II, Boston, 1838. A full translation in
   French, by Mme. Ch. Moureau de la Meltière, came out in 1837 in
   Paris. The first complete translation into English, from the
   German edition by the scholar Karl Lachmann (Berlin, 1826), was

published in Berlin in 1848 by Jonathan Birch, the pen name of an English clergyman. This was followed by Lettsom's more widely accepted translation two years later (T).

2. Carlyle translated the first two strophes as follows:

We find in ancient story, Wonders many told
Of heroes in great glory, With spirit free and bold
Of joyances, and high-tides Of weeping and of woe,
Of noble Reckon striving Mote ye now wonders know.

A right noble maiden did grow in Burgundy,
That in all lands of earth Nough Fairer mote there be;
Chriemhild of Wormans she hight; She was a fairest wife;
For the which must warriors a many lose their life.

II. PROSE

A. The Language

IDEOLOGICAL ANALYSIS OF THE TENSES
IN SPANISH CONJUGATIONS
Prologue

Bello's study was first published in Valparaíso
in 1841 by M. Rivadeneyra in pamphlet form. A reprint
with notes by Juan Vicente González was published by
Imprenta Corser in Caracas in 1850, the same edition
was reproduced by Leocadio Gómez in Madrid in 1883.

For an appraisal of Bello's study, see
"Introducción a los estudios gramaticales de Andrés
Bello" by Amado Alonso, in Bello's <u>Obras</u> <u>completas</u>,
Vol. IV, Caracas, 1851.

As to its date, we have only Bello's own words
when it was published in 1841 to the effect that he had
had it "buried" for more than thirty years. It must
therefore be earlier than 1810, the date of his
departure from Caracas when he was twenty eight. This
means it was a work of his youth, yet "the most
original and profound of his linguistic studies,"
according to Marcelino Menéndez Pelayo.

I reproduce the prologue.

To the director and teachers of
the National Institute of Chile
The author

After the work of Condillac, Beauzée, and other eminent
philosophers on verbal analysis, a desire to base that part of
grammatical theory on principles other than those recommended by
them will seem either presumptuous or foolhardy. I urge you,
however, to consider these principles of mine with an open mind,
deciding whether they explain these seemingly complicated and
irregular parts of speech satisfactorily, and whether the same can
be said of the others. Whatever enlightened decision is made I
shall accept.

Misgivings that my theory, once studied carefully, might be
considered groundless or inaccurate do not trouble me. In it, or at
least in its basic principles, I believe I see all the makings of

truth and soundness; and while I realize what appeal the illusions of the imagination have, I still hold firmly to a conviction born of an earlier study and consistently confirmed by the later observations of many years. What I fear is that my readers may lack the patience to accompany me through all the details of a necessarily meticulous analysis and hasten to reject it without having understood it.

There will also be many who will consider this analysis inapplicable to the general study of Spanish grammar. I think otherwise. Notwithstanding the fact that reading good authors gives certain exceptional minds a sensitivity that frees them from the study of rules; notwithstanding the fact that the very analogical instinct that creates language is often enough to show proper sentence structure and proper usage of noun and verb inflections.

I believe many errors would be avoided and the written language would be used more accurately and precisely if greater attention were given to what happens in the mind when we speak. A subject which, apart from its practical value, is interesting philosophically because of the subtle mental processes it reveals, unimaginable in the everyday use of a language.

Few things help more to develop the faculties of the mind, to make them quicker and more nimble, than the philosophic study of language. Learning a language has been mistakenly construed to be the work of memory alone. A sentence cannot be constructed nor one language translated into another without delving into the most intimate relationships of ideas, without making a microscopic examination, so to speak, of their accidents and changes. Nor is this type of study so devoid of appeal as those unfamiliar with it think.

The subtle, fleeting analogies on which the selections of verbal forms hinges (the same might be said of other parts of speech), rests on a marvellous chain of metaphysical relationships bound together with surprising order and precision, when one considers how totally indebted they are to popular usage, the one and only maker of language. The meanings of verbal inflections appear to be haphazard, everything seemingly arbitrary, irregular and subject to whim. But under the light of analysis the apparent disarray vanishes and in its place emerges a system of general rules susceptible to statement in strict formulae, that can be combined and taken apart like those of algebra and that operate with absolute uniformity.

This is precisely what led me to think that the only bonafide value of verb forms, as far as their temporal meaning is concerned, is the one I give them, the only one that faithfully represents the facts, i.e., the different uses of verb inflections as practiced by correct speakers. No explanation can be credible when each piece of data is separate and independent, serving itself alone, and the data as a whole have no common bond uniting them in a dynamic relationship, and when the exceptions are constantly at odds with the rules.

As soon as all data work together smoothly, anomalies disappear, and variety is understood to be nothing more than unity transformed in accordance with constant laws, then we are entitled to think the problem has been resolved and we have a real theory, i.e., an intellectual vision of reality. Truth is essentially harmonious.

Convinced that the difficult, yet interesting explanation I plan to make of language, rests on firm ground, I decided to remove this work from the darkness where I had it buried for more than thirty years and to publish it after a severe revision during which some illustrations were added and a few changes made. I am encouraged by the hope that sooner or later people of intelligence will examine it and perhaps adopt and improve upon its ideas.

I again urge those who read this analysis not to condemn it hastily before they have understood it. Objections will occur in the very first pages that will later be satisfactorily resolved. At least, I hope so. The nomenclature will seem strange; but if the reader finds it has the merit of providing in each name a full definition, more than a definition, a formula in which the mental actions for which each verb tense is a sign by the combination and arrangements of the parts, I flatter myself that they will judge it preferable to the ones given in our grammars.

This analysis of the tenses is limited specifically to Spanish conjugations, but I am certain its method and principles are applicable with some changes to other languages and have given examples of this in some of the notes accompanying the text.

INDICATIONS ON THE CONVENIENCE OF SIMPLIFYING AND STANDARDIZING ORTHOGRAPHY IN AMERICA

This article was first published over the signature of G. R. and A. B., the initials of Juan García del Río and Andrés Bello, in the Biblioteca Americana, London, 1823, pp. 50-62, and reprinted in Repertorio Americano, London, October 1826, vol. I, pp. 27-41, with some additions and changes. I reproduce the second version.

The reader may consult the study by Angel Rosenblat entitled "Las ideas ortográficas de Bello," the prologue to Obras completas, vol. V, Caracas, 1951, and "La ortografía de Don Andrés Bello," a report of the editorial commission written by Oscar Sambrano Urdaneta, in Revista Nacional de Cultura, No. 74, Caracas, May-June, 1949.

One of the most interesting studies for man is the language of his native land. Its cultivation and improvement constitute the foundation of all intellectual advancement. Minds are molded by tongues, the author of Emile tells us, and thoughts tinted the color of language.

Following the Spanish conquest of the New World, the Indian languages have gradually perished, and though some are still preserved integrally among the independent tribes, including those touched by civilization, Spanish is the prevailing tongue in the new nations formed from the dismemberment of the Spanish monarchy and doubtless will gradually force all others to disappear.

The cultivation of Spanish partook of every flaw in the educational system of the times. While awkward to say so, among the majority of the American population admittedly not five in a hundred knew their own language grammatically and hardly anyone could write it correctly. Such was the effect of the plan adopted by the court in Madrid for its colonial possessions, and indeed the inevitable result of Spain's own backwardness.

Among the means of polishing a language and expanding and universalizing all branches of enlightenment, few are more important than simplifying orthography. Upon this rests the more or less easy acquisition of the two primary skills on which all the edifice of literature and science rests, reading and writing. According to the Spanish Academy, orthography enhances a language, preserves its elegance, specifies the true pronunciation and meaning of words, and clarifies the meaning of the written word, making the written language a true and safe repository for law, art, science, and all thought left to posterity by educated men and scholars in every profession. From the importance of orthography springs the need to simplify it. The plan or method that should be followed in making changes for this purpose is the subject of the present article.

We do not have the temerity to think the reforms suggested by us will be adopted at once. We know full well the prerogatives of prejudice and habit, yet nothing is lost by mentioning and submitting them now for discussion by thinking people so they may be amended if need be or their introduction hastened, and the way paved for the literary bodies that must set new educational directions in the Americas.

For the purpose of furthering the reforms mentioned, we shall examine the methods used by several writers of the Academy itself, following the latest 1820 edition of the treatise on Spanish orthography 1/, and therefrom deduce our own.

Antonio de Nebrija laid down the orthographic principle that each letter must have a distinctive sound and each sound be represented by one letter alone. All orthographic change should move in that direction. Putting Nebrija's idea into practice, Mateo Alemán made pronunciation the only standard for writing, to the exclusion of usage and origin.

Juan López de Velasco set off in another direction. Believing that pronunciation alone should not prevail and following Quintilian's advice that "nisi quod consuetudo obtinuerit, sic scribendum quidque judico quomodo sonat," 2/ he stipulated that the language should be written as simply and naturally as it is spoken, yet without unsavory innovations. Gonzalo Correas, however, spurning this encroachment of custom as authority (not without reason), set out to correct one of the most awkward irregularities in the Spanish alphabet by substituting k for hard c and q. Other ancient and modern writers have recommended further changes. All concur in the aim of making Spanish writing uniform and easy, but opinions have varied on the means.

As to the Spanish Academy, we regard its work as indeed remarkable. Comparing the status of Spanish writing when the Academy first set out to simplify it with its present situation, we are at a loss as to what to praise most, whether the openmindedness (a quite different spirit from that which generally inspires these bodies) with which the Academy sponsored and introduced helpful changes itself, or public meekness in adopting them both in the Peninsula and abroad.

Its first work of this kind, as the Academy itself tells us, was the prologue to the first volume of its Dictionary; since then, it has been gradually simplifying writing in the several editions of its Orthography. We do wonder whether it might not have been well to introduce all the changes at once, raising the alphabet to the peak of perfection of which it is capable and making it wholly consistent with the principles of Nebrija and Mateo Alemán.

What certainly would have been desirable was for all the editions to have followed a consistent, uniform plan, and for each innovation to have been a step in the direction of the goal envisaged, without pointless detours. But we must remind ourselves that the transactions of this kind of body cannot be so systematic nor its principles so stable as those of an individual. Thus, giving the Academy its due for the good it has done and for the general direction of its efforts, its shortcomings must rightly be regarded as inherent to the nature of a philological society.

In 1754, the Academy added (in its own words) a few letters peculiar to the language that had been omitted earlier and were needed to complete the alphabet. It also made other changes deemed desirable to make writing easier by lessening dependence on origins. In the third edition of 1763, it stipulated the rules governing accents and did away with the double s. In the four successive editions of 1770, 1775, 1779, and 1792, it did nothing but augment the list of words whose spelling was uncertain.

In 1803, the Academy made way for the letters ll and ch in the alphabet as representatives of the sounds pronounced in llama, chopo; and eliminated ch when it had the value of k, as in christiano, chimera, using c or q instead, accordingly, and doing away with the circumflex accent that for purposes of differentiation used to be placed over the following vowel. It also banished ph and k; and to soften pronunciation omitted some letters in words where usage so indicated, such as b in substancia, obscuro; n in transponer, etc., and substituted s for x in others, as in extraño, extranjero.

The 1815 edition (identical to the 1820 edition) added other important changes, such as the unqualified use of c in combinations with the sound of ca, co, cu, bequeathing q merely to combinations que, qui in which u is mute. The diaeresis used for purposes of differentiation in eloqüencia, qüestion and similar words thus became superfluous. This innovation was a big step (though we wonder whether it might have been preferable to do away with the mute u in quema, queso. But we feel it was inconsistent and erratic to omit only the initial or middle harsh x, as in xarabe, xefe, exido, and retain it in the final position as in almoradux, relox, where its value is the same.

Worst of all was the substitution of g for x before the vowels e, i only, otherwise j. Why this gratuitous variety of usage? Why not substitute j, such a convenient letter because of its uniform value, for harsh x before every vowel instead of g, an equivocal, awkward sign that sometimes has one sound and others another? The Academy system tends manifestly to do away with g itself when it equals j; therefore, the new practice of writing gerga, gícara is a superfluous stage, a step that could have been avoided by writing jerga, jícara once and for all. The other changes were to do away with the circumflex accent in examen, existo, etc., because of the unified value x began to have in this position; and writing (with some seemingly unnecessary exceptions) i insted of y when the letter was a vowel, as in ayre, peyne.

The Academy observes that a great drawback to improving orthography is the irregular pronunciation of c and g combinations and syllables with other vowels, and that this is why children have trouble learning to syllable. Even so, it does not correct this anomaly. Antonio de Nebrija wanted to leave the sound and function of k and q to c; Gonzalo Correas endeavored to give this to k at the expense of the others; other writers endeavored to give the less harsh sound to g and pass on all hard guttural pronunciation to j. This would avoid the use of u when mute, as in guerra (gerra), and the diaeresis in others, as in vergüenza (verguenza). The Academy, however, says that in such a far-reaching reform, it preferred to allow learned use to lead the way and to authorize it at a later, better time.

This circumspect procedure is perhaps inevitable in a body zealous of protecting its sway over public opinion, the individual is in a position to be bolder, and when his use coincides with the progressive plan of the Academy, already authorized by general consensus, it cannot be said this freedom causes confusion. Quite the contrary, it paves the way and hastens the time when standardized writing in Spain and the Americas will display a degree of perfection now unknown anywhere in the world.

The Academy laid down three fundamental principles for the development of orthographic rules: pronunciation, regular use, and origin. Of these, the only essential, bonafide one is the first, the concurrence of the other two is an irrelevance that could only be tolerated for the sake of necessity.

The very Academy that allows them contains contradictions in more than one page of its treatise. In one place it says that none of the rules is so general as to be invariable; that pronunciation does not always govern how words should be written; that usage is not always common and regular; that origin is often not a straightforward matter. In another place, that pronunciation is a principle deserving more attention because with writing being the image of words and words the mirror of thought, it seems that there should be the closest correlation between letters and sounds and, consequently, writing should resemble speech and pronunciation. In one place, it states Spanish has broad discrepancies in writing, mainly because bad habits and poor learning or incorrect instruction in principles have led to confusion in pronunciation of some letters with others, such as b and v, and c and g; j and g also sound alike. In other passages, it states that pronunciation makes it difficult to know whether vaso should be written with b or v, and that the way they are pronounced the words vivir, vez, could be written with b.

Of words taken from other tongues, some (according to the Academy) have retained their original characters, others have dropped them and assumed those of the adopted language; even words from old Spanish have undergone change. It likewise says that many times origin cannot be the general rule, especially in the present state of the language, because gentle pronunciation or force of habit has prevailed.

Finally, the Academy says that correct writing poses many problems because pronunciation or a knowledge of etymology is not enough but common, regular usage to the contrary must also be determined, in which case (it adds) this must prevail as the arbiter of language. These problems, however, largely disappear and the way to orthographic reform will become clear if we recall what the craft of writing and the object of orthography are.

The highest degree of perfection in writing and the goal towards which all change should aim is a precise correlation between the elemental sounds of a language and the signs or letters used to represent them, so that each elemental sound has one letter standing for it invariably and each letter stands just as invariably for one sound.

Some languages cannot aspire to this ultimate degree of orthographic perfection. While tolerating sound transitions, and, if the term is admissible, half-tones (which are essentially a large number of elemental sounds), a great many new letters would have to be introduced in order to perfect their orthography and a new alphabet formed, quite different from the one they have today, an undertaking to be regarded as impossible. In the absence of this expedient, the values of their letters have been multiplied, and false dipthongs, i.e., complex signs representing simple sounds, developed. English and French are in this position.

Fortunately, one of the qualities of Spanish is that it has few, well differentiated and distinct elemental sounds. It is perhaps the only European language with no more elemental sounds than letters. Thus, the way to orthographic change is clear and evident: <u>if a sound is represented by more than two letters, select the one that represents that sound alone and substitute it for the others</u>.

Etymology is the great source of confusion in all European alphabets. One of the greatest absurdities that could have been introduced into the craft of drawing letters is the rule that says we must define their origin in order to put them on paper. What is more senseless than to make the pronunciation of peoples who lived two or three thousand years ago the norm for the written word of today, meaning our pronunciation will apparently be the lodestar for the orthography of people two or three thousand years hence? Looking up its etymology to see how to write a word is really nothing else. Let no one reply this is done only when the sound allows freedom of choice between two or three letters. Do away, reason dictates, with superfluous signs and salvage only the ones that deserve preference because of their unity of value.

Assuming we always knew the etymology of words with different spellings in order to write them accordingly, the spelling suggested by word origin would still be misleading. Anyone seeing <u>philosophia</u> who thought it was written that way by the Greeks would be roundly mistaken. The Greeks wrote the sound ph with a single letter which may have originated <u>f</u>. So by writing <u>filosofía</u> we are much closer to the original word and not the way the Romans were forced to do it because of their different <u>f</u> sound.

The same applies to <u>Acheos</u>, <u>Achiles</u>, <u>Melchisedech</u>. Neither the Greeks nor the Hebrews wrote <u>ch</u> because that sound was represented with a single specific letter. What grounds in etymology do people have then who say Hebrew or Greek words should be written the way the Romans did? As far as <u>usage</u> is concerned, we call this standard abusive when it conflicts with reason and the convenience of people who read and write. Some will clamor against changes so obviously suggested by the nature and purpose of writing, alleging <u>they are ugly</u>, <u>that</u> <u>they</u> <u>are</u> <u>offensive</u> <u>to</u> <u>the</u> <u>eye</u> and that <u>they</u> <u>are</u> <u>shocking</u>. As if a single letter could be becoming in some combinations and unbecoming in others!

All these statements, if they have any sense at all, merely mean that what they set out to reprove is something new! What does it matter if something is new if it is useful and desirable? Why must we force something that could be improved to stay the same? If what was useful had always been rejected because it was new, what would the present state of the written language be? Instead of writing letters, we would be drawing hieroglyphics or tying quipu knots.

Etymology and the rule of custom should not work against substituting a letter that most naturally or most genuinely represents a sound, provided the new practice does not conflict with the established values of the letter or letter combinations. For example, j is the most natural letter for the initial sound in the words jarro, genio, giro, joya, justicia, and has no other value in Castilian, a claim that cannot be made on behalf of g or x. Then why not always write this sound with j? For the uneducated, it makes no difference whether we write genio or jenio. Only learned men will find the innovation odd, but they will approve of it if they consider how it will help simplify the art of reading and stabilize writing. They know the Romans wrote genio because they pronounced guenio, and will acknowledge that once we changed the sound we should also have changed the sign used to represent it. But it is still not too late, for nothing stands in the way of substituting j for g in such instances except the etymology, which few people are familiar with, and the special use of certain vowels, which should be subordinated to more general usage in the language.

The same is true of initial z in zalema, cebo, cinco, zorro, zumo. But even though c in Spanish is the most natural sign for the initial consonant sound in casa, quema, quinto, copla, cuna, we still think it cannot take the place of the combination qu when u is mute before e or i because this new value of c would conflict with the use already assigned it in front of those vowels. It would only cause confusion to write arrance, escilmo instead of arranque, esquilmo.

It would seem most appropriate then to begin by making an exclusive province of z the soft sound it now shares with c, and once the public (the illiterate public, with whom most care should be taken) becomes used to pronouncing c like k at all times, then will be the time to substitute it for the combination qu, unless the complete elimination of c is preferable (and perhaps it would have been best), replacing it with q in the hard sound and z in the soft sound.

Likewise, g is the natural sign for the ga, gue, gui, go, gu sound, but even so we cannot substitute g for the combination gu when u is mute because of the conflict with the value of j before the vowels e, i. It is best then at the start never to use g with the value of j.

Another feasible reform is the removal of h (except of course in the ch combination), and of mute u accompanying q; the substitution of i for y whenever y is not a consonant, and the rr to represent the hard sound in rrasón, prórroga, reserving the single r for the soft sound found in arar, querer. Another reform, though one for which the way must be paved, is to delete mute u after g before e, i.

Let us take note in passing how much usage in the language has changed with respect to these letters. The writers of old (and we cite them to defend what they condemned rather than continue the wise reforms they started) had almost done away with the unvoiced h by writing ombre, ora, onor. Thus, Alfonso X, who began each of his Partidas with a letter from his name (Alfonso), started the fourth one with the word ome (inadvertently written home by the editors, according to Tomás Antonio Sánchez). Later scholastic pedantry, which is worse than ignorance, instead of imitating the writers of old and banishing the superfluous sign once and for all, instead of relying on reason as earlier writers had done and not the vain ambition of displaying their Latin, restored the h even in words where it had long been forgotten.

We have made y a sort of short i using it as a subjunctive vowel in dipthongs (ayre, peyne) and in the conjunction y. Conversely, medieval writers frequently used it as an initial letter, writing yba, yra, from which the practice may have evolved of using it as a capital i in handwritten documents. This practice was admittedly outrageous yet its modern substitute is no better.

As to the initial rr, we see no reason to condemn it. Writers of old doubled no initial consonants, nor do we. The rr, visibly a double consonant, actually stands for a sound that cannot be split in two and should be regarded as a single one, no different than ch, ñ, ll. Had those who reproach the innovation lived five or six centuries ago, and been so inclined, we would write levar, lamar, lorar today on the pretext of not doubling an initial consonant, and our written language would be indebted to them for one more complication.

We now submit our draft reforms to the enlightened sectors of the American public, in the order we believe they should be introduced:

First Epoch:

1. Substitute j for x and g whenever x and g have the guttural Arab sound.
2. Substitute i for y whenever the latter is merely a vowel.
3. Eliminate h.
4. Write with rr all syllables having the strong sound pertaining to this letter.
5. Substitute z for soft c.
6. Do away with mute u after q.

Second Epoch:

7. Substitute q for hard c.
8. Eliminate mute u after g.

Some will wonder why we fail to substitute simple signs for the two sounds supposedly represented by x and write ecsordio, ecsamen, or eqsordio, eqsamen. But we are not certain the x breaks down precisely into either cs, as almost everyone claims or gs (perhaps closer to the truth), as thought by a few. If we are to believe our ears, we would say the x stands for an incipient reciprocal change of the two elemental sounds and that the former particularly is much softer than the regular c̲, k̲ or q̲ sound and rather closely resembles g̲.

In the past x̲ equalled c̲s̲ but also in the past z̲ equalled d̲s̲; z̲ has so weakened that no trace of a compound sound remains; x̲, unless we are mistaken, has begun to weaken in a like manner. Orthography, whose purpose is not to correct pronunciation but to be its bonafide representative, should, if we do not deceive ourselves, keep this letter. But this is a point which we submit willingly not to scholars but to keen observers who trust their prejudices no more than their ears.

It is our contention that once this system is fully installed, the number of letters in the alphabet should be cut from the twenty-seven the Academy indicated in the publication mentioned earlier to twenty-six, and their names changed as follows:

A, B, CH, D, E, F, G, I, J, L, LL, M, N,
a, be, che, de, e, fe, gue, i, je, le, lle, me, ne,

Ñ, O, P, Q, R, RR, S, T, U, V, X, Y, Z.
ñe, o, pe, cu, ere, rre, se, te, u, ve, exe, ye, ze.

The letters c̲ and h̲ would thus be removed from our alphabet, the former because it is ambiguous and the latter because it has no meaning; mute u̲ and use of the diaresis would be out; the r̲ and r̲r̲ sounds would be represented with appropriate distinction and clarity; and the consonants g̲, x̲, y̲ would each have the same value consistently. The only area left for observing etymology and usage would be the choice between b̲ and v̲, a matter not within the jurisdiction of orthography as such but of orthoepy, because the latter has the exclusive function of indicating proper pronunciation, while that of orthography is to depict it.

In order for the simplification of writing to further, in so far as possible, the art of reading, the names of the letters would have to be changed as we have done, because acting as a guide for those beginning to syllable, the name itself of each letter must be a reminder of the value each combination of syllables should be given.

In naming the letters we have also discounted the usual difference between those that are mute and semivocal, which is of no use nor is there any basis for it in the sounds themselves nor in our customs. We call initial consonants b̲e̲, c̲h̲e̲, f̲e̲, l̲l̲e̲, etc. (with no initial e̲) and e̲r̲e̲ and e̲x̲e̲ (initial e̲) ones that can never begin a word nor, consequently, a syllable. The result is that when they are between two vowels they form a syllable with the preceding vowel not the one after. Actually, the natural way to separate the syllables in c̲o̲r̲a̲z̲ó̲n̲, a̲r̲a̲d̲o̲, e̲x̲o̲r̲d̲i̲o̲ is c̲o̲r̲-a̲-z̲ó̲n̲, a̲r̲-a̲-d̲o̲, e̲x̲-o̲r̲-d̲i̲o̲. Therefore, readers should not have the combinations r̲a̲, r̲e̲, r̲i̲, r̲o̲, r̲u̲ nor x̲a̲, x̲e̲, x̲i̲, x̲o̲, x̲u̲, which are very difficult to pronounce because they really do not exist in the language.

We have already said enough, although longwindedness on an issue concerning general education, whose purpose is to further and spread the art of reading in countries where unfortunately it is so uncommon, should be tolerated more than on any other issue. We could easily have written a more entertaining article, however, the principal aim of this newspaper is the promotion of art, knowledge and useful inventions, particularly those most dictated by the status of society in America.

The orthographic innovations adopted by us are few in number: Substitute j for harsh g; i for the vowel y; z for c in words whose root is written with the former, and join the soft r and x to the preceding vowel in the division of lines. These are all the changes we have dared to introduce for now. We will set forth later our thoughts on accents, capital letters, abbreviations and marks of punctuation.

We will be content if anyone examining our principles impartially concurs that superfluous letters should be removed from the alphabet, rules set that no two letters should have the same sound, the rule of pronunciation adopted as a general principle, and normal usage accommodated thereto without neglecting origins. This appears to be the simplest and most natural system. Should we be wrong, we hope our readers' indulgence will excuse an error born merely of our zeal for the propagation of knowledge in America, the only way to establish freedom based on reason and with it the benefits of civil education and public prosperity.

NOTES

1. Ortografía de la lengua castellana. 1820 (A).

2. "I believe one should write in the way one speaks, unless custom has it otherwise".

ANCIENT USE OF ASSONANT RHYME IN LATIN POETRY OF THE MIDDLE AGES AND IN FRENCH POETRY, TOGETHER WITH OBSERVATIONS ON ITS USE TODAY

This study was first published in El Repertorio Americano, II, London, January 1827, pp. 21-33. Bello's work was virtually transcribed, with no citation of origin, by Eugenio de Ochoa in the prologue to Tesoro de los romanceros y cancioneros españoles, Paris edition, 1838, pp. xxiii-xxix.

This is a perfect index of Bello's research on ancient literary history, to which he devoted so much attention during the years of residence in London (1810-1829).

One of the peculiarities of Spanish poetry most difficult for foreigners to sense and appreciate, whose beauty eludes even those who learned the Castilian tongue at their mother's breast, is assonant rhyme, a rhyming scheme that joins two seemingly opposite things. More finely textured than consonantal or full rhyme, now prevalent all over Europe, it is still so popular that poems sung by the common people for their own amusement and joy usually rhyme in assonance.

Nor is this confined to the Peninsula. The assonant crossed the Atlantic with the language of Pizarro and Cortes, it took root in the Spanish settlements in the New World and is one of the strings of the American lyre today. The assonant influences the rhythm of the Colombian and Peruvian yaraví just as it does the ballad and seguidilla of Spain. The gaucho on the southern pampa and the plainsman on the banks of the Apure and Casanare, rhyme their couplets in assonance the same as the dandy in Andalusia or the peasant in Extremadura or the Mancha.

Today this metrical scheme is the exclusive province of Spanish versification. But, has this always been so? Did the assonant originate in the language of Castile? Or did the Castilian troubadors and bards have predecessors and teachers in this as in other matters pertaining to the art of rhyme?

The former opinion has almost universal acceptance today. Far from challenging the assonant as a product of the Peninsula, it is taken for granted that this rhyming pattern was barely known or used beyond its boundaries. Except for some Italian imitations of not too distant date, who ever heard of poems rhymed in assonance other than those composed by Spaniards?

Despite this, scholars in recent times have traced if not the assonant itself at least its monorhythmic structure (I mean the practice of keeping many consecutive lines in a single rhyme) to the Arabs. In my opinion, the justification for this is very weak. The Arabs, it is said, usually gave the same desinence to every verse in a composition, the Spaniards have done the same in their ballads. If the rhyme now seems to be every other line, it is because we divide what used to be one line into two, in other words, what we now call verses used to be hemistichs. So, they add, there is a palpable similarity between the Castilian ballad and that particular type of Arab composition.

The truth is, however, that monorhythmic versification (assonated or not) is much older in Europe than we think, preceding either the birth of the Castilian tongue or the Moslem invasion. The earliest compositions in which the rhyme follows a regular pattern, sought not for the sake of incidental embellishment, are monorhythmic, viz., the final Instruction of Commodianus, the plebian poet of the third century, and San Augustine's psalm against the Donatists composed in the fourth century.

The Latin cantinela in which the Franks celebrated the victories of Clotar II over the Saxons were apparently monorhythmic also. All the verses still preserved have a uniform ending. A fragment of this cantinela is in Bouquet's collection and cited by virtually everyone who has dealt with the origins of French poetry, including M. de Roquefort. 1/ With the exception of one distich alone, the other cantinela, composed in 924 for the Modena garrison when the city was threatened by the Hungarians and copied from Muratori by Sismondi 2/, was also monorhythmic. The most noteworthy part is that all these compositions were either written by unlearned poets or addressed for plebian use, which shows how common this rhyming practice was among the nations of Europe from early Christian times.

The assonant was not used in monorhymes from the start. The oldest assonated compositions are Latin, and in them (at least those I have seen) the assonants are always couplets, one verse rhyming with the one after, or the hemistichs in each verse rhyming internally. The Rhythmica of Saint Columban, founder of the monastery at Bobbio, found in the fourth epistle of the Epistolarum Hisbernicarum collected by James Ussher, 3/ is of the first type. Since this saint flourished in the late sixth century, the assonant can be regarded as at least that old.

The most common practice, however, was to rhyme the hemistichs in assonance. I could easily cite several opuscules from the time of Saint Columban up to the thirteenth century that follow this pattern. In order not to disturb the rest of authors long since forgotten in the libraries, I will mention only one who suffices for many.

That is Donizo, an early twelfth century Benedictine monk from Canossa whose renowned Life of the Countess Mathilda is cited by everyone who has explored the civil and ecclesiastical history of the Middle Ages. This very long Life is written in hexameters, in all of which both hemistichs in each verse rhyme in assonance (save only one or two passages by another pen transcribed by the author), as follows:

Auxilio Petri jam carmina plurima feci.
Paule, doce mentem nostram nunc plura referre,
Quae doceant poenas mentes tolerare serenas.
Pascere pastor oves Domini paschalis amore
Assidue curans, comitissam maxime, supra
Saepe recordatam, Christi memorabat ad aram;
Ad quam dilectam studuit transmittere quendam
Prae cunctis Romae clericis laudabiliorem,
Scilicet ornatum Bernardum presbyteratu,
Ac monachum plane, simul abbatem quoque santae
Umbrosae vallis: factis plenissima sanguis
Quem reverenter amans Mathildis eum quasi papam
Caute suscepit, parens sibi mente fideli, etc.

This sample of Latin assonants in such an old, unquestionably authentic work appears to me to be decisive. Leitnitz and Muratori, each printed editions of the Life of Mathilda in their collections. The surprising thing is that with the rhythmic scheme followed by Donizo so evident, neither of them noticed it. Consequently, the new readings proposed to clarify some of the obscure passages, at times violate the rules of assonance consistently observed by the poet.

Passing now from the medieval Latin poets to the trouveurs (following the example of M. de Sismondi and other scholars, this is the name I give the French poets of the langue d'oui to differentiate them from the troubadors of the langue d'oc who versified in very different taste and style); passing on to the trouveurs, we find assonance widely used in the chansons de gestes or epic narrations of wars, travels and chivalry towards which the French from the time of the Merovingian kings were greatly inclined.

The method was to rhyme every verse in assonance, taking one and keeping it up for some time, then another, and so forth, as a result of which the poem was divided into several monorhythmic stanzas or strophes with an indeterminant number of verses. Briefly, the rhythmic scheme was the same as in the old Castilian of the Cid, a work whose plan, nature and even language was a faithful imitation of the French chansons de geste, 4/ inferior in the regularity of its meter and the poetical quality of the descriptions but surpassing them in other qualities.

Much would have to be said of the influence of the trouveurs on early Castilian poetry and the troubadors on the second phase. Nor is this surprising, in view of the relations and close, frequent contact between the two nations. Overlooking the ties between the two ruling families and the many French ecclesiastics who occupied the chairs of metropolitans and bishops and inhabited the monasteries in the Peninsula, who can be unmindful of the many lords and knights from France who joined the Christian armies of Spain against the Saracens, led by fanaticism of the times, covetous of the spoils of a nation whose wealth and culture were often extolled in the songs of the trouveurs themselves, or who went there to settle with their household?

A jongleur was ever present in a lord's retinue to entertain
the latter with chansons de geste or the French fabliaux,
boisterous tales in verse, or their lays, love songs and tales of
chivalry in a serious vein of which some excellent pieces are still
preserved. This was the origin of the name juglar, later given the
jesters in the palaces of princes and great lords. During the time
under discussion, they were called in Spanish joglares, in French
jongléors and menestrels, in English minstrels, and in low Latin
joculatores and ministrelli, itinerant musicians who wandered from
fair to fair, from castle to castle, and from one local pilgrimage
to another reciting adventures of war and love to the tune of the
rote and vihuela.

Their cantinelas were the major pastime of the people, taking
the place of public spectacles, which were limited to tournaments,
jousts and the mystery or miracle plays occasionally performed in
the churches. The particularly famous French chansons were
translated into every European language. Roland, Reinaldos,
Gawain, Oliver, Guy of Burgundy, Fierabras, Tristan, Guenevere,
Isolde, the Marquis de Mantua, Partinuples, and many other
personages from the old Spanish ballads and books of chivalry had
already provided themes for the trouveurs. Having borrowed the
subject, it was logical to imitate the metrical patterns as well,
especially assonant rhyme, which in twelfth and thirteenth century
France was almost wholly limited to the poems of chivalry.

Earlier I referred to the cantinela by Clotar II. This name
in Latin was given to what the French called a chanson de geste, in
Castilian cantar, a narrative poem. The same name was given the
major sections of a long poem, later called cantos. 5/ Judging
from Clotar's cantinela or epic poem, monorhyme was customary in
such works and it was natural for poets to rhyme their verses in
assonance because, being easier, it was best suited to the
monorhythmic structure.

Whether the assonant originated in the dialects of the people
or was first heard in the Latin of the cloisters is difficult to
ascertain; I tend to the former belief. The monastic poets, in my
view, did no more than absorb the rhythmic forms that amused the
people into the meters and cadence of classical verse.

Anyone who heedlessly thinks we are talking about modern-day
French will cry out against the idea of assonants in French, which,
with its abundance of different, yet similar, almost imperceptible
vowel sounds, is not receptive to this type of rhythm. That French
was not always the language we know today is self-evident. Born
from Latin it passed through many centuries of change and
corruption to reach its present state. Before fragilis and
gracilis became frêle and grêle, they had to go through the
intermediate forms fraïle and graïle, pronounced like Castilian
baile. Alter did not suddenly become autre (otr); there was a time
when the French pronounced this dipthong au like the Spanish do
auto and laure.

Old French pronunciation must inevitably have closely
resembled Italian and Castilian with all the dipthongs dissolved
and the syllables en, in, voiced in the way handed down in the
other languages derived from Latin. This is precisely what we see
in French assonated poetry, all of which predates the fourteenth

century. The closer we are to the origins of French the more we see it. When pronunciation changed, use of the assonant stopped. Many of the old poems in assonance had to be reworked into full rhyme, thus accounting for the multitude of variants according to the date of the manuscripts involved.

It would be tedious to catalogue the poems of chivalry still preserved in full (or in long enough fragments to be able to judge their metrical pattern) in which assonance is clearly in evidence, governed by the same rules observed in Spanish verse. A simple yet conclusive sample will suffice, taken from a very old poem composed (judging by its language and character) in the early days of French. It is an account of a legendary trip made by Charlemagne and the twelve peers to Jerusalem and Constantinople. A manuscript of the poem is in the British Museum 6/ and was first published by M. de la Rue,7/ although what he says about its versification convinces me he missed its scheme of assonance.

The rest of the French critics who have set about to elucidate the poetic antiquities of their language were guilty of the same oversight, no doubt because of the difference between old French pronunciation and that of today. M. de la Rue, a justly esteemed antiquary to whom we owe so much excellent data on the origins of French language and literature, saw a great affinity between the language in this composition, the laws written on the order of William the Conqueror, and the psalter he also had translated.

Below are two passages copied by me from the manuscript preserved in the British Museum; in the first, the poet describes the lodgings offered Charlemagne by Hugo, the alleged emperor of Constantinople:

> Saillent li escuier, curent de tute part.
> Ils vunt as ostels comreer lur chevaus.
> Le reis Hugon li forz Carlemain apelat,
> lui et les duzce pairs; si s'trait a une part.
> Le rei tint par le main; en sa cambre les menat
> volvite, peinte a flurs, e a perres de cristal.
> Une escarbuncle i luist, et clair reflambeat,
> confite en un estache del tens le rei Golias.
> Duzce lits i a bons de cuivre et de metal,
> oreillers de velus et lincons de cendal;
> le trezimes en mi et taillez a cumpas, etc.
> Par ma foi, dist li reis, Carles ed feit folie,
> quand il gaba de moi para si grande legerie.
> Herberjai-les her-sair en mes cambres perrines.
> Si ne sunt aampli li gab si cum il les distrent,
> trancherai-leur les testes od m'espee furbie.
> Il mandet de ses humes en avant de cent mile,
> Il lur a cumandet que aient vestu brunies.
> Il entrent al palaiss entur lui s'asistrent.
> Carles vint de muster, quand la messe fu dite,
> il et li duzce pairs, les feres cumpainies.
> Devant vait le emperere, car il est li plus riches
> et portet en sa main un ramiset de olive, etc.

There is a noticeable similarity between these verses and the poem of the Cid. Both show that it was customary from the start to rhyme every line in assonance, not just the even lines the way

Spanish does today. Even when the verses were short, the assonant was continuous, not every other line. Evidence of this is the twelfth century lai of Aucassin e Nicolette in its only worthwhile edition published by Barbazan in his collection of fabliaux, 1808, and grotesquely altered elsewhere by people insensitive to its metrical pattern who have attempted to reduce it to regular rhyme.

Enough, however, of stirring around in these dusty papers of remote eras. I shall conclude with a few observations on assonant rhyme and its modern-day use.

In the opinion of some people, this rhyme is too easy, appropriate only for dramatic dialogue and the simple quasi familiar style of the ballad. But no matter how easy it is, it could never be as easy as free verse. I however do not agree that the assonant perfected by seventeenth century Spanish poets does not demand great skill.

The ease of the rhymes is lessened greatly by the need for repetition, the prevailing practice of avoiding consontal or full rhyme, which in some endings is very recurrent, and the higher degree of correlation demanded between the pauses in assonant verse and those dictated by the sense of the poem. Some assonants too are extremely difficult, with only a versifier skilled in using all the resources available to the language able to sustain them for a long time.

Of the three types of rhyme used in European languages --alliterative 8/, consonant, and assonant--the least pleasing in my opinion is the former, as Cicero correctly observed: notatur maxime similitudo in conquiescendo. Of the other two, full rhyme is preferable for couplets, cross-rhymes or other combinations. Assonance, however, is not only the most appropriate but the only one pleasing to the ear in long stanzas or totally monorhythmic compositions. Consonant rhyme is equally perceptible and pleasant in all languages; but just as alliteration is better suited to the Germanic dialects where consonant groups prevail, so assonance is more appropriate for languages such as Spanish that have an abundance of full, sonorous vowels.

Assonance has, if I am not mistaken, one advantage over other types of rhyme. Without becoming tiresome and monotonous and depending on what vowels are used, it gives a composition a certain special flavor, perhaps because the unique quality each vowel possesses is too weak to be perceived but acquires body and makes itself felt with repetition. I may deceive myself but it seems to me some vowels are better than others for certain effects. If there is any truth in the qualities grammarians assign to vowels, which must apply to Spanish particularly because of its fullness and clarity, 9/ this cannot help but be so. One sound or another may indeed move a person in a particular way because of casual and therefore misleading associations.

What I do think quite true is that the more difficult assonants are, the more pleasing their effect per se, apart from any connection with idea or feeling. In other words, the pleasing effect of a meter or rhythm is proportional to its difficulty; or less familiar, yet not totally foreign, final sounds are more pleasing to the ear, or the repetition of these final sounds offsets and tempers an overabundance of others in a language.

I would risk one more observation, submitting it, like all else, to the judgment of intelligent readers. Modern Spanish poets have failed to take full advantage of the different colors and qualities of assonance to give their works the zest of variety, or else have imposed too severe restraints on themselves when they use assonant rhyme. A single assonant rhyme is justified in lyric ballads, _letrillas_ and other short compositions, but must a whole _canto_ in an epic poem, or the whole act of a play that may have over a thousand verses, have a single assonance also? Far from having a pleasing effect, this constant drumming of a single assonance is genuine torment, lacking even the merit of difficulty.

Harder still is a skillful sequence of several assonants than the endless repetition and reliance on a few steadfast endings which the practitioners of this tedious uniformity use without respite. When metric unity was added to the theater, although neither prescribed nor observed by antiquity, the variety of rhymes so delightful in the comedies of Lope and Calderón might at least have been salvaged. Why not shift from one assonance to another in impromptu episodes, in sudden mutations in the players, sentiments or styles? This fourth unity has contributed much to the lassitude, weakness, and lack of harmony exhibited with few exceptions by the Spanish theater of today.

NOTES

1. De l'état de la poésie française dans les XIIe et XIIIe siècles,p. 362 (A).
2. Littérature du Midi de l'Europe, chapter 1 (A).
3. James Ussher (or Jacobo Usserius), Veterum Epistolarum Hibernicarum Sylloge, 1632 (T).
4. The author of the Cid so named it for that reason: "Aqui s'compieza la jesta de mio Cid el de Bivar" (A).
5. This is the sense in which it is used in the Cid: "Las coplas deste cantar aqui se van acabando" (A).
6. Biblioth. Reg. 16 EVIII (A).
7. Rapport sur les travaux de l'Académie de Caen, cited by M. de Roquefort, De la poésie française, chapter III (A).
8. Alliteration is the repetition of the same initial consonant in two or more nearby words, as in these verses by Ennius:
   Nemo me lacrimis decoret, neque funera fletu
   Faxit. Cur? volioto vivus per ora virum.

Ennius and Plautus were particularly fond of this sing-song rhythm, later improved upon and subjected to regular rules by the poets of the northern nations, especially Denmark, Norway, and Iceland (A).
9. "Fastum et ingenitam hispanorum gravitatem, horum inesse sermoni facile quis deprehendet, si crebram repetitionem litterae A vocalium longe magnificentissimae, spectet... sed et crebra finalis clausula in o vel os grande quid sonat" (Is Voss. De poematum cantu et viribus rhythmi) (A).

PRINCIPLES OF ORTHOLOGY AND METRICS

Prologue to the 1835 Edition

Bello published the first edition of this work in Santiago, Chile, in 1835 in the Imprenta de la Opinión. He later prepared two new editions with major additions in 1850 (Imprenta El Progreso), and in 1859 (Opinión), the latter was the last one prepared personally by Bello.

See the study by Samuel Gili Gaya entitled "Introducción a los estudios ortológicos y métricos de Bello," the prologue to Obras completas, vol. VI, Caracas, 1955.

Since each nation among those speaking the same language has its own peculiarities of pronunciation, orthology is a necessary study everywhere for people intent on speaking correctly. It is not enough for words and sentences to be right unless they are enunciated with the proper sounds, quantities and stresses.

Orthology is absolutely necessary in order to deter what would otherwise be a rapid degeneration of language. The more languages there are, the greater the problems of such forceful tools of civilization and prosperity as communication and human commerce. People whose station in life would preclude them from revealing any tinge of vulgarity or ignorance in their speech must be familiar with orthology. Neglecting it makes an orator dull, perhaps even ridiculous, and his audience disdainful. Orthology should be the first step for anyone hoping to write poetry, or at least in reading it, to experience the mental enjoyment derived from the portrayal of nature and moral behavior, so helpful in improving and polishing manners.

In the past, this essential art has been entrusted to parents and to teachers, who generally have no precise norms and are more likely to harm a child's pronunciation by their example than to correct it by their admonitions. However, the importance of orthology has at long last been acknowledged and it can no longer be ignored in the branches of learning required for the education of a man of letters, orator, poet, politician, or teacher.

It is in the hope of furthering their study that I submit this brief treatise to the young of America. I believe they will find it has all they need, so that by learning the rules and seeing how they are practiced in good dictionaries and universally regarded works of verse and prose, they will little by little acquire correct, elegant speech habits.

On controversial questions I note the opinions of orthologists and if I take sides or propose something new, this is not done as reproof of someone else. Teachers using my text for their orthology lessons are free to make any changes they wish and to accommodate it to their personal views on controversial points, which fortunately are neither many nor very important. For instance, I prefer the pronunciation substituir and transformar, but will not deem a speaker incorrect who drops the b in the former and the n in the latter, as many educated people do today whose learning I respect.

Differences in usage are inevitable in these confines, so to speak, of the different schools of thought, nor could this easily be avoided except under the sway of an authority using force rather than persuasion, an authority incompatible with literary freedom and one that, were it to exist, would be more harmful than beneficial. In letters, as in art and politics, freedom is the true mother of progress.

Some rules of orthology (like syntax and orthography) are based on word origin and are inapplicable without a knowledge of other languages, which students cannot be assumed to have. Still, they ought not to be omitted from an endeavor the purpose of which is to investigate the fundamental principles and rules of good pronunciation, both those that can be grasped by less learned observers and those that per se can only help scholars and literary associations who are responsible for regularizing the language. It behooves the teacher to select the subjects in an elemental treatise that are accessible to his pupils and to avail himself of the others, if he deems them helpful, to decide difficult cases which beginners cannot resolve alone.

In addition to the orthology, which covers the rules on stresses and quantities commonly called prosody, I thought it well to include a treatise on metrics. Prosody and metrics are generally combined because they touch upon and illustrate one another reciprocally.

In metrics, I give a complete but brief analysis of our pattern of versification and the real principles or components of meter in Castilian poetry, which in this respect has a great affinity with the verse of almost all nations today. It was impossible for me to perform this analysis without encountering the disputes that have divided humanists for centuries over syllabic quantities, the purpose of stress, and the measurement of verses.

After carefully reading not a few of the writings on this subject, I accepted the view that appeared to have the evidence of the ear most clearly in its favor. Unless I am mistaken, this surpasses all others in its simple, easy way of explaining how verse is measured, the different type of verse, and the peculiarities of both old and modern rhythms. These and other clarifications and debatable issues are in the appendices. If mingled with the texts, they would interfere with the didactic explanations addressed to the young.

I will not conceal the fact that my views are in absolute opposition to two eminent men of letters, one a translator of Homer and author of an excellent literary treatise, the other commendable for the first elements of <u>orthology</u> published in the Castilian tongue, a work filled with original observations and the fruits of long years of study. Because the authority of these two writers is of such moment, it was most urgent to show where they were not right. If I am wrong, the cause of letters will be served by refuting my arguments and presenting, more clearly and satisfactorily than in the past, the true theory of prosody and metrics of the Castilian tongue.

It remains only to express my gratitude to the government of Chile for the generous support given this work. I hope its usefulness will meet the expectations of a patron so zealous of the advancement of letters, as well as my own fervent desire to see generalized throughout the Americas the cultivation of our splendid tongue, today the common heritage of so many nations.

FOREWORD TO THE EDITION OF 1850

Santiago, March 1, 1850

In the second editon major revisions have been made to clarify some parts of the first edition which I thought required it and also to fill some blanks. In addition, I thought the number of examples, too few in the previous edition, should be enlarged. Subsequent study has only confirmed my convictions on the fundamental points of my theory of prosody and metrics. In this regard the two editions virtually conform with one another.

FOREWORD TO THE EDITION OF 1859

Santiago, March 1, 1859

Apart from not a few purely verbal and orthographic revisions, this third edition has some relevant new examples, a more logically organized explanation of some of the points, a theory of a sort of popular rhyme which I do not believe has been considered earlier, and a few other less important additions that do not essentially alter the ideas set forth in the original edition.

GRAMMAR OF THE SPANISH LANGUAGE FOR AMERICAN USE

Prologue

The first edition of the <u>Grammar</u> <u>of</u> <u>the</u> <u>Spanish</u> <u>Language</u> <u>for</u> <u>American</u> <u>Use</u> appeared in Santiago, Chile, in April 1847, published by El Progreso printing house, Plaza de la Independencia, 9. It was numbered as follows: xii, one page of erratas, and 334 pages of text and notes.

Seven editions of this work were published during Bellos's lifetime, the seventh in Valparaíso in 1864 by the Imprenta y Librería del Mercurio de Santos Tornero. The sixth and seventh were exact reproductions of the fifth edition, 1860, the last one revised by Bello.

See Amado Alonso, "Introducción a los estudios gramaticales de Bello," the prologue to Bello's <u>Obras completas</u>, vol. IV, Caracas, 1951.

Although I would rather not have deviated from the usual nomenclatures and explanations in this Grammar, there are matters of usage in Castilian that I thought could be defined in a more complete and more accurate fashion. Some readers will call such changes unnecessary or attribute them to an excessive effort on my part to say something new. The reasons alleged to uphold the changes will show, at least, that I made them only after mature consideration.

The most adverse reservation, because of its continuing sway over fairly learned individuals, is that faulty definitions, bad classifications, and false concepts pose no problem in a grammar, provided the rules governing good usage are properly spelled out. I believe these two things are irreconcilable, that usage can only be accounted for correctly and faithfully by analyzing and developing the very principles behind it, that strict logic is an indispensable prerequisite of all learning, and that it is in the first awakenings of the intellect when it is most urgent to train the mind not to content itself with words alone.

The speech of a people is an artificial system of signs, in many ways different from other systems of the same sort; thus, each language has its own theory, its own grammar. We ought not apply to one idiom the principles, terms and analogies that to some degree summarize the practices of another.

The very word idiom 1/ tells us that each language possesses its own spirit, its own physiognomy, its own idiomatic constructions. A grammarian would be derelict in explaining his own language who merely says what it has in common with another, or (worse yet) assumes similarities where differences alone exist--major radical differences.

General grammar is one thing, the grammar of a given language is another. It is one thing to compare two languages and another to consider one language per se. If it is a question, for instance, of Spanish verb conjugations, the forms, meanings and use of each one must be enumerated as if there were no other language in the world than Spanish. This approach is compulsory when explaining the rules of the only language they know to children, their native tongue. It is this focus that I have sought to adopt and I would ask people of discernment, to whose judgment I submit my work, to do the same, discarding particularly any reminiscenses they have of Latin.

In Spain and other European countries, an overzealous admiration for the language and literature of Rome gave Latin overtones to almost every creation of the mind. This was the common tendency during the epoch of the restoration of letters. Pagan mythology still provided the images and symbols of the poets, and the Ciceronian period was the hallmark of style for the writers of classicism. It was not surprising then that Castilian nomenclature and grammatical canons were taken from Latin.

If circumstances had given Greek ascendancy over Latin as the ideal prototype for grammarians, our declensions would probably have five cases instead of six, our verbs would have both a passive and a medium voice, and aorists and pastperfect futures would not have been absent in Castilian conjugations. 2/

The signs of thought clearly follow certain general rules which, being derived from those that control thought itself, govern all languages and constitute a universal grammar. But, if one excludes the resolution of thought into sentences and sentences into subjects and objects, the existence of nouns to express things directly, verbs to refer to predicates, and other words to modify and define nouns and verbs so that with a limited number of each, every possible concrete and abstract object can be named with all its perceived or imagined qualities. If we except this fundamental fabric of language, there is nothing I see that we are called upon to recognize as universal law from which no language would be free.

There can be more or fewer parts of speech than in Latin or the Romance languages. Verbs can have genders and nouns tenses. What could be more natural than for a verb to agree with its subject? In Greek that was not only allowed, it was common for the plural of neuter nouns to agree with verb singulars. In the mind, double negatives automatically cancel one another out. This is almost always so in language as well. Still, there are situations in

Castilian when two negatives do not make an affirmative. Thus we should not translate the meaning of ideas into the accident of words lightly.

Not a few errors have been made in philosophy by assuming that language is a faithful image of thought. The same overdrawn assumption has taken grammar in two directions, both wrong with some thinkers reasoning from the copy to the original and others from the original to the copy. In language, what is conventional and arbitrary covers much more terrain than is commonly thought. For beliefs, the whims of the imagination, and innumerable casual associations must clearly cause a vast discrepancy in how languages succeed in describing the innermost happenings of the soul, a discrepancy that grows as languages increase the distance from their common origins.

I am willing to listen patiently to any objections to what might appear new in this grammar, even though on second glance what sometimes looks like innovation on my part is no more than restoration. My idea of cases in declensions is the old bonafide concept. By endowing infinitives with the nature of nouns, I am only developing an idea fully stated in Priscian, "Vim nominis habet verbum infinitum; dico enim __bonum__ __est__ __legere__, ut si dicam __bona__ __est__ __lectio__."

I have, however, avoided any dependence on authority. For me, the only unimpeachable authority as far as a language is concerned is the language itself. I do not feel sanctioned to divide what language itself has made one nor to relate what it differentiates. I regard the analogies of other languages as no more than accessory evidence. I accept practice as given by the language without imaginary ellipses, without explanations other than those that simply account for use by virtue of use itself.

This was my reasoning. As to the aids I have used, I should mention especially the works of the Spanish Academy and the grammar of Vicente Salvá. I regard the latter as the most plentiful collection of Castilian expressions, as a book no one who hopes to speak and write our native language correctly should fail to read and consult freely. I am also indebted for some ideas to the talent and wisdom of Juan Antonio Puigblanch in his passing treatment of philological questions in his works. Nor would it be fair to overlook Garcés, whose book, considered a mere glossary of Castilian words and phrases of the classic age, illustrated with appropriate examples, is, I believe, undeservedly discredited today.

After such a major work as Salvá's, the only thing I thought missing was a theory to exhibit how the language develops, uses its inflections, and constructs its sentences free from some of the Latin traditions that are not at all appropriate. By __theory__ I do not mean metaphysical speculation. Mr. Salvá rightly reproves ideological abstractions such as those of one author he mentions, advocated to validate what usage proscribes. I avoid them, both when they conflict with usage and when they go beyond mere observance in the language.

I would reduce the philosophy of grammar to a portrayal of usage by means of simpler, more intelligible formulae. Grammar cannot nor need it base these formulae on any intellectual processes other than those that really and truly govern usage. But, the intellectual processes that actually do govern usage, or stated another way, the exact value of word inflections and combinations, are a necessary subject of inquiry. Any grammar that ignores them will not perform its function properly. Just as a dictionary gives the meaning of source words, so must a grammar explain the value of inflections and combinations, not merely isolated primary value but the secondary and metaphorical values if they have come into general usage.

This is the exclusive and at the same time limited area of grammatical speculation. If I have ever gone beyond these limits, it has been but a brief digression when dealing with the alleged ideological bases of a theory or when the chances of grammar revealed an unusual mental process. Such transgressions are so rare, on the other hand, that it would be too exacting to label then inopportune.

Some have said this grammar is too difficult and obscure. Experience in Santiago has indicated it was more so for people burdened by doctrines from other grammars who disdain reading mine carefully to familiarize themselves with its language, than for pupils using it to learn their first notions of grammar.

A common misconception makes us think that studying a language as one must in order to speak and write it correctly is an easy matter. Many grammatical points cannot be grasped in early years. I have therefore thought it best to divide the book into two terms, the first limited to the least difficult, most necessary notions, and the second expanded to cover those parts of the language requiring more developed minds.

I have used different typeface for each and included both in one treatise not only to avoid repetition but also to give first-year teachers the benefit of explanations intended for the second if they should need them. I also believe these explanations will not be entirely lost on beginners, as they progress any difficulties in understanding will gradually disappear. In this way also teachers are free to add to their elementary-level lessons anything from the next course they believe appropriate, depending on the ability and progress of the students. In the footnotes, I call attention to some of the corruptions in popular speech in America so they may become known and can be avoided, and have clarified some points with observations requiring a knowledge of other languages.

The accumulation of examples may at times seem profuse but this was only done when it was a matter of comparing corruptive innovations with usage by recognized writers, to discuss controversial issues, or to explain some of the processes in the language I thought had not been emphasized enough in the past.

It was also my view that a national grammar should not overlook forms and utterances that have disappeared from everyday language, either because poets and even prose writers still have recourse to them or because one must be familiar with them to fully understand the best works of the past. An explanation of how these terms are used incorrectly in some quarters and the wrong meaning given them in others was also deemed advisable. Should I be the one in error, may my mistakes stimulate better equipped writers to undertake the same task more successfully.

I do not pretend to write for the Castilians. My lessons are for my brothers, the people of Spanish America. I believe the language of our forebears should be preserved in the purest state possible as a providential means of communications and fraternal bond between the nations of Spanish origin scattered over the two continents. I do not, however, advocate excessive purism. The prodigious advancements in art and science, the propagation of culture and political revolutions are a daily inducement for new signs to express new ideas. Brand-new words taken from foreign languages and the languages of antiquity no longer shock us when not manifestly unnecessary or a reflection of some writer's affectation or poor taste.

Something else is even worse: to expand the meaning of familiar words or phrases. This multiplies the amphibology that plagues all languages because of the many meanings given a single word, perhaps more so those most commonly used given the virtually infinite number of ideas that has to be accommodated to a necessarily limited number of signs. The worst of all evils, and one that if not curbed will deprive us of the advantage of common language, is the influx of neologisms in syntax, inundating and bedeviling the language and converting it into a horde of irregular, unrestrained and rude dialects; embryos of future tongues which during a long process of development could turn America into what Europe was like during the twilight of Latin. Chile, Peru, Buenos Aires, Mexico would end up speaking their own language, that is, several languages, like Spain, Italy, and France, where provincial tongues prevail alongside several other languages, hindering the spread of enlightenment, lawmaking, government administration, and national unity.

A language is like a living organism, its vitality depends not on the constant relationship of elements but on the systematically uniform functions they carry out, from which the form and nature that differentiates the body as a whole emanate.

Whether or not I have exaggerated the danger, this has been my principal inducement for composing a work which in many ways is beyond my powers. Intelligent readers who honor me by examining it attentively will realize the care I have taken in demarcating, so to speak, the limits observed by good usage in the midst of the freedom and ease of its idiomatic constructions, in taking note of the most prevalent corruptions found today, and in stating the essential difference between Castilian syntax and foreign constructions that somewhat ressemble it and which we are used to imitating without a due degree of discernment.

It is not my intention in recommending the preservation of Castilian, to label everything peculiar to the people of America spurious and corrupt. Castilian utterances exist here that are outmoded in the Peninsula and subsist traditionally in America. Why ban them? If general practice in America calls for a more analogical verb conjugation, what reason would we have for preferring one that has accidentally prevailed in Castile? If we have formed new words from Castilian roots, according to the regular recognized processes Castilian has used and continues to use to increase its wealth of expression, why should we be embarrassed by them?

Chile and Venezuela are just as entitled as Aragón and Andalusia to having their change digressions tolerated when backed by the uniform, genuine custom of learned people. This is much less harmful to accuracy and purity in the language than the borrowings from French that have blemished the most highly regarded works of the Peninsular writers of our time.

I have set forth my principles, my plan and my purpose, and justly acknowledged my debt to those who have gone before. I have pointed to ways yet unexplored and may not always have given the necessary instructions for the deduction of exact generalities. Once again, if all I propose seems unacceptable, my hope would be satisfied if some part of it is and that it might benefit a branch of learning which, if not the most engaging, is at least one of the most necessary.

NOTES

1. In Greek, peculiarity, nature of its own, characteristic style (A).

2. The declensions of Latin imitators remind me of the modern-day painter who dressed his subjects in ruffs so his canvases would look like the old masters (A).

PROLOGUE TO THE POEM OF THE CID

This was published in Bello's Obras completas, vol. II, 1881, as the preface to the posthumous edition of Bello's long work on the Poem of the Cid, to which he devoted many years of activity. Bello probably wrote the Prologue after 1862 when he saw the publication of his work as a forthcoming, possible reality. In it he summarizes his thought on the venerable epic poem of early Castilian literature. See my book La épica española y los estudios de Andrés Bello sobre el Poema del Cid, Caracas, 1954.

Many years ago I had the idea of bringing out a new edition of the Poem of the Cid, published in Madrid in 1779 by the royal librarian Tomás Antonio Sánchez, in volume I of his Colección de poesías castellanas anteriores al siglo XV. I was prompted to do so by both the interest this production of Spain's Middle Ages awakened in England and Germany shortly thereafter and in France and Spain later, and by the sadly corrupt state of the text prepared by Sánchez.

Widely diverse opinions existed on the merit and antiquity of the work. Some scholars considered it the best of all Spanish epic poems. For others it was no more than a fleshless chronicle written in a primitive language and extremely rude, formless verse. Some assumed the poem had been written a few years after the hero's death, others thought it no earlier than the only known manuscript used by Sánchez, found in a monastery in Vivar near Burgos.

I

One must start by inquiring into the real date of the manuscript. The last verses of the Poem say that "Per Abbat lo escribió en el mes de Mayo, en era de mill e CC...XLV años."[1] After the second C, however, according to the editor's testimony, there was an erasure and a blank space as if it might have been filled by another C or, not uncommon in dealing with similar dates, the conjuction e. This second assumption is inadmissible. What purpose could there have been for erasing such a common, relevant word? Was the copyist so tediously scrupulous in his use of words? It is not inconceivable that, having accidentally put in one letter too many, he might have erased it. But what is most likely is that someone else erased it, as Sánchez suspected, to make the manuscript look older and more venerable, a conjecture borne out both by the handwriting, which Sánchez judged to be fourteenth century, and by the later opinions of Pascual de Gayangos and Enrique de Vedia, translators of Mr. Ticknor's History of Spanish Literature.2/

After their examination of the manuscript, they made the following statement in one of their footnotes (vol. I, p. 496): "As to the date of the manuscript, it was undoubtedly written in MCCCXLV, from which someone erased a C to make it look older; if there had been an e instead of a C, as some assume, the erasure would not have been so large. We have examined this point carefully and scrupulously with the original manuscript in view and have not the slightest doubt left on this matter."

The era MCCCXLV corresponds to 1307 A.D. As generally known, in those times era meant the Spanish era, which added thirty-eight years to the Christian era. The distinguished antiquary Rafael Floranes, with a view to supporting his personal conjecture on the authorship of the Poem, assumed that the era mentioned in the manuscript was not the Spanish but the Christian era. This, however, apparently contradicts the custom of the times, according to which the latter was generally accompanied by a phrase such as "Era or Year of the Encarnation, or the Birth of Christ."

II

When was the Poem composed? It is doubtless much older than the manuscript. I am inclined to regard it as the earliest, chronologically speaking, of the surviving body of Castilian poetry. This judgment presupposes that the primitive features of the Poem are not portrayed in the Vivar manuscript. Rather, the manuscript portrays the Poem as distorted by the jongleurs who recited it and copyists who certainly did the same as in other works of the past: accommodate it to the successive changes in the language by removing, adding or altering as they pleased, until it reached its present mutilated, vitiated condition. Not much intelligence is required to discover blanks, interpolations, transpositions and the substitution of one epithet for another here and there, to the detriment of the Poem's rhythm and rhyme. Poetry addressed to the people at large experienced this type of corruption more than any other, either in the copies that were made or in the oral transmission.

There was unquestionably at least one poem celebrating the exploits of the Cid dating from the mid-twelfth century. The Latin Chronicle of Alfonso VII, written in the second half of the twelfth century, contains a list in verse of the soldiers and military leaders who took part in the Almería expedition. When mentioning Alvar Rodríguez de Toledo, the Chronicle recalls his grandfather Alvar Fáñez, a companion of Rui Díaz whose exploits were celebrated in epic poems and who was commonly known as Mío Cid:

Ipse Rodericus Mio Cid saepe vocatus,
De quo cantatur, etc.

Thus, the triumphs of Rui Díaz were being recited and he was being called Mío Cid, a name repeated all through the Poem, by the second half of the twelfth century at least. Mr. Ticknor, based on these verses, conjectures that the ballads which began to appear in printed collections in the sixteenth century, many inspired in the exploits of Rui Díaz, were known and recited as early as the second half of the twelfth century. But his conjecture strangely neglects to include the Poem of the Cid with its frequent, habitual use of the epithet Mío Cid, which I do not recall having seen in any of the old eight-syllable ballads celebrating the Campeador.

Those romances, which the famous Anglo-American historian was the first to call by the English word ballads, composed in eight-syllable verse with every other line in assonant or full rhyme, were apparently unknown in this form prior to the fifteenth century. I understand no old manuscript has been uncovered containing ballads written in this style. It is true that they no doubt came from the long verses used in the Poem of the Cid, in Berceo's compositions, in the Alexander, etc., originating with the practice of writing the two hemistichs of the longer verse on two separate lines.

But ever since then they were regarded as two different meters, the long verse commonly known as the alexandrine and the romance verse the octasyllable. There were no grounds for finding any vestige of the latter in the Chronicle of Alfonso VII with its vast difference in language and style from the older narrative poem, even though some passages imitate the Gesta de Mío Cid as edited by Sánchez, but always in the sense of modernizing it.

The word romance has had different meanings in Castilian, apart from its primitive yet still prevalent meaning of vulgar Latin. It was used to denote all types of poetic compositions. Berceo called his Loores de Nuestra Señora a romance (stanza 232) and the Arcipreste de Hita, his collection of devout, moral and satirical poems (stanzas 4 and 1608). In Spain, as in France, it was customary to call the oldest historical or chivalresque epics romances as well as gestas and cantares de gesta.

The Poem of the Cid itself is called a gesta and its major divisions cantares. Therefore, the word romances meant either metrical compositions of any type or form, or epic poems specifically. The old ballads of the cancioneros and romanceros collections were printed later. Finally, in the twelfth century came the composition in eight-syllable verse with alternating assonance of the subjective lyrical ballads which our poets have continued to cultivate down to the present day, albeit displaying better rhythm and a more elevated style.

The foreign critics so laudably zealous in studying old Castilian poetry have not always had the acumen, nor should this have been expected, to discern these two periods in the eight-syllable romance, nor to realize that the old ballads were considerably distant from the old narrative poetry of Castille as found in the authentic poems of the thirteenth century.

Argote de Molina and Ortiz de Zúñiga, cited by Tomás Antonio Sánchez (note to verse 1016 of the Arcipreste de Hita) and by Mr. Ticknor (History, I, p. 116) speak of two poets, named Nicolás de los Romances and Domingo Abad de los Romances, who were with Saint Ferdinand during the conquest of Seville and were given repartimientos in that city. Supported by the preceding considerations, I do not believe the word Romances in their last names refers specifically to the eight-syllable verses compiled in the cancioneros and romanceros but to metrical compositions in general. The meter of a cantiga attributed by them to Domingo Abad, from which some verses are copied, in full-rhyme pentasyllables, helps prove this.

What some have believed is a less equivocal indication of greater antiquity in the Cid is the irregularity of its meter. But the negligence of the copyists has had a bearing on this, notable examples of which are cited in this edition and in the accompanying notes. Furthermore, if we regarded this as a certain way of determining the date of a work, the Arcipreste de Hita would have to be assumed to predate Gonzalo de Berceo; and the Crónica rimada, published recently in volume XVI of the Biblioteca of Rivadeneyra, to have preceded the Poem of the Cid itself, despite the indubitable reasons that speak for its later date.

Simplicity and disarray in phrasing and construction are indicators of even less value. The structure of Berceo's verse is generally more correct and a little more artificial, but this could be due to other circumstances such as how learned the author was, particularly what knowledge he had of Latin which would presuppose certain notions of grammar.

It would be reckless to say that the Poem as we know it, was precisely the one or one of the ones, alluded to in the Crónica of Alfonso VII, even overlooking the unquestionable corruption of the text, and considering the Vivar manuscript as merely an incorrect transcription of an earlier work. But I believe it very likely that by 1150 an epic poem or narration of the Cid's deeds was being recited in the long verses and simple, truncated style of the kind preserved in the Poem, regardless of its errors. A narration, though intended for recitation, written and listened to as a historical account and a repository of traditions, the proximity of which to the hero's time meant it was not far removed from the truth.

With the passage of time and following the usual process of the beliefs and songs of the people, this account underwent continual change and interpolation that exaggerated the deeds of the Castilian hero and assimilated legendary tales which quickly moved into the chronicles and what was then reputedly history. Each generation of jongleurs had, in a manner of speaking, his own peculiar edition in which both the language and the traditional legend took on new forms. The present Poem of the Cid is one of those editions and represents one of the successive phases of that very old epic poem.

We had set out to verify the date of that edition. Should we not dispense with purely orthographic changes, the retouching of phrases and words to align them with the status of the language in 1307, and a few other innovations having no bearing on the substance of the events, or the typical nature of the expression and style, the Poem would have to be considered somewhat earlier than the manuscript. But, in the midst of its infidelity, the manuscript doubtless reproduces a work many years older.

The primitiveness of the meter as compared to Berceo is no proof of this. From what has been said, as an indicator it is worth little. Nor is the greater antiquity of the words and phrases in Mío Cid in comparison to Berceo and other thirteenth century writers, because such an assertion lacks support. Anyone taking the trouble to glance at the glossary with which I shall conclude this edition will see, alongside the vocabulary and phrases from Mío Cid, the same forms as they appear in Berceo, Alexander, the Castilian version of the Fuero Juzgo, and other works regarded as postdating Mío Cid. They generally are closer to their Latin origins and therefore apparently point to greater antiquity. For now, I will make only a few observations:

1. The Cid has no articles other than the present-day el, la, lo, los, las. The Alexander sometimes uses ela instead of la, elo instead of lo, elos instead of los, elas insted of las.

> Creyeron a Tersites ela maor partida (Stanza 402)
> Por vengar ela ira olvidó lealtat (668)
> Alzan elo que sobra forte de los tauleros (2221)
> Fueron elos troyanos de mal biento feridos (572)
> Quiérovos quántas eran elas naves cuntar (225)
> Exian de Paraiso elas tres aguas sanctas (261)

We see the same thing in the Castilian version of the Fuero Juzgo: "E por esto destrua mas elos enemigos extrannos, por tener el so poblo en paz." "De las bonas costumpnes nasce ela paz et ela concordia entre los poblos." In his edition of the Alexander, Sánchez unwittingly splits these old articles into e la, e lo, etc. One need scarcely note their immediate derivation from the Latin illa, illud, illas, illos. They are intermediary forms between Latin forms and those in the Poem of the Cid.

2. Several different verbs had been combined with the verb meaning "to be" in Latin: fui, fueram, fuero, fuerim, fuissem, doubtless have a different root than es, est, estés, este, estote, eram, ero, essem. It is probable that sum, sumus, sunt, sim, come from a third root. The Castilians augmented this heterogeneity by adding still another element taken from the Latin verb sedeo. The earlier a writer is, the more frequently this verb appears and the closer its proximity to the Latin form.

In Berceo we find the forms seo (sedeo), siedes (sedes), siede (sedet), sedemos (sedemus), seedes (sedetis), sieden (sedent). There is no vestige of this in the Cid, whose present indicative is always very similar to the modern form: so, eres, es, somos, sodes, son.

In the imperfect indicative, the Cid resembles Berceo: sedia, sedías, or sedie, sedies, or seia, seias, or seie, seies, derived from sedebam, sedebas, plus era, eras. The Arcipreste de Hita still preserves the subjunctive seya, seyas (sedeam, sedeas). In the Cid we consistently read sea, seas.

The infinitive in Berceo is usually seer (sedere); in the Cid it
is always ser, a contraction probably no earlier than the thirteenth
century. What in Berceo is seere, seeria or seerie, in the Cid is
seré, seria, serie. The contraction seré, seria, serie is sometimes
present in Berceo when required by the meter but the double e
prevails, with, I believe, no example in the Cid.

This inclusion of the Latin verb sedeo meaning "to be" in
Castilian is a very old phenomenon found in the earliest known
documents and privileges: the privilege of Avilés still has the pure
Latin form sedeat, later seya and finally sea. No forms taken from
sedeo subsists in modern-day Spanish other than the infinitive ser
(from which seré and seria were formed) and the present subjunctive
sea, seas.

3.   A tense of the Latin conjugation not in Mío Cid but still
found in Berceo is the tense ending in ero (fuero, potuero):

   Si una vez tornaro en la mi calabrina,
   Non fallare en el mundo señora nin madrina (S. Orian, 104)

   Ca si Dios los quisiere e yo ferlo podiero,
   Buscarvos he ocorro en quanto que sopiero (Miracles, 248)

The proximity of the verb forms to their Latin origins may
occasionally be due to the relatively rapid degeneration experienced
by the mother tongue in different provinces of the Peninsula. But
whatever the reason may be, an affirmation of the greater ostensible
antiquity attributed to the language of the Mío Cid is likewise
inadmissible.

Some observers say rather plausibly that the Poem could only
have been composed when many Castilian words had not yet
dipthongized the vowel o into ue, when morte was not yet muerte and
forte not yet fuerte. We thus see fuer (for) v. 1405, and fuert
(fort), v. 1353, etc., assonating in o. The copyists, giving the
words their own pronunciation and writing them in that fashion, thus
destroying the assonance, reveal they were working with originals
that were outmoded by the time they were transcribed.

But this alone is not sufficient reason to presuppose Mío Cid
was written before Berceo's works. Nowhere in Berceo's copious
production do words in ué rhyme with words stressed in ó, the former
rhyme with one another only, apparently indicating that in Berceo's
time o had still not been converted into the dipthong ue. Stanza
263 of the Vida de San Millán has cuesta, repuesta, puesta and
desapuesta; stanza 83 of the Loores de Nuestra Señora rhymes huerto,
tuerto, puerto and muerto. Obviously the substitution of the
original vowel o for the dipthong ue would keep the full rhyme
intact.

This unvarying practice in Berceo makes it plausible to think
that the step from the vowel to the dipthong had still not been
made. No other writer follows the same procedure: in the Loor de
Berceo (anonymous) cuento rhymes with ciento, and similar full
rhymes are occasionally found in the Alexander and still more often
in the Arcipreste de Hita.

Another observation made by some critics as evidence of changes made in the text according to the Vivar manuscript concerns the assonance of penultimate stressed vowels with final stressed vowels, such as mensaje, partes, grandes, with lidiar, canal, voluntad, and bendiciones, corredores, ciclatones, with Campeador, sol, razón. They concluded the poet must have written lidiare, canale, Campeadore, razone, endings close to the Latin origin and therefore older.

The fact is, however, that the earliest poets in the language did not take the final e of grave words into account for the assonance, probably because its pronunciation was weak and muffled, like the mute e in French. It is inconceivable that son, dan, ya (sunt, dant, jam) were ever pronounced sone, dane, yae, with a final e that would have alienated these words from their origins rather than bringing them closer. In prose words we constantly come upon ovier for oviere, quisier for quisiere, podier for podiere, dond for done, part for parte, grand for grande; but never mase for mas or mais, dae for da, dane for dan, nor yas for ya, written by the collectors of ballads in the sixteenth century.

Their anxiety to restore the lost assonance made them add a final e to acutely stressed words when they should really have dropped it from words stressed on the final syllable and written part, cort, corredor's, infant's. In this way their written versions would have approximately represented the old, weak, muffled sounds made fuller and more robust by later Castilian.

This extraneous e never appears in the cancioneros except at the end of a verse where the collectors thought it was needed for the assonant rhyme. The presence of the e would not make the Poem of the Cid any older than many of the ancient ballads, such as:

> Moriana en un castillo
> Juega con el moro Galvane;
> Juegan los dos a las tablas
> Por mayor placer tomare.
> Cada vez que el moro pierde,
> Bien perdía una cibdade;
> Cuando Moriana pierde;
> La mano le da a besare;
> Por placer que el moro toma
> Adormecido se cae, etc.

(Rivadeneyra, Biblioteca de Autores Españoles, vol. X, p. 3)

Although arguments concerning Mío Cid's antiquity that hinge on the simple or rude quality of the language and the Poem's irregular meter deserve consideration, I believe one must acknowledge that they are not always conclusive. The degree of culture possessed by the poet and the fact that this genre of poetry meant for the people, could not help but adapt itself to the simplicity and primitiveness of the listeners in an incivilized time when the modern languages were in an early stage of development, have a bearing on these qualities.

The truncated, often unconnected phrases are characteristic of both French and Spanish epic poems and are still preserved in our old ballads. A certain reminiscense of them can even be sensed to a certain degree in the ballads of the seventeenth century. In addition, as mentioned earlier, the general proximity of the words to their Latin origins is partly accounted for not so much by the age of the writers as by dialect. It is an uncontestable fact that Latin degenerated and words themselves changed at a fairly fast tempo in the different kingdoms and provinces of the Peninsula.

Judging by word forms, I believe Mío Cid may have been composed in the first half of the thirteenth century, although closer to 1200 A.D. than 1250. This conjecture gains strength as we go from the evidence of outward form to substance. The fables and historical errors that abound point to the passage of at least a century from the time of the hero's life to that of the Poem.

The epic in twelfth and thirteenth century Spain was history in verse written without discernment and teeming with the popular rumors that have distorted the exploits of famous heroes in all ages, particularly (and even more so) in generally primitive eras. Its listeners (few could read outside the cloister) regarded it as a substantially true account of the protagonist's life or principal adventures. But legendary traditions are not born nor do they gain credence all at once, especially those that presuppose complete ignorance of real history and are at odds with it on points that would not be lost upon contemporary observers or their immediate descendents.

Such is the case in the Poem of the Cid of the legend of the marriage of Rui Díaz' daughter to the Infantes of Carrión and everything thereafter up to their marriage with the Infantes of Aragón and Navarre. Quite obviously, the author of the Poem was unaware of the high station of Doña Jimena, the wife of the hero, and the real names and marriages of his daughters. The Infantes of Carrión are as apocryphal as those of the no less famous Infantes of Lara.

Early exaggeration of the number and scope of the exploits of such a famous, popular leader would not be surprising, but one can hardly conceive that shortly after his death when one of his grandchildren sat on the throne of Navarre, a great granddaughter was married to the heir of Castile. Some of his companions in arms were perhaps still living and many of their immediate descendants were scattered all over Spain, his wife's blood ties to the ruling family should be unknown in Castile or that his youngest daughter had married not an imaginary Infante of Aragón but a sovereign count of Barcelona who died thirty two years after his father-in-law.

Some will tolerate the subterfuges resorted to by Berganza and others in order to reconcile the poetic tradition of the Cid with history, by assuming the Cid married twice and that his daughters had two different names. But this totally unfounded, gratuitous assumption, is unable to overcome the veracity of the ballads, chronicles, and epic poems which refer to a single marriage of the Cid and give one name alone to each daughter. In the Notes, I shall endeavor to separate what is history from fable in the popular traditions about the Cid Campeador and refute the arguments of people who, conversely, find nothing reliable in anything written about Rui Díaz and even doubt he ever existed.

The judgment suggested by a comparison of poetic account with historical fact, is partially validated by a chronological item in verse 1201 that mentions el rey de los Montes Claros, a title given by the Spaniards to the princess of the Almohades sect and dynasty. This sect did not appear in Africa until well after the beginning of the twelfth century, nor did it take part in events in Spain until the mid-twelfth century. Thus, an author writing at that time, or shortly thereafter, could not have committed the anachronism of making them contemporaries of the Cid and Yusuf, the Miramamolin of the Almoravides dynasty which they destroyed.

Padre Risco, in Castilla, p. 69, mentions an opinion of the distinguished antiquary Rafael Floranes and calls attention to the fact that the Repartimiento de Sevilla of 1253, published by Espinosa in his history of that city, included the names of Pero Abat, a cantor of the royal clergy. Floranes, according to Padre Risco, became convinced that this was none other than the author of the Poem, considering the date, his occupation, and the good taste of Alfonso IX and the holy king Ferdinand, his son.

Accordingly, Per Abbat is not the name of a mere copyist but of the author himself, and the date in the manuscript is the date of composition, not of the copy. But would that date then be 1207, which corresponds to the era MCCXLV, apparently that of the manuscript, or 1307 corresponding to the era MCCCXLV, the only acceptable one according to the above interpretation?

The former date did not suit Floranes who was led by another piece of information we will speak of later to think the Poem of the Cid had been written before 1221. The latter date, however, is too far away from the time of the repartimiento. To surmount this difficulty, Floranes assumed that the era mentioned in the manuscript was the Christian era, not the Spanish era, which has thirty-eight years less. According to Floranes then, the Poem was composed in May of the year 1245.

This opinion has had few followers. Militating against it are the traces of greater antiquity provided by the Poem itself, which, strictly speaking, are not absolutely decisive, and the highly suspicious erasure and conversion into the Christian era in a way at odds with the general custom of the period. The similarity of names is not a strong enough argument against such serious obstacles.

Instances involving similar names, without personal identity, were commonplace in Spain where there was little variety in the first names used, many being hereditary and firmly rooted in some families. Aside from this, the very wording of the manuscripts points to its being a copy. One month (as Sánchez observed) was time enough to transcribe the Poem but not to compose it.

Floranes placed particular emphasis on the following verses at the end of the Poem:

> Ved qual ondra crece al que en buen ora nació,
> Quando señoras son sus fijas de Navarra e de Aragón.
> Oy los Reyes de España sos parientes son.
> A todos alcanza ondra por el que en buen ora nació. 3/

Sánchez' edition reads todas instead of todos, a manifest error either in the manuscript or by the printer. This adjective can only refer to reyes.

These verses appear to indicate the Poem was composed after all the ruling families in Spain had intermarried with the descendants of the Cid. Rui Díaz' blood ascended the throne of Navarre through García Ramírez, the Cid's grandson, who recovered the dominions of his elders in 1134. It entered the royal family of Castile in 1151 with the marriage of Blanca de Navarra, the daughter of Don García Ramírez, to Don Sancho, son of the emperor Don Alonso and heir apparent to the throne.

From Castile it was conveyed to León in 1197 by Doña Berenguela, the daughter of Don Alonso of Las Navas, the son of Sancho and Blanca, and to Portugal by Doña Urraca through her marriage to the Portuguese monarch Alonso II whose reign began in 1212. The relationship with the kings of Aragón did not take place until 1221 when Jaime el Conquistador married Berenguela of Castile. According to Rafael Floranes' conclusion, the Poem must therefore have been composed after 1221.

But this argument must be viewed for what it is worth. The real date of composition should not be deduced from the verses mentioned using actual historical data but rather the poets' own mistaken notions of history, whatever they were. If the poet thought the Cid's descendants had married into the dynasty of Aragón as early as the eleventh century through the alleged marriage of one of his daughters to an Infante of Aragón, then obviously the real date of the link between the two families cannot be helpful in determining when the Poem was written.

With this date repudiated, the others admittedly have litte ground to stand on. If the poet believed the Cid's blood had ennobled two of the principal Christian thrones of Europe--Aragón and Navarre--since the eleventh century, many intermarriages between the several ruling families in the Peninsula would have justified his vaguely deducing that within the space of eighty or a hundred years all of them must have formed a link with the Campeador's descendants, with no consideration of specific marriages or epochs. All that can be validly deduced from the verses in question would be a mere repetition of what was said earlier: a rather long period of time must have elapsed between them and the death of the Cid, in order for so many exaggerated or false events to have been accepted as truth.

On the other hand, I am inclined to think the Poem was not composed much later than the year 1200 and might even have been written a few years earlier, to judge by the fables injected therein which lie, so to speak, half-way between historical truth and the sweeping fictions of the Crónica general and the Crónica del Cid, both composed somewhat later. The language, as found in the Vivar manuscript is, of course, not so remote, but we have already explained the reason why.

We have no conjecture to make at all on the authorship of this venerable monument of the language, except the one made by Rafael Floranes which has not prospered. All things considered, the Poem of the Cid was the work of many generations of poets, each one of whom shaped his own particular text, reworking earlier ones and embellishing them with exaggerations and legends that found a willing reception in national pride and credulity. Development of the legend continued until it was finally rendered in the <u>Crónica</u> <u>general</u> and the <u>Crónica of the Cid</u>, whose authority was such that later additions made up to the seventeenth century were held to be figments of the imagination and not incorporated into the traditions reputed to be historical in nature.

III

We must still classify this composition and determine its place among the poetic productions of the European Middle Ages. Sismondi calls it the oldest known epic poem in a modern language and compares it unhesitatingly with those of Pulci, Bojardo, and Ariosto. But we would classify it on a more limited scale with the legends in verse by the trouveurs that bear the name of <u>chansons</u>, <u>romans</u>, and <u>gestes</u>. The author himself declared its lineage and kind when he entitled it a <u>gesta</u> in the beginning of the second section or <u>cantar</u> of the <u>Poem of the Cid</u>:

   Aqui s'compieza la Gesta de Mio Cid el de Bivar (v. 1103)

Thus, the real title of the Poem is <u>La Gesta de Mío Cid</u>, and the genre to which it belongs is then the <u>gestes</u> or <u>chansons</u> de geste. The affinity between the <u>Poem of the Cid</u> and the ballads of the trouveurs, not in theme alone but also in style and meter, is so clear that anyone who reads them carefully could not help but notice it.

As to the poetic merit of the Poem, we miss in the <u>Mío Cid</u> some of the ingredients and embellishments customarily thought essential in the epic, and in all poetry for that matter. There are none of the marvellous adventures or supernatural agencies that were the soul of the old ballad or narrative poem in their best epochs, no bouts with love, no similes, no picturesque descriptions. In these respects, <u>Mío Cid</u> is not comparable to the best known ballads or epic poems of the trouveurs. But it does have other appreciable, truly poetic qualities. The natural flavor of the dialogue, the animated portrayal of customs and character, its pleasing candor of expression, its spirited movement, the Homeric sublimity of some passages, and (what is noteworthy for that age) the tone of gravity and decorum that reigns virtually throughout the Poem, give it, in our judgment, a place among the top productions of the emerging modern languages.

The text has suffered immensely in the hands of copyists, who must bear a large share of the blame for its coarseness and disarray. Studying the language of the author and of his models, a tone all its own will be perceived and passages at first sight, crude and graceless, will be found that glow with unexpected elegance. In narrowing the age of the Poem we do not consider it an authentic, virtually contemporary chronicle, as Sismondi, Bouterwek, and Southey do. For that very reason, we feel the poetic intention and imagination of the Castilian trouveur are to be even more highly applauded.

I believe the presence of several different meters in La gesta de Mío Cid has gone unnoticed in the past. The predominant form is probably the fourteen syllable alexandrine found in Gonzalo de Berceo, but there is unquestionably a frequent mingling of the hendecasyllable and occasionally, nine-syllable verse. The rules governing these types of three meter verse as observed in La gesta must first be examined.

The alexandrine verse in its true form was the one used by the trouveurs, and was composed of seven-syllable hemistichs if the final syllable was unstressed or six syllables if stressed. There is never a synaloepha between the two hemistichs. Samples taken from the trouveurs are compared below with alexandrine verses from Mío Cid.

> Tranchairai-lur les testes/od m'espée furbie.
> Alcándaras vacías/ sin pielles e sin mantos.
>
> Par son neveu Roland/tire sa barbe blanceh/
> Cid, en el nuestro mal/vos non ganades nada.
>
> Li reis Hugon li forz/Carlemain apelat.
> Doña Ximena al Cid/la mano l'va a besar.

In both hemistichs the stress falls on the sixth syllable, in which case the final syllable of the verse may be stressed or unstressed, In Castilian the stress may also be on the second from the last syllable:

> Resucitest' a Lázaro/ca fue tu voluntad.

The hendecasyllable of the ancient poems was taken from the decasyllable of the trouveurs, composed of two parts I shall call hemistichs, although each had a different number of syllables. French verse usually has a stressed final syllable; Castilian, a stressed penultimate syllable, but both count the syllables up to and including the final stress. Therefore, the eleven or nine-syllable Castilian meter is the same as the French ten or eight-syllable meter. To avoid making awkward distinctions, I shall call the French verses by the names used in Castilian.

The hendecasyllable of the trouveurs had two hemistichs, one of five syllables if the last was unstressed, or four if stressed, the other was just like the alexandrine hemistich. The same was true in Castilian.

> Totes les dames/de la bone cité.
> Sueltan las riendas/e piensan de aguijar.
>
> Qui descendites/en la Virge pucele.
> Rachel e Vidas/en uno estaban amos.
>
> Blont ot le poil,/menu, recercelé.
> Fabló mio Cid/de toda voluntad.

Nine-syllable verse, whether in French or Castilian, had nine syllables if unstressed and eight if stressed.

Mut la trova curteise e sage
Bela de cors e de visage.
Ha menester seiscientos marcos.

Se si fust que jeu vus amasse
E vostre requeste otrelasse.
Besan la tierra e los piés amos.

Nuls ne pout issir ne entrer.
Es pagado e davos su amor.

Nine-syllable verse is rare in the Poem of the Cid, while
hendecasyllables are frequent, sometimes many in succession, as in
verses 1642-1646. The crónica rimada, despite its extreme
irregularity, probably made worse by the copyists, has the same
three types of verse intermingled.

One verse form usually prevailed from beginning to end in
French narrative compositions, either the alexandrine as in the
Voyage de Charlemagne à Jerusalem, hendecasyllable in Gerardo de
Viena and in Garin le Loherain, or nine-syllable verse as in all the
poems of Wace and the lays of Marie de France. We also have a
sample of eight-syllable verse in Aucassin et Nicolette.

The identity of the three Castilian meters with the French is
beyond any doubt. This then is a manifest sign of affinity between
La Gesta de Mío Cid and the French compositions of the same genre.

Another equally strong indication is the monorhythmic structure
in assonance. This rhyming arrangement was an arbitrary matter.
Why is there no interior rhyme as in Donizo's Life of Mathilda, or
each verse rhymed with the next as in Wace and Marie de France, or
four-verse stanzas as in Berceo and the Alexander? If both the
Castilians and the trouveurs composed in monorhymed strophes, one
group of poets must have been imitating the other. Therefore, it
was the jongleurs who imitated the trouveurs, who predated them by
centuries.

Since the matter of versification in the Cid has been touched
upon, I would note before going further that the way syllables were
counted in all primitive poetry was quite different from how it was
done in later epochs when concern for form usually jeopardized
substance. Thus, versification became progressively more precise
and regular, longer cadences gradually took over and rhythm was
finally subjected to a kind of strict, measured harmony that ended
up being monotonous and annoying.

This gradual refinement is especially apparent in the manner of
counting the syllables. Primitive poets (and popular versifiers are
always that kind) use the synaloepha and synaeresis very freely. In
the ancient poets seer is sometimes a two-syllable word and
sometimes monosyllable. The same is true of Díos, vío (normally
accented on the í). The mute sound of final unstressed e meant it
could be dropped or not counted in the middle of a verse. The
following verses were perfect alexandrines:

Vio puertas abiertas ë uzos sin estrados.
Díos qué buen vasallo si oviese buen señor.

Mezió Mio Cid los hombros e engramëo la tiesta.
Comö a la mi alma, yo tanto vos queria.
El diä es exido, la noch' querie entrar.

Just as these were perfect hendecasyllables:

Yo mas non puedo ë amidos lo fago.
Pasó por Burgos, al castiellö entraba.
En poridad fablar querria con amos.
En aques' dia en la puent' de Arlanzon.

Another cause of apparent irregularity was the arbitrary use of the definite article before a possessive pronoun. The poet said <u>sus fijos</u> o <u>los</u> <u>sus</u> <u>fijos</u>, <u>mi</u> <u>mugier</u> o <u>la</u> <u>mi</u> <u>mugier</u> indifferently, <u>but</u> the copyists kept it or dropped it without taking the meter into account the way the poet presumably would have done.

IV

The only old manuscript extant of such a unique work is regrettably the Vivar codex, which has pages missing and others that have been retouched, according to Sánchez, by an unskilled hand, perhaps the reason for some of its harmful errata. Reduced to that manuscript (or rather the Sánchez edition thereof) and anxious to publish the Poem as completely and accurately as possible, we had somehow to make up for the lack of other manuscripts or printed editions by turning to the Crónica of Rui Díaz which Fr. Juan de Velorado took from the archives of Cardeña and published in 1512.

This is a compilation of earlier chronicles, including the present Poem. Many of its chapters follow the Poem step by step, usually in substance only, although occasionally word for word with minor alterations, or even whole series of verses. There are other passages that are versified in the manner of the Poem. Judging by their location they apparently belong to the missing pages, if not taken from other old compositions in honor of the same hero; several evidently existed, even earlier than the one we know. At any rate, the Crónica provides a rather extensive commentary of the part of the Poem that survives and abundant materials to fill in somehow what was lost.

With this idea in mind and convinced that the Poem in its original entirety ranged over the whole life of the hero, according to the traditions current at the time (in that century the epic, as we indicated earlier, was ostensibly historic and no one was concerned about its unity and the separation of legendary elements), we decided to preface the work with a brief account taken word by word from the Crónica of the principal exploits of Rui Díaz before his exile, to complete what was missing and further an understanding of what follows.

A comparison of both works, a study of their language and that of other old works, plus attention to the context have led me, as if taken by the hand, to a true reading and interpretation of many passages. Nevertheless, I have made only those corrections that seemed sufficiently probable, informed the reader whenever this was done, and saved for the notes any that were somewhat conjectural or venturesome.

As to the orthography, I have adhered to the Vivar manuscript (as given in the Sánchez edition) whenever it was not manifestly defective or there was no risk of jeopardizing correct word pronunciation. The changes are limited to writing c for ch, j for i, 11 for l, ñ for n or nn, etc., when indicated by the corresponding sounds, such as arca, ojo, lleno in place of archa, oios, leno.

Indeed, these words were never sounded in the latter mode. If they were spelled that way it was because in the time of the copyist the letters in our alphabet had less settled values than now. We might have represented the pronunciation of the author more faithfully by writing pleno, or plegar, plorar, etc., the way we often read in Berceo and occasionally even in the Cid, but it cannot reasonably be assumed that each word was pronounced just one way. There are some that still vary, depending on the fancy or convenience of a speaker or writer. The closer we are to the early days of a language, the less stability we will find and the great freedom there is to choose one form or another.

Apart from the variants, the notes include everything I thought might be useful to clarify obscure passages, to isolate what is authentic from what is legendary and fanciful, to explain briefly Middle Ages customs and historical or geographical issues related to the text, to show similarities of language, style and concepts between the Poem of the Cid and the epics of the old French poets, and finally, to proclaim the real spirit and character of the composition and spread some light on the origins of our language and poetry.

The latter objective is more appropriately developed in the appendices on the Middle Ages ballad or epic and on the history of the language and Castilian versification. Perhaps I shall be accused of reaching into matters not directly related to the edition of the Poem itself. However, they are all connected with the genesis and development of a beautiful section of modern literature, one of whose earliest efforts was the Poem of the Cid.

The work ends with a glossary in which an attempt has been made to fill in some blanks and to correct some inadvertencies of the first edition. The greater the authority of Tomás Antonio Sánchez, the greater the need to refute some of his opinions and explanations that I thought wrong. This in no way detracts from the high opinion he so justly deserves nor does it affect the gratitude owed him by all lovers of our letters for his appreciable efforts.

Some will judge my own efforts with this work futile and of no importance to the matter, others will find much to reprehend in its execution. I am supported by the example of scholars from all nations, who in recent times have devoted themselves to shedding some light on their ancient literary monuments. The obscure nature of some of the points I have dealt with will partially excuse my errors.

1. "Per Abbat wrote it in the month of May in the era of MCC...XLV."

2. Ticknor, George, History of Spanish Literature, New York, 1849, translated as Historia de la literatura española by Pascual de Gayangos and Enrique de Vedia, Madrid, 1851-56 (T).

3. "Behold to him on our propitious born
    What honor falls! His daughters have become
    The queens of Aragon and Navarre;
    His relatives today are kings of Spain.
    To him on hour propitious born hath come
    In all things honor." [Translation of A. M. Huntington, Poem of
                                   the Cid, II, New York: Putnam (1902)
                                   verses 3724-3729].

LETTER TO MANUEL BRETÓN DE LOS HERREROS

When he was nearly 82 years old, Andrés Bello decided to write a long letter to Manuel Bretón de los Herreros, which I call "Bello's Cidian testament" and which is a notation of the principal subjects covered in his research on the Poem of the Cid. Bello probably felt death close at hand and was reluctant to have the results of more than half a century's research lost. The text of the letter was provided by Miguel Luis Amunátegui Aldunate in Vida de Don Andrés Bello, Santiago, 1882, pp. 166-171.

Santiago, Chile, June 18, 1863

Don Manuel Bretón de los Herreros
Secretary of the Spanish Royal Academy

Sir:

I have just learned in the press that the Spanish Royal Academy is involved in several important undertakings on the language and literature of Spain; two of them attracted my attention particularly, a Dictionary of old words and phrases, and a new edition of the Poem of the Cid with notes and glossary.

Having spent much of my life on studies of this kind, it occurred to me, perhaps presumptuously, that I might be able to provide some indications to the Academy that might assist in the aims it so zealously proposes and which are of such evident benefit to Castilian letters.

As to the Dictionary, I believe some of the twelfth or thirteenth century literal versions of the Vulgate in Castilian cited by Padre Scio in the notes to his translation of the Bible, provide one of the best means for its development. These manuscripts, according to Padre Scio, who describes them in a concluding note to his Introduction, are in the Escorial library.

The relevant ones are those he marked A, numbers 6 and 8. I am familiar only with short fragments of the manuscripts included in the notes, and they have been very helpful to me in understanding the oldest works in Castilian. The glossaries of Tomás Antonio Sánchez leave not little to be desired and, if that scholarly philologist had had those old versions available, he might possibly have filled in some of the blanks, particularly in his meager glossary of the Poem of the Cid, and would have explained some words more successfully. I shall cite one example. Verse 13 of the Poem says:

Mezió Mio Cid los ombros, e engrameó la tiesta.1/

Sánchez conjectures that the verb engramear, which he apparently had never heard of, meant to raise or to lift up. But that is not so, it means to shake, to move, to toss, as shown many times in the Escorial manuscripts. Thus, in their translation of Commotione commovebitur terra (Isaiah 24, 19) manuscript 6 says "Engrameada será la tierra con engrameamiento."2/ In the same manuscript Fluctuate et vacillate (Isaiah 29, 6) is translated "Ondeat vos e engrameat"3/, and Concussa sunt from Ezekiel 31, 5, is rendered "Se engramearon"4/ in the same manuscript.

I know of no more abundant source of materials for the Dictionary and, while these manuscripts are probably not unknown to the Academy scholars entrusted with this undertaking, I felt nothing was lost by pointing them out even at the risk the Academy may find my suggestion superfluous. A Dictionary with timely, well selected examples accompanying the definitions, would make for varied, interesting reading, unlike the bare, arid glossaries of the same sort with which I am familiar.

As to the Poem of the Cid, or Gesta de Mio Cid, the title used by its author, I take the liberty of informing you for what it may be worth that I have a not insignificant number of notes and disquisitions aimed at explaining and shedding light on this composition, which has so attracted the attention of scholars in England, France, and Germany and is of such evident importance, as you are not unaware, in literary history, particularly the medieval epic.

My intention was to suggest the many necessary or probable corrections required by the text, to show the true nature of its versification. Which in my opinion has not been adequately determined, thus enhancing the primitive, rude character of the text, and also to supply some of the missing verses which detract from its merit. For this and other purposes I have made an exacting comparison of the Poem with the Crónica del Cid published by Fray Juan de Velorado, and would also have compared it with the Crónica general attributed to Alphonse the Wise, but have unfortunately been unable to lay hands on it. One of the most important additions I was considering is described below.

The Vivar manuscript used by Tomás Antonio Sánchez had pages missing and not just a few as Sánchez imagined. The Poem having been, I believe, a full account of the life of the Campeador according to popular tradition, it is not creditable that some of his most memorable deeds before he was exiled, which became the theme of an infinite number of old ballads, should be missing. These include the famous duel of young Rodrigo that led to his marriage to the legendary doña Jimena Gómez, the seige of Zamora and all the events related thereto, and the oath of Santa Gadea.

But how to go about filling in these ill-fated blanks? The chronicles, with their occasional watered-down fragments of the Poem (disjecta membra poetae), do not provide us with enough material despite some long sections in which the alexandrine versification of the Gesta is self-evident. The sample quoted below is on the oath of Santa Gadea, which if available in full would no doubt be a very beautiful, truly Homeric passage.

Among the magnates of Castile, it was Rodrigo de Vivar who dared take the oath of Alphonse VI, accompanied by twelve peers acting as witnesses, that he had had no part in the death of his predecessor, king Don Sancho, an oath which the privilege of Castile said had to be repeated three times. Rodrigo administered the oath in the following terms:

> --Vos venides jurar por la muerte de vuestro hermano,
> Que non lo matastes, nin fuestes en consejarlo?
> Decid: Sí, juro, vos e esos fijosdalgo,
> E el rey e todos ellos dijieron:--Sí juramos.5/

Rodrigo again spoke:

> --Rey Alfonso, si vos ende sopistes parte o mandado,
> Tal muerte murades, como murió el rey don Sancho.
> Villano vos mate, que non sea fijodalgo.
> De otra tierra venga, que non sea castellano.
> --Amén, respondió el rey, e los que con él juraron.6/

The device of changing the assonant for the repetition of the oath is an apt one, bringing to mind the two versions of the message from the Eternal Father in octaves 11-15 of the first canto of Tasso's Jerusalem.

> Es ora Mio Cid, el que en buen ora nació,
> Preguntó el rey don Alfonso e a los doce buenos omes:
> --Vos venides jurar por la muerte de mi señor,
> Que non lo matastes, nin fuestes end consejador?7/
> Repuso el rey e los doce:--Ansi juramos nos.
> Hi responde Mio Cid; oiredes lo que fabló:
> --Si parte o mandado ende sopistes vos,
> Tal muerte murades, como murió mi señor.
> Villano vos mate, ca fijodalgo non.
> De otra tierra venga, que non sea de León.
> Respondió el rey:--Amén; e mudósele la color.
> --Varon Ruy Diez, por qué me afincades tanto?
> Ca hoy me juramentastes, e cras besáredes mi mano.
> Repuso Mio Cid:--Como me fizieredes el algo;
> Ca en otra tierra sueldo dan al fijodalgo,
> E ansí farán a mí quien me quisiera por vasallo.8/

Anyone comparing these verses with the prose in the relevant chapters of the Crónica will see how small and natural the changes made by me are, yet they still probably fail to reproduce all the archaic color of the original. In all that follows up to the place where the Chronicle matches the first verse of the Poem, there are frequent traces of versification. Particularly worthy of mention is the colloquy of Ruy Díaz with his followers after he had been ordered into exile:

E los que acá fincáredes, quiérome ir vuestro pagado.
Es ora dijo Alvar Fáñez, su primo cormano:
--Convusco iremos, Cid, por yermos e por poblados;
Ca nunca vos fallescerémos en quanto vivos seamos.
Convusco despenderemos las mulas e los cavallos,
E los averes e los paños,
E siempre vos serviremos como amigos e vasallos.
Quanto dijera Alvar Fáñez todos allí lo otorgaron.
Mio Cid con los suyos a Vivar ha cavalgado;
E cuando los sus palacios vió yermos e desheredados....9/

The first verses of the Gesta de Mio Cid, in the mutilated
form they have come down to us, clearly follow:

De los sos ojos tan fuertemientre llorando,
Tornaba la cabeza e estábalos catando.
Vió puertas abiertas....10/

The assonant is the same and the los in the second verse of the
Gesta clearly refers to the palace in the prior verse given in the
Crónica, which then follows the Gesta faithfully for several more
chapters.

In view of the foregoing, I believe no one will dispute me when
I say that all these pieces belonged to a single work, the Gesta de
Mio Cid. I do not pretend that the text of the chronicle and my
hypothetical changes are a precise restoration of the Gesta although
they may be so occasionally. My purpose was to show how the poetic
form had been converted into prose and at the same time how useful
the chronicles can be in completing, correcting and interpreting the
Poem.

I should not dissemble my disagreement with those scholars who
regard the eight-syllable ballad to be the early form of the ancient
alexandrine, which in their opinion is merely the merger of two
eight-syllable verses. Just the opposite, I believe the
eight-syllable ballad originated from the alexandrine or long
verses so prevalent in early Castilian versification. In the first
place, everyone acknowledges that there is no codex extant with
Spanish epic poetry in eight-syllable verse prior to the fifteenth
century.

But samples of long verses divided into two hemistichs,
characteristic of narrative poems, are old and well-known in
thirteenth and fourteenth century works. Second, in the poems of
the French trouveurs, in my opinion the model for the Spanish poets,
the rhyme in assonance, unlike the eight-syllable ballad, is never
alternating but continuous, even when the trouveurs employed
eight-syllable verse. Witness the story of Aucussin and Nicolette
in volume III of Barbazan's collection.

The Academy may make whatever use it pleases of these
explanations. For me it would be enough for the Commission to bear
them in mind even though it were to dismiss them if considered
unfounded. At the same time, I would be highly gratified if the
Commission would review some of the major writings I have worked on
with a view to publishing a new edition of the Gesta de Mio Cid, an

enterprise begun forty years ago and now impossible for me to finish. If the Academy accepts this humble tribute, I would make it immediately available and submit the entire work to your judgment.

I hope you will do me the honor of answering this letter if your many duties permit you to do so.

May the Lord keep you for many years,

Very truly yours,

Andrés Bello

NOTES

1. My Cid shrugged his shoulders and tossed his head.

2. The earth will be moved exceedingly.

3. Move and shake.

4. They were shaken.

5. You came here to swear concerning the death of your brother
    That you neither slew him nor took counsel for his death?
    Say, "Yes, I swear," you and these hidalgos,
    And the king and all of them said, "Yes, we swear."

6. King Alfonso, if you knew of this thing, or gave
    command that it should be done,
    May you die even such a death as king Don Sancho
    By the hand of a villain, one who is not a hidalgo
    From another land, not a Castilian.
    "Amen," responded the king and the knights who were
    with him as well.

    The remainder of Bello's letter, with the exception of the last three substantive paragraphs, closely follows the wording of part of his Notas a la crónica published posthumously in Obras completas de Don Andrés Bello, II, Santiago, Chile, 1881, pp. 82-84. The Spanish verses quoted are from his transcription of the Crónica del Cid (T).

7. Berganza read "end consejador" in the manuscript of the Chronicle preserved in San Pedro de Cardeña, instead of "en consejardo," the reading in the printed chronicles, which breaks the assonance (A).

8. When My Cid, who on hour propitious was born, asked King Don Alfonso
    and the twelve knights;
    You came to swear concerning the death of my lord.
    That you neither slew him nor took counsel for his death?
    May you die by the hand of a villain, not a hidalgo,
    From another land, not from Leon.

127

And the king responded, "Amen"; and his color changed.
"Ruy Diaz, why dost thou press me, man?
Today thou swearest me, and tommorow thou wilt kiss my hand.
My Cid replied, "When you do something for me;
In another land they pay a hidalgo a wage,
And so shall any who wants me for a vassal."

9. "And the Cid sent for all his friends and his kinsmen and
    vassals, and told them how king Don Alfonso had banished him
    from the land, and asked of them who would follow him into
    banishment, and who would remain at home. Then Alvar Fáñez,
    who was his cousin-german, came forward and said, Cid, we will
    all go with you, through desert and through peopled country,
    and never fail you. In your service we will spend our mules,
    and horses, our wealth and our garments, and ever while we live
    be unto you loyal friends and vassals. And they all confirmed
    what Alvar Fáñez had said. My Cid with his friends rode to
    Vivar, and when he saw his palaces deserted and emptied...."
         Translation from Robert Southey, The Chronicle of the
    Cid, 1808, New York: Heritage Press, 1958, p. 51, with
    the exception of the last sentence which is not in
    Southey's translation.

10. His eyes grievously weeping
    He turned his head and looked back upon them
    He saw doors standing open...

B. History of Literary Criticism

SUMMARY OF THE HISTORY OF VENEZUELA
Fragment

In 1810, the Calendario manual y guía universal de forasteros en Venezuela para el año de 1810 was published in Caracas in the country's first print shop, Gallagher and Lamb.

The author of the work, which was left unfinished, was Andrés Bello. Most of the Calendario is taken up by the Summary of the History of Venezuela which Bello wrote expressly for that edition. The Calendario is today a rare edition, with only three known copies existing in the world. The intricate bibliographic problem posed by Bello's study was examined by me in the Resumen de la Historia de Venezuela by Andrés Bello, Caracas, 1946. I later published a facsimile edition of the Calendario, once it was located, in El primer libro impreso en Venezuela, Caracas, 1952, with a preliminary study.

The epoch when the civil restoration of Venezuela began must be dated in the late seventeenth century. At that time, with the conquest over and the population pacified, religion and politics assumed a task launched by the heroic deeds of men driven by greed, if the truth be told, yet who left for posterity examples of valor, prowess and perseverance that history may never see repeated.

One of the factors that helped give lasting consistency to the political system of Venezuela was the failure of the mines discovered early in the conquest. This forced the conquistadors to turn their attention to sounder, more useful and more beneficent pursuits, agriculture being the most obvious in a country possessed of all the blessings nature could provide. Spain encouraged farming and industry in Venezuela; hence, property rights accessory to the conquest soon became of prime importance.

The privilege of filing property claims was held by the cabildos. The governors alone were responsible for sanctioning them. This system probably increased land ownership considerably. The ratio of land area to population was huge, but proximity to the cities, the provision of irrigation and of facilities for transporting farm commodities inevitably ended in disputes over ownership, which had to be settled by legal means or referred to the jurisdiction of the tribunals. Under a measure taken without due premeditation, these suits were remanded to the Spanish court; as a result, and contrary to the sovereign's will, farming was dealt a mortal blow.

Ownership cf the land became the subject of innumerable controversies, involving enormous expenditure and dissension that continues to the present day. Misgivings concerning cost, plus delays in airing their rights at such a distance, made the Venezuelans decide either to waive their claims or to hold the land without title, thus jeopardizing national progress on the one hand or their own heirs on the other. Realizing this, the Court issued an order in 1754 granting the audiencias final authority in all land matters.

To correct past abuses, all landowners were ordered to submit their deeds to the commissioners of the tribunal. Those that had been granted by the governors were approved, provided the owner had not gone beyond the bounds of his concession; land on which no deeds were submitted reverted to the crown. Landowners who had violated their boundaries were compelled to purchase the extra land from the king at a moderate price or to surrender it together with any products and improvements made thereon.

These first steps towards legal ownership in Venezuela were the consequence of other earlier measures taken on behalf of the original holders of the land. Under a royal decree of 1687, the Indians distributed in the encomiendas of the conquistadors were freed from personal service and left subject to the clergy alone. Once able through the Church's beneficent ministry to become a part of society, they enjoyed every right granted under Spanish law, a fact our detractors have chosen to ignore. The making of a complete code immediately after the discovery of strange new lands and the establishment of such novel civil institutions, were superhuman efforts that should only have been expected in the course of time and as circumstances permitted.

Europeans and Americans who regard other colonies as no more than a temporary home and source of wealth for the mother country, enjoy under the protection of our laws everything that makes man cherish the soil under his feet. Three centuries during which many cities were built in America that rank with the best in Europe will remain a permanent tribute to the policies, prudence and wisdom of a government that managed to retain its influence without jeopardizing the progress of lands so far from its center of authority.

Venezuela at first lacked the appeal other areas had for Spain. Its mines did not entice Spanish fleets and galleons to its ports and much time went by before its farm products entered Spain; once development of the land began, its commodities were sought on every market. Cacao from Caracas was worth more than the cacao from the country where it originated. Nations without metal or the precious ores that attracted the attention of Europe from the early times of the discovery of America profited little from the policies of Spain. Venezuela with cacao alone was of not much significance in the mercantile system of the new world.

Government attention centered fully on Mexico and Peru, which absorbed all that Spanish industry turned out. Venezuela was scarcely able to say it had any contact with the mother country. For many years cacao from Caracas reached Spain through third nations only, which, in supplying their Venezuelan neighbors what was needed for the comforts of life, kept Spain from trading in the commodity directly.

These clandestine arrangements forced the people engaged therein to elude inspection by the customs house. It was to the former that Puerto Cabello owed its existence, to the detriment of Borburata, the regular port for Venezuelan trade with the Peninsula. Naturally endowed to dock and careen the whole Spanish navy, Puerto Cabello was selected by the Dutch from Curaçao as the anchorage where they disembarked their goods and took on cacao. For a long time the port town, the nucleus of which was a few dilapidated huts belonging to smugglers and fishermen, looked more like a colony of Holland than a Spanish possession.

The government attempted to bring the law to that community of men whose occupation and ways must have posed a constant threat to the peace. Their outlawry and the Dutch general's own private interest, however, meant the government's designs were so stubbornly opposed that it abandoned any plans to submit the huts of Puerto Cabello to its authority. They soon became an asylum of impunity and a general warehouse for the Dutch colonies on the coast. Except for cacao, Venezuela had nothing to draw the vessels from the Peninsula into its ports. The Dutch however, were careful to siphon it off, thus placing under the monopoly of need a country with no other source of supply for its agriculture than the warehouses of Curaçao, and no other outlet for its commodities or port of entry for the proceeds of their sale than Puerto Cabello.

A political arrangement more surprising than accountable finally put an end to that situation, while again turning Venezuela into a useful yet scandalously abusive monopoly that was instrumental in raising agriculture out of its infancy. Under the leadership of the Guipuzcoan Company, the country made its first steps in the direction of progress; Spain received an area of trade that had been unjustly usurped, and Puerto Cabello became a major city, the largest port on the coast.

This mercantile venture, which was perhaps responsible for the see-saw rhythm in the political restoration of Venezuela, was the most memorable act of the reign of Philip V in America. Notwithstanding the invectives hurled at it by Venezuelan public opinion, the Company provided undeniable momentum to the machinery implanted by the conquest and turned the evangelical zeal of the people into an orderly force. The conquistadors and the conquered peoples, joined by a common language and a common religion into a single family, saw their efforts for the motherland prosper in a land earlier tyrannized by the Dutch monopoly.

The farming activity of the Basques revived the conquistadors from their state of rejection and, under the auspices of law, put the indolent natives to work. Since 1700 Spain had made but five ruinous expeditions to Venezuela; in 1728, ships of the Company sailed into the ports of Spain and filled its warehouses with the very cacao earlier received from foreign powers.

Cacao was not the only commodity that helped develop Venezuelan farming; new crops increased yields and brought the land to a level of production justified by the fertility of its soil and the beneficent climate. The Aragua valleys underwent a rebirth with the additional income provided their owners through the efforts of the Basques, who were joined in their endeavors by Canary Islanders. The experiments with indigo made by don Antonio Arvide and don Pablo Orendain gave that commodity a prominent place in the European market.

Once the growing and processing of indigo were successfully introduced, the valleys of Aragua attained a degree of wealth and population scarcely evident in the most hardworking nations. From La Victoria to Valencia the scene was one of plenty and happiness. A traveler wearied by the harshness of the mountains separating the area from the capital was captivated by the joys of rural life and welcomed everywhere with generous hospitality. There was nothing in the valleys that did not tempt him to prolong his stay: indigo and sugar were on all sides and at every step a Venezuelan landowner or Basque tenant disputed the honor of providing him all the comforts of the rural economy. Under such favorable conditions, towns sprang up out of nowhere.

La Victoria quickly rose to its present position from a poor town sheltering Indians, missionaries and Spaniards scattered in the mines of Los Teques; Maracay, barely a village forty years ago, now has all the appearance and advantages of a farming town and its surroundings are witness from afar to the industry of its people. Turmero too is indebted to indigo and the king's tobacco plantations for the growth that has made it one of the principal towns of the government district of Caracas; Guacara, San Mateo, Cagua, Guigue, and many others still in their infancy, owe their existence to the influence of the agricultural genius that protected the valleys of Aragua. The shores of Lake Valencia are alive with crops that year after year provide a large part of its subsistence to the capital.

The scene we have just described will always justify the early years of the Company in the face of the valid objections lodged against its final years until its extinction. The initial effort of the Guipuzcoan Company strengthened Venezuela's ties with Spain and furthered its relations with other parts of the hemisphere. Mexico, Havana and Puerto Rico bought cacao more advantageously and production increased under the momentum of the exports and markets acquired by the Company. Population grew with the influx of agents, clerks, employees and laborers from Vizcaya and the Canary Islands, shipping and stevedoring came into being, crops were improved and new ones introduced, and the people of Venezuela redoubled their efforts towards a new order of prosperity as domestic demand multiplied.

Interior communication with neighboring kingdoms and provinces was furthered. Cattle from the immense, bountiful plains of Venezuela entered Santa Fe by way of the Meta, in exchange for Colombian emeralds and the goods turned out by that country's incipient industry, which matched the needs of a new-born country. For the first time Europe realized there was more in Venezuela than cacao when it saw Company vessels loaded with tobacco, indigo, hides, dividivi, balsam and other exotic goods.

Such were the effects that would always make the Guipuzcoan Company a valuable institution, assuming such agencies are of any use at all when society no longer needs the support required in its infancy. Venezuela was quick to realize its strength. Its first action was to get rid of the obstacles that kept it from standing alone.

The outcry reached the ears of the monarch, despite the resistance of selfishness and passion, and forced changes in the Company that would leave scarcely a trace of its original appearance. Still, its preponderance made a mockery of all the precautions taken by Charles III to reconcile Company interests with those of his subjects in Venezuela and those of his exchequer. The Company was so corrupt that genuine, sound reforms had to be considered.

The deathblow was sounded with the establishment of an intendancy in Caracas whose leader, acting with integrity and fearlessness, launched a movement that weakened the mercantile colossus. Despite this, the latter withstood repeated attempts to topple it by the Venezuelan customs authorities and citizenry for several years, finally succumbing to a blow dealt by a most zealous and enlightened minister who managed to reconcile the opposing interests.

The year 1788 will always be a memorable date in the political restoration of Venezuela, inseparable from the memory of the monarch and minister who brought down with august munificence the barriers that stood in the way of Venezuela's advancement. When all America was proclaiming thanksgiving for the freedom of commerce decreed in 1774, one of the Spanish monarchy's finest dominions was being crushed under a government monopoly that operated despite the desires of the king and the opinion of a minister aware of the legitimate interests of his nation.

The complaints of subjects worthy of a better fate soon reached his receptive ear and Venezuela took the place intrigue and selfish interest had denied her in the monarch's heart. Assisted by such beneficence, its arrested prosperity miraculously expanded, the harvest began from a tree actually planted by the Company, though it had begun to wither in its evil shadow. Everything changed in Venezuela. The influence of mercantile freedom was particularly evident in agriculture. Landowners were given additional resources under a new system of planting previously unkown crops. Earlier, the French islands had supplied Europe with its coffee, but no sooner did Caracas enter the market than it commanded the same price as Martinique, Santo Domingo and Guadalupe.

Future generations of Venezuelans will always be grateful to the prelate who successfully stamped the epoch of his spiritual government with political prosperity. The name of Mohedano will evoke those of Blandin and Sojo, followers of his example who promoted one of the major commodities that is now an essential part of Venezuelan agriculture. Failure would have ensued if a political event had not brought attention to their work.

The calamities that befell the French colony in Santo Domingo meant the sudden loss to European commerce of the major share of coffee from the Antilles, in the wake of which coffee and its growing processes were moved to the mainland. The Chacao Valley became the center of efforts throughout the province devoted to this new branch of agriculture. Soon all the mountains and hills, which until then had preserved the primitive qualities of creation, were stripped, planted and covered with coffee.

For the first time, man and his crops penetrated and walked on the inaccessible heights surrounding the capital of Venezuela. The valleys of Aragua, earlier covered by the luxuriant green of the indigo tree, and the peaks and slopes where pumas and serpents once roamed, were symmetrically covered with coffee. People who earlier failed to conceive of any productive property except in the valleys and along river beds suddenly discovered they had immense areas of land that could be profitably planted. Laborers redoubled their efforts to realize a return on such a rapid turn of fate. Work multiplied ownership and people became productive landowners overnight, who never would have been without the prospect opened to the province by the planting of coffee.

Spain was not alone in welcoming the development of this part of its dominions. Foreign nations prospered legitimately from commerce with Venezuela, free of the burdens of the clandestine monopoly imposed by Holland in early colonial times. The good fortune of having an intendant whose knowledge of economics later made him prime minister enabled the province and its friends in the Antilles to benefit reciprocally from a trade based on convenience and organized with political foresight. The excess food commodities extracted from Venezuela's soil went to neighboring islands. Our ships sailed under the most prudent conditions, loaded with cattle, fruit and grain and came back with a cargo of implements and manpower for the promotion of agriculture.

The new relationships propagated knowledge, attracted wealth, and introduced new rural industries. The east concentrated on growing cotton, which was shipped from Cumaná and boosted Venezuelan trade, cattle from the lowlands stimulated growth of the port of Barcelona and Coro, Guyana was given new life with tobacco from Barinas, sought as a favorite for consumption and European trade. Even the political events that deprived Spain of one of its best possessions in the Antilles helped expand farming in Venezuela.

Immigrant landowners from the island of Trinidad and farmers who fled the constant lack of rainfall in Margarita worked the land in the valleys of Güiria and Guinima. Nature, politics and hard work, assisted by the election of another intendant whose talents and economic knowledge together with a finely attuned criterion as to the local circumstances of the country, helped him make use of the favorable conditions in the province and to perpetuate his memory through actions that gave this part of Spain in America its present stability and won him the fame that took him to one of the highest posts in the government.

Such was the development of political policy in the administration of the conquest, settlement and restoration of a country that stretches from the flooded plains of the Orinoco to the barren shores of the Hacha, one of the Spanish monarchy's most plentiful and interesting possessions, and such the events with which its people bound together as one family by the interests of a fatherland, matched the efforts of the government to raise Venezuela to the rank reserved for it by nature in South America.

Three centuries of unflagging loyalty would clearly suffice to accredit the reciprocal relationship making one hemisphere inseparable from the other; but circumstances reserved for Venezuela the satisfaction of being one of the first countries in the New World to pronounce spontaneously and unanimously an oath of eternal hatred for the tyrant who attempted to cut loose these close bonds. Thus, giving the final and greatest proof of its people's conviction that their peace and happiness lie in maintaining the relations to which all America owed its existence and growth for so many centuries.

On July 15, 1808, the circle of Venezuela's glories will close when it recalls the patriotism with which, to the eternal opprobrium of perfidy, this splendid part of its patrimony swore to live in continued unity, loyalty and peace with the Crown of Castille.

HOW TO WRITE HISTORY [1]

This article appeared in El Araucano, 912, Santiago, on January 28, 1848. Bello included it in his Opúsculos literarios y críticos, publicados en diversos periódicos desde 1834 hasta 1849, Santiago, 1850, pp. 144-153. See "Don Andrés Bello enseña a los chilenos a narrar la historia nacional", by Domingo Amunátegui Solar in Anales de la Universidad de Chile, semestre I and II, Santiago, 1939.

"There is no worse guide for history than the systematic philosophy that sees things not as they are but as they conform to one's own system. As to the followers of that school, I would cry out with Jean Jacques Rousseau, "Facts! facts!" —Carlos du Rozoir.

Historians educated in eighteenth century concepts let themselves become too preoccupied by the philosophy of their time.... They treated facts with the disdain of right and reason, doubtless a fitting way to revolutionize minds and governments but much less suited to the writing of history. History can no longer be written in the service of a single idea. This is not what our century wants; rather, it demands to be told everything, that nations as they were in different epochs be redepicted and explained, and that each past century be given its real place, coloring and meaning.

This is what I have tried to do with the great event the history of which I have undertaken. I have consulted only original documents and texts, both to individualize the different incidents in the narrative and to describe the people and groups that were a part of it. Indeed, I have taken so much material from those texts that I flatter myself little is left. National traditions of peoples less familiar to us and ancient popular poetry have provided me with many indications of the character, sentiments, and ideas of men in the times and places to which I shall convey the reader.

As to the account itself, I have adhered as closely as possible to the language of the ancient historians, contemporaries or near contemporaries of the facts. Whenever I have had to generalize because available information was inadequate, I have tried to validate my statements by reproducing what originally led me to them by induction. I have preserved the narrative style throughout, so the reader would not suddenly be jumping from an account of ancient date to present-day commentary and to avoid a dissonant tone in the work caused by mingling fragments of chronicles with disquisitions on a particular theme.

I likewise felt that by narrating rather than dissertating, even in expounding events and general results, I would be able to endow society as a whole and its individual members with a sort of historical existence, and find some of the human interest in the political destiny of nations that is automatically inspired by the simple details of the fortunes and adventures of single individuals.

I thus plan to present the national struggle that followed the conquest of England by the Normans settled in Gaul, in as individualized a fashion as possible. 2/

Sismondi announced his plan to write the history of France up to the time of Louis XVI and concluded his work with a philosophy of the history of France in the following terms:

If life and health remain with me to conclude this task I have imposed upon myself, I shall ask from these thirteen centuries the lesson in the social sciences they hold for us. I shall above all attempt to make known that successive progress of the condition of nations, their internal organization, their state of wellbeing or restlessness, which we ought to regard as the grand result of public institutions, and which alone can teach us to distinguish with certainty what merits our consideration or our censure.

I should also say a few words on the method I have followed in working on ancient documents. I flatter myself that at first glance no reader will hesitate to acknowledge that this history is not, like many others, a compilation made from other compilations. My work begins and ends in the originals, according to the advice given me earlier by the great historian Juan de Muller. I have sought history in its contemporaries, as it appeared to them.... I always cite the sources so the unbiased reader can verify my work and form his own judgment with the same data used by me for mine. 3/

History has no value apart from its lessons on how to make men happy and virtuous, and facts are important only to the extent that they represent ideas. Yet it is also true that facts are easily subdued by the desire for order and that instances will always be sifted from the chaos of events to support the most foolish theories. I have seen the truth twisted to serve a lie a thousand times.

The glibness so frequent in superficial writers has convinced me more than anything else how useful it is to individualize and how important it is to examine the least little circumstance scrupulously. Perhaps it will be thought I give too detailed attention to comparatively insignificant facts, include many that might well have been left out, and might still have covered the great lessons of history and developed the principles I would engrave on the memory of the reader in four volumes instead of sixteen.

Had I proceeded that way I would have selected the facts instead of recording them, and the conclusions would then have depended not on the facts per se but on the spirit presiding over their selection. Nay, I wanted the reader to have the history of Italy as something separate and apart and be able to go over it and contemplate it from all sides. I have not concealed the feelings experienced by me in my encounters with it, but wanted to allow the reader to make his judgments independently. Here are the facts; if another interpretation fits them, it can be used. 4/

Villemain 5/ was unforgiven of Robertson for leaving out details from his Introduction to the History of Charles V 6/, and presenting them later in the form of notes or background documents.

That Introduction is much praised and admired, and it indeed has a serenity of reason, a well realized distribution of parts, a certain regularity and progress that pleases the mind. But it is followed by one whole volume of notes. Robertson will say, for example, that a certain barbarous people, invaders of civilized Europe, possessed the highest degree of war-like violence and fanaticism. That is what he places in the text; but the features, the factions of that savage ferocity, the singular depiction of the barbarian's encampment, the crowd milling around a savage bard entoning martial songs, the women and children weeping because they cannot follow their children or fathers into combat, all those details related by the Roman ambassador Prisco, still possessed of the terror he felt when he saw them led off to the Byzantine court, all that is relegated by Robertson to the notes and should be in his book.

They have one thing in common [the Greek and Roman historians], even Salustio with the regrets of his frustrated ambition concealed under the veil of a disheartened, bitter philosophy: their talent as storytellers. For all of them, the narrative was their end or means, and they presented it with openhearted simplicity or under the inspiration of vivid and profound feeling. If they had an opinion to support or a moral to emphasize, its color was in the narration. Whether the facts took place before them as in a play or whether they attempted to get to their root and discover therein a knowledge of men and nations, they always succeeded in depicting them as they themselves saw them. They had studied something real and lived it, copying for them was a work of the imagination.

How did Tacitus do it, of all those men the one who most helped make human thought lofty and robust, whose words will forever move souls withering under despotism, who seemed to savor the only consolation left to men by tyranny and baseness, the satisfaction of knowing them and scorning them? What was his secret? How does he move men with his opinions? How does he demonstrate general cause or particular motives? He does it by narrating. As witness to his judgments, he depicts scenes and protagonists before our eyes. Our spirit can capture profound judgments, profound reflections in the form of living images. Is this man a philosopher with his grave and severe lessons? Or is he a politician, exhibiting the wheels of government before us? Or an orator formally accusing Tiberius and Seyanus? No, he is not. He is (to quote Racine) the greatest of all painters of antiquity.

Perhaps the epoch in which we live is destined to restore narration and return it to its old place of honor. Never has there been such curiosity for a knowledge of history. For more than thirty years we have been living in a world shaken by many different prodigious events, nations, laws, and thrones have filed before us in such a way; the near future must find the solution to such large issues that the study of history is fast becoming the primary way of spending leisure and reflection. As the existence of each one, large or small, is now tied to the vicissitudes of our common destiny; since life, fortune, honor, vanity, what we do, even our opinions, in short, a citizen's whole condition depended on happenings in his country and the world over, and still do, attention has turned almost wholly to the history of nations.

This is what philosophy has done. What causes and what effects are more worthy of tracing to their origins? Poetry itself captivates us only when it tells us that which offers so many wonders, stirs such lively emotions. Drama seems to be devoted to reproducing historical scenes alone. The once frivolous novel, given such eloquence by the depiction of great passions, has been absorbed by the interest in history, told not to recount the adventures of individuals but to show them as real, living witnesses of a country, an epoch, a point of view. People want the novel to reflect the private life of a nation; is not its private life always the secret memoirs of its public life?

We are tired of seeing history turned into a docile, paid sophist ready to lend itself to all the proofs each one wants to squeeze out of it. What is asked of it are the facts. What we want to know as observed in the details and movement of this great drama in which we are actors and witnesses, is what nations and individuals were like before our time. History must evoke and resurrect them before our eyes. 7/

This is what our most distinguished contemporary historians say, virtually all of them, combining example and doctrine, have given the world instructive, interesting histories, perhaps the most seasoned fruits of modern literature. They all agree on the importance of facts and consider telling the living social drama the substance and soul of history. Our authority is worth very little (no matter how much Mr. Chacón, a biased judge in this matter, has exaggerated it). Therefore we had to validate sound doctrines by drawing on names of renown. In the pages we selected (the first that came to hand) it is easy to see that what Mr. Chacón calls the beaten path is the one and only path of history, as he himself implied in the first lines of his Prologue, and that only through the facts about a nation, individualized, living and complete, can we get to the philosophy of its history.

Yet there is a need to distinguish two kinds of philosophy of history. One is just the science of mankind in general, the science of moral and social laws, independent of local and temporal influences as necessary indicators of the intimate nature of man. The other is, comparatively speaking, a concrete science which deduces the spirit characteristic of a race, nation, or epoch from the facts pertaining to them; in no other way than from the facts about an individual can we deduce his character, his temperament.

This enables us to see an idea gradually develop in each race and assume the different forms that are impressed on a country and an epoch. An idea that when fully developed and its potential for assuming new forms is spent, its purpose fulfilled, gives way to yet another idea that will go through the same stages and also eventually perish. Not unlike the way an individual has hopes and aspirations that change constantly from the cradle to the grave, with new instincts that call him to new goals unfolding in each stage of life.

The general philosophy of history, the science of mankind, is the same everywhere in all eras; progress made by one nation is useful to all nations and becomes a part of the common heritage over which all of them have dominion. It is like the theory of attraction or the theory of light in the natural sciences. The laws of physics and chemistry operated the same way in the antediluvian world as they do now in ours. They work the same in Europe as in Japan, discoveries in physics and chemistry made in England and France become a part of the common heritage of nations all over the earth. Even so, the general philosophy of history cannot lead us to the particular philosophy of history of any one nation in which many causes and effects combine with the essential laws of humanity to modify the physiognomy of individual nations just like those that merge with the laws of matter to modify the geography of a country.

How could the whole body of European science tell people what our hills, valleys and rivers are like, what kinds of vegetation there are in Chile, what the Araucanians or the Pehuenche tribe look like, without direct observation? Doubtless very little. The same is true concerning the general laws of mankind. Any attempt to deduce from them the history of a particular nation is like a European geometrician trying to draw a map of Chile in his own study using the theorems of Euclid alone as a guide.

This is the concept of the philosophy of history held by Victor Cousin, the philosopher who has best expressed its importance, its components and its scope. He contends the philosophy of history is the philosophy of the human spirit applied to history. It therefore presupposes history, and in such a way that the former must be tested and guaranteed by the latter so we can be certain it is the exact expression of human nature and not a deceptive system that misleads once put into practice.

This philosophy should take everything into account; it should examine the spirit of a people in their climate, laws, religion, industry, art, wars, letters and science. How could it do this without presenting all the facts about that people, all the successive forms in every function of their intellectual and moral life?

Let us look at how Cousin depicts that vast, grandiose endeavor and then say whether it can be understood without a full exposition of the facts, the working material of the philosopher. Let us see the stuff human nature is made of by applying his principles to war. "Would you know what a man is worth?" this eloquent writer asks us.

Watch him in action; there he puts forth all the good there is in him, so also the virtue of a people makes its appearance on the field of battle. The philosophy of history must follow him there....

The organization of armies, even tactics, are of importance to history. Look at how the Athenians and Lacedemonians fought; all of Athens and Lacedemon were present there. Do you remember the organization of that small Greek army of 30,000 men which, commanded by a young man, advanced into the East to Bactriana? That was the redoubtable Macedonian phalanx, the configuration of which alone was the symbol of the rapid and powerful expansion of Greek civilization and embodied all the impetuosity, celerity and irresistible ardor characteristic of the spirit of Greece and of Alexander. The Macedonian phalanx was organized for rapid conquest, to break through and penetrate everything. It had irresistible momentum but little internal force, little weight and duration.

But look now at the Roman legion, it stood for all of Rome. A legion was a great whole, an enormous mass that overwhelmed everything in its path, in no danger of being dissolved, so compact was it, so vast and so full of inner resources. In sight of a legion we feel we are in the presence of an irresistible power, one that will endure and sweep away the enemy, replace him, occupy his land, settle there and take root. The Roman legion is a city, an empire, a small self-sufficient world. Its organization lacks nothing. In a word, a legion was an army organized not only to subdue but to possess the world; its character was consistency, weight, duration, permanence. It was the spirit of Rome. 8/

If philosophy must consider each component of a nation, is it not clear that there must first be a history of that nation, a history if possible that depicts it in its entirety, vitally and dynamically? We are embarrased to stress such an obvious truth.

Mr. Chacón was right when he said that the world of science is one. The scientific advances made by each nation, each man are part of the common heritage of mankind. Still we should clarify matters. Philosophical works done in Europe do not provide us with the philosophy of the history of Chile. It is up to us to do this through the only legitimate process there is, induction. This does not mean we regard a knowledge of what the Europeans have done is useless even when dealing only with our own history. The philosophy of European history will always act as our model, as a guide and method; it paves the way for us but does not free us from treading the same path.

Our young friend will allow us to say that the comparisons with which he sets out to uphold some of the ideas in the Prologue have more fantasy than logic. "What would we think" (I quote him) "of a scholar who told us not to avail ourselves of European railroads because Chile must begin on the road of discovery from the simple path of the mule cart until it reaches the railroad? What would we think of a scholar who said Chile should not avail itself of European dramatic art and all its excellence, because it should start, like Europe did, with the rude mysteries?.... What would we think of a scholar who said Chile should not take advantage of Europe's machinery but start out, like Europe did, with the coarsely woven cloth and hose of our ancestors?"

The truth is that these same propositions, if slightly modified, would not be at all absurd. There is a certain path that must always be traveled, albeit at a fairly fast tempo. A nation need no longer produce a James Watt in order to have railroads but it would have to have begun not with a highway but at least a narrow path connecting one hut with another. Would Mr. Chacón take the railroad to our colony in the straits? Would he put a lace or silk factory in Araucania? And would it be necessary perchance to wander afar to find nations to whom the mystery plays of the Middle Ages would be better suited than Racine's tragedies or Victor Hugo's dramas?

But this is not where the paradox lies. The comparisons used by Mr. Chacón are not right for the issue in hand. A machine can be transported from Europe to Chile and produce the same effect in Chile as in Europe. But the philosophy of the history of France, for instance, accounting for the separate manifestations of the French people in different epochs of their history, has no meaning when applied to the history of the Chilean people.

The only way it might be helpful to us is in charting our own work properly when, with the facts about Chile before us in all their circumstances and details, we sit down to uncover their inner spirit, the variety of ideas and the metamorphosis of each one in the different epochs of Chile's history. Otherwise, the work of Mr. Lastarria, who said in his prologue he intended to give us the philosophy of our history, would have been in vain.

In another number we will continue to develop these ideas and demonstrate how the Bosquejo histórico is as its title indicates a strictly historical work, even though some points and interpretations appeal for support by the facts. We cannot close, however, without answering the charge that accuses the Commission of exclusivism and intolerance because it felt the study of the history of Chile should begin with a clarification of the facts. If this judgment, which was modestly stated in the form of a hope, is an act of intolerance, literary criticism is doomed.

Villemain wanted Robinson, instead of describing the facts in general statements, to individualize them and depict them. Let us then protest against that wish as an act of exclusivism. What else might have been said if, instead of justly esteeming the Bosquejo histórico as Mr. Chacón himself admits, and awarding it the prize, the Commission had vested itself with inquisitorial powers and banned it?

The same freedom one writer has to publish according to the dictates of his conscience and intelligence, another writer has to examine and criticize that work according to his own particular knowledge and understanding.

NOTES

1. This article and the next were written against the background of a
    controversy over a prize in history awarded by the School of
    Humanities of the University of Chile in 1847. The prize went to
    José Victorino Lastarria for his work entitled Bosquejo histórico
    de la constitución del gobierno de Chile durante el primer período
    de la revolución, with some reservations voiced by the Commission
    as to the documentation of some of the author's findings. Jacinto
    Chacón, an admirer of Lastarria and author of the prologue to the
    Bosquejo histórico, countered with a defense of Lastarria's
    theories and an attack against the Commission. Bello refutes him
    in these articles (T).

2. Thierry, Augustin, Histoire de la Conquête de l'Angleterre par les
    Normanda, de ses causes et de ses suites, Paris, 1825 (T).

3. Simonde de Sismondi, J.C.L., Histoire des Français, Paris,
    1821-1844, 31 vols. The quotation is from the introduction to
    Part I, The French under the Merovingians, translated by William
    Bellingham, London, 1850, pages xxxix-xl (T).

4. Simonde de Sismondi, Histoire des républiques italiennes du moyen
    âge, Zurich, 1807-1809, 8 vols. (T).

5. Villemain, Abel Françoise (1790-1870), French classical and
    literary historian (T).

6. Robertson, William (1721-1793), an American historian. Bello
    refers to his View of the State of Europe, a study prefixed to The
    History of the History of the Reign of Charles the Fifth,
    Philadelphia, 1770, 3 vols. (T).

7. Baron de Barante (1782-1866), a French historian and author of
    Histoire des ducs de Bourgogne, etc., Paris, 1824-1838, 12 vols.
    The quotation is from the introduction (T).

8. Cousin, Victor, Introduction to the History of Philosophy, a
    series of lectures delivered and published in Paris in 1828.
    Bello's quote is taken from the ninth lecture (T).

HOW TO STUDY HISTORY

This article appeared in El Araucano, 913, Santiago, February 4, 1848. Bello reproduced it in his Opúsculos literarios y críticos, publicados en diversos periódicos desde 1834 hasta 1849, Santiago, 1850, pp. 154-160.

Because of the controversy raised by this article, Bello had to publish the following note in El Araucano, 915, February 18, 1848:

Science of History. "We would not say another word about this matter if not impelled to do so by a letter published in the Progreso of February 11. We found it very strange that its author might imagine we had a hidden intention of damaging his reputation. Our only purpose in this controversy has been to defend the vote of the Commission responsible for judging the work by J. Victorino Lastarria, in favor of which we also voted in the School of Humanities when it concurred in the Commission's decision. We are by no means unaware of Jacinto Chacón's qualifications as an instructor of history at the National Institute. Quite the contrary. We have always done justice in the past, and will continue to do so, to his ability, knowledge, and assiduous commitment to the cultivation of letters, which we should like to see more generally imitated."

It must be said, although Mr. Chacón set out from the beginning of his first article to settle the matter (which in our judgment was already clear), he instead seems to have driven it out of all proportion. The Commission, after duly praising the Bosquejo histórico, said that not enough data were available for it to accept the author's assessment as to the nature and leanings of the parties involved in the Chilean Revolution.

It quite rightly thought that general outlines developed without a clear, composite picture of all the events, the people and the material trappings of history involved, have the drawback of allowing much room for theory and in part distorting the truth. A failing, the Commission added, common to every work in which all the background used by the author in making his judgments is absent. It was the Commission's hope that studies would first be made to clarify the facts. "The theory explaining those facts will come along immediately, treading firmly on familiar ground."

It is not then a matter of whether the ad probandum method, as Mr. Chacón calls it, is good or bad per se, nor whether, strictly speaking, the ad narrandum method is better. It is merely a matter of finding out whether the ad probandum method, or more clearly, the method that investigates the innermost spirit of the facts about a nation, the idea they embody, their future direction, is appropriate for the current status of the history of Chile as an independent nation, a history which is still to be written.

Only a few essays have yet been published, and they far from give the picture as a whole, let alone exhaust their own limited goals. Which of the two methods should we start with to write the history of Chile? The one that supplies the background or the one that deducts results? The one that sheds light on the facts or the one that discusses and summarizes them? The Commission thought the former. Was it justified in its opinion or not? This and this alone is the issue that should have been settled. Each method has its place, each is good in its time, and there are also moments when, depending on the judgment or talent of the writer, one can be used instead of the other. The issue is merely one of order and relative convenience.

With that settled, it is simple to see that the quotation from Barante, which Mr. Chacón regarded as decisive support for his argument, has no bearing on the matter under discussion. In the presence of the great historical works done by his contemporaries, Barante said no single direction is exclusive, no single method compulsory.

Our position is the same as his. When the public has a huge mass of documents and history books available, a historian can easily start a new work based on those documents or histories, and either follow the method involving an inductive approach, like Guizot in his History of Civilization, or else the narrative method used by Augustin Thierry in his History of the Norman Conquest of England.

A nation's history found only in incomplete documents that are scattered hither and yon and in vague traditions that need to be weighed and assessed, makes the narrative method compulsory. If anyone denies this, let him cite a single general or specific history that was begun otherwise. Furthermore, in his own approach, Barante himself makes no secret of his preference for a philosophy that springs spontaneously from the facts related in their entirety and in their natural colors, over a method presented in the nature of theory or premeditated system which always raises the fear that history may unwittingly be twisted to accommodate a preconceived notion. The latter, according to Cousin, vitiates history. See Barante's introduction to his History of the Dukes of Burgundy and particularly the history itself, an admirable web of original testimony with no philosophic pretense whatever.

It is not our intention to say there is or should be a strict division between the two methods, which we might call narrative and philosophic. The thing is that the philosophy, which in the former blends with the narrative and rarely makes a direct appearance, is the major part of the latter, to which the facts are subordinated. The facts themselves are not touched upon nor dwelt on except as needed to demonstrate the cause and effect relationship. This leaves room in between for innumerable shadings and halftones, samples of which could easily be found in contemporary historians.

The judgment of the Commission is not preclusive nor its preference absolute. One only need read its report to realize that the arguments adduced by the author of the Prologue are beside the point, they challenge what no one said or had in mind. The decision of the Commission touched no issue on which literary opinion is divided, as he assumes. It expected—not expected—it hoped we would be given the premises before the conclusion, the text ahead of the commentary, the details before they had been condensed into generalities. It is impossible to state more modestly a judgment more consistent with the experience of the world of science and the doctrine of recognized authors who have written on the history of science as such.

Indeed, assuming the issue were debatable, the Commission, had it come out on one side of the controversy, would merely have been exercising a right protected by literary privilege. Is it perchance illicit for a person willing to use his intelligence to choose between one opinion or another the one he thinks more reasonable and justified? And is this man the champion of literary freedom who forces us to suspend our judgment on controversial issues and state no ideas not bearing the imprint of universal approval?

Mr. Chacón summarizes the origin and development of European history beginning with the Crusades, a gratuitous summary as far as the matter in hand is concerned and one not altogether accurate. He begins with Froissart whom he places at the head of a number of chroniclers "who in the twelfth and thirteenth centuries mixed history with legend, the ballads of Charlemagne and King Arthur with the deeds of chivalry."

Mr. Chacón forgets that Froissart flourished in the fourteenth century and seems unaware that the ballads of Charlemagne and King Arthur had begun to contaminate history sometime before the first Crusade. Judging by this account, it might be thought that in the early period of the French language (which was not rightly the language of the troubadors), there were no true historians, actual witnesses to the events of the Crusades, such as Villehardouin and Joinville.

Be that as it may, Chacón parades a procession of chroniclers, historians and philosophers of history before our eyes, beginning with Froissart and ending with Hallam. "Are we being asked," he wonders, "to step backwards; are we being asked to close our eyes to the light from Europe, not to take advantage of the progress made in the science of history by European civilization, as we do in other arts and sciences, but instead to rewalk the same path from the chroniclers on down to the philosophy of history?".

The answer to this question is not difficult. One can hardly go backwards when he has bearly placed his feet on the ground. We are not asking for the chronicles of France to be written all over again; how could the history of Chile, which has not yet been done, be set back? So that once it is done, philosophy can give us an idea of each personnage and each historic event (our own, that is), treading with a firm step on familiar ground? Must we look to Froissart, Comines, Mizeray or Sismondi for the history of Chile? The real step backward would be if we began where the Europeans left off.

To assume we are being asked to close our eyes to the light from Europe is pure oratory. It was never anyone's idea. What is expected is that we will open our eyes wide to the light but not expect to find what is not nor can be there. Let us read and study European history books. Let us watch the specific spectacle unfolded and synthesized in each from one milestone to another. Let us accept the examples and lessons they contain, an issue perhaps given the least amount of thought. Let us use them as a standard and guide for our own works of history. Can we discover Chile with its own particular achievements, its own characteristic physiognomy, in those books? This is the job for Chilean historians, whichever method they use. Open the best-known studies made according to the dictates of the philosophy of history. Do they give us the philosophy of the history of humankind?

The nation of Chile is not mankind in abstract, it is humankind under specific forms, as specific as the country's mountains, valleys and rivers, as its plants and animals, as its races, as the moral and political conditions in which our society was born and flourishes. Do those works provide us with the philosophy of the history of the nation, of an epoch? Of England under the Norman conquest, of Spain under the rule of the Saracens, of France during its revolution?

There is nothing more interesting or instructive. Yet, let us not forget that the Chilean of the time of independence, the man who is the protagonist of our history and our particular philosophy, is not a Frenchman, Anglo-Saxon, Norman, Visigoth or Arab. He has his own spirit, his own features, and his own peculiar instincts.

THEMES OF HISTORY AND GEOGRAPHY

Let us admit we are to blame for having found some passages of the Prologue inconsistent or obscure. Actually the trick used by Mr. Chacón to reconcile them in his first article did not elude us, but the idea seemed too at odds with common sense to attribute it to him. We dare not charge him with it even now and prefer to think that (doubtless our own fault) we never understood him.

We apologize to our readers. We have prolonged to the point of tedium our defense of a truth, of an obvious principle many regard as trivial. But we hoped to address the young. Our youth has taken up the study of history expectantly; we have just seen brilliant evidence of their progress, and we would like them to fully grasp the real mission of history so they may study it productively.

We should especially like to caution them against an exaggerated sense of servility to the science of European civilization. There is a sort of fate that subdues new-born nations to those that went before. Greece subdued Rome; Greece and Rome subdued the modern states of Europe when the revival of letters took place, and we are being drawn along now more than is proper by the influence of Europe, whose freedom of thought we should imitate at the same time we avail ourselves of its enlightenment.

Not too long ago European poets looked to pagan history in search of images invoking the muses in which neither they nor anyone else believed. A rejected lover would address devout appeals to Venus to move the heart of his beloved in a kind of poetic solidarity similar to what Mr. Chacón apparently expects in history.

Likewise, we must not value philosophic nomenclature too highly; generalizations with little or no inherent meaning per se for a person who has neither contemplated human nature in history nor the primitive, original historians. We are not talking here of our own history alone but of history as a whole. Young men of Chile! learn to judge for yourselves; aspire to independence of mind. Go to the sources, or at least the streams closest to them. The very language of the primitive historians, their ideas, even their prejudices and fabulous legends are a part of history and not its least instructive and true part. For instance, do you want to know what the discovery and conquest of America was like? Read the diary of Columbus, the letters of Pedro de Valdivia and Hernán Cortés. Bernal Díaz will tell you much more than Solís and Robertson. Inquire into each civilization in its works, ask each historian to produce his guarantees. That is the first philosophy we should learn from Europe.

Our civilization, too, will be judged by its works, and if European civilization is copied slavishly even to the extent of what is inapplicable, what will a Michelet or a Guizot think of us? They will say America still has not loosened its fetters, it follows in our footsteps blindfolded, no ideas of its own, no original thought, nothing characteristic filters through its works. It mimics the forms of our own philosophy but misses its spirit. Its civilization is an exotic plant that has still not imbibed the juices of the earth that sustains it.

One more final observation. What goes by the name of philosophy of history is a science in swaddling clothes. If we are to judge it by Cousin's program, it has scarcely taken the first steps on a long road. It is still an unstable science, the faith of one century is anethema to the next, the philosophers of the nineteenth century have turned their back on those of the eighteenth, the ideas of the most lofty one of all, Montesquieu, are accepted only with reservations.

Has the final term been reached? Posterity will say. The philosophy of history is still a tournament with the parties at loggerheads. Which will have the final victory? Science, like nature, feeds on ruins. Whereas systems are born, develop, wither and die, science lifts itself above the spoils in luxuriant splendor and stays eternally young.

STUDIES ON VIRGIL, BY P. F. TISSOT

This concerns the two-volume work by Pierre François Tissot published in Paris in 1825. Bello's article first came out in El Repertorio Americano, I, London, October 1826, pp. 19-26, and was apparently based on an article by Juan Bautista Amado Sansón de Pongerville which appeared in the Revue Enciclopédique, Paris, January, 1826.

The great writers of the century of Louis XIV knew the full value of the literary treasures of antiquity, evident in their many successful borrowings from them. Yet, an appreciation of the sublime concepts of the ancients was wanting in that period. Worse still was the following century, by which time the fact that the ancients had been the creators and models of the very beauty that was so greatly admired had been forgotten. Whether accidentally or on purpose, a few noteworthy authors sometimes dared deride them and cast them into outer darkness.

With the ancients spurned, careful usage of their sacred language ended and literature lost one of its most effective resources. If a critic still mentioned the writers of antiquity, it was merely to sacrifice them to the glory of his contemporaries. This is the most serious charge that can be made against the seventeenth century, which perhaps lacked no more than a thorough knowledge of antiquity to place it on a par with its predecessors.

One literary figure known for a number of fine productions set out to follow the trail marked by Quintilian, but frequently forgot his purpose as the acclaim of a frivolous audience drew him away from his master. Furthermore, La Harpe was imbued with the literary opinions of his time, and little versed in the Greek and Roman authors, he judged them and the moderns by the system of the school to which he belonged.

Justice always has its day. Scarcely half a century has passed and many of La Harpe's maxims have already been revoked. His treatise on literature, with its unfailing taste, easy elegance, and the cleverness of an author who had been the pupil of Voltaire, neglects the writers of antiquity and evidences throughout the continuing sway of reason over great minds.

Powerful causes have subsequently intervened, which have given criticism better insight and afforded custom and politics great influence over literature. The crises around them stirred men's minds; the unfolding, endless struggle of human passions was watched with curious eyes. The habit of thought united with the need to put ideas to work, led to improvements in the art of forceful expression. Political events, in changing the course of human thought, created a liking for serious study. Thus, our sphere of learning has broadened, truth has regained its sway over the arts, taste (inseparable from reason) has become more demanding, and man has learned by experience to judge things for himself. The friends of letters, having been brought back to nature, gave antiquity its due and recognized that the true way to surpass the writers of the day was to equal those of old.

M. Tissot, a successful man of letters qualified to assess progress in the arts and to guide young intellectuals, was selected by the foremost poet of the century and distinguished interpreter of Virgil to be his successor. 1/ M. Tissot did justice to the trust of his predecessor when he launched on his new career, and students touched by the muses were indebted to him for the development of talents that make them now the hope of our literature. None left his side without a strong desire to devote to arts and letters the enthusiasm he had awakened.

After long dedication to teaching, M. Tissot returned to a quiet life of reflection, intending to serve letters from his study as he had from his university chair. The translator of Juan Segundo's Besos and Bucólicas, wrote his Studies on Virgil. The simple title given this major work might make one think it deals with the Aeneid alone. The author's plan, however, like that of Quintilian, embraced the full range of literature. He naturally chose as his vantage point the work of the great imitator or writers before him and model for those who followed.

Thus, M. Tissot found a suitable means for establishing the relative nature of the literary productions from Homer to Virgil and from Virgil down to the modern-day. In his work he not so much judges as compares. When he analyzes the creations of antiquity, he contrasts them with modern works of the imagination. His learned investigations reveal the borrowings of one genius from another in all their forms. Nor does he limit his contrast to works bearing an analogy with the epic; with profound insight he moves into didactic to cyclical poetry, the drama, legend, and the novel. In short, he covers the different branches of literature that sprouted from the same stock and are nurtured by a single source.

The Studies on Virgil should thus be regarded as a complete and highly interesting treatise on ancient and modern literature. The author has created a method as original as it is clever and enjoyable. He avoids the aridity of the scholastics and the blind admiration of the commentators. Outspoken yet fair, he carefully notes the beauty and shortcomings of the great masters and puts them to successful use.

Above all, he possesses the secret of communicating his enthusiasm to his readers. M. Tissot's style, moving and truthful though florid, is never at odds with the ideas of the writers he brings on stage. We can almost hear them confiding the revelations of their muses to him. But, let us allow the professor himself to develop his ideas on the relationship between the great writers of all times and of all nations:

Adding the wealth of the present to the treasures of the past, perpetually contrasting and comparing the principal writers of the world, it was my hope to avail myself of the progress of enlightenment and the authority of such great minds to reveal the religion of truth and beauty in all its glory, imbued with all the qualities that have earned our respect. After several epochs of splendor, this religion has now dimmed and become lost in shadow as the human mind surrenders itself to skepticism and the dual poles of incredulity or idolatry.

The Asia of olden times was the cradle of that religion. Egypt, land of mystery, revealed it to a few jealous servants who concealed it from the common herd. The Greeks intermingled it with their fables while remaining true to its nature and laws. Orpheus, Linos, and Muse, felt its first sparks of insight as a heavenly gift. Hesiod was raised to great heights. Homer, his heart pierced and creative genius captivated, may still be its high priest despite the mantle in which it is sometimes enfolded to silence the murmurings or reason. Tucidides and Xenophon rendered it pure hommage. Schylo dealt with it in unequal, sublime commerce. Sophocles was virtually always its worthy interpreter. Euripides, harboring it intuitively, lacked literary conscience and too often profaned it.

Plato, after soaring heavenward on its wings, later followed his imagination and became lost in the region of the clouds. Aristotle, more reposed and austere, worshipped the science of truth and beauty all his life; his unsurpassed wisdom still holds lessons for all men. Sublime instinct and vocation bound Demosthenes to that religion forever. Cicero, destined to be its minister and interpreter, learned it in studying philosophy and gave eloquence an irresistible allure. Lucretius possessed the power and love of truth and beauty, but, to serve them better, lacked a more flawless style and better taste, above all.

Terence was a loyal pupil of truth and beauty and though more aware and wiser than Plautus had no equal power of imagination. When Virgil confronted nature face to face, when he drew from his own studies or from within himself, he was the Raphael of poetry, the most faithful portrayer of truth and beauty. Give this religion to Ovid and he would be one of the world's best poets. Like Euripides, he realized his failings but clung to them relentlessly. This religion requires taste and enlightenment, which were absent in Lucan and Juvenal, who were its unwitting transgressors.

Dante, Shakespeare, and Milton, after offering it the incense of their genius, offended it irreverently, insulting sound reason; yet their century has a greater share of the blame than them. Buffon, the Aristotle, Pliny, and Plato of our day, had the religion of truth and beauty thoroughly etched on his soul. Why then, with his devotion to magnificence, did he not use that eloquent heedlessness of nature, so full of grace, as his model? Buffon is like a king who never forgets his dignity, the Louis XIV of writers, his flaws are embedded in his character. He was probably thinking of himself when he said, "Style is the essence of man."2/

An active mind, a superior intellect overruled by a stronger imagination, and first-class eloquence, did not always save Rousseau from occasional rhetoric and sophism. He gauged the noble simplicity of the ancients; one wishes he had followed their example in other ways. An emulator of Richardson, he far from equals him in how faithfully the latter imitated the language of women. Yet the love of truth and beauty burned steadily in his soul, fed by the flame of his enthusiasm and immense yearning for fame. Had his soul been nurtured like Fenelon's, his literary conscience would have shown the courage required by the sacrifices a writer should call upon himself to make.

Nature gave Voltaire the reason of Locke, the dramatic eloquence of Euripides, the variety of wit found in Fontenelle, Pope and Hamilton, the satiric originality of Lucian, the urbanity of Horace, the festive lightness of Ariosto, and the brilliant facility of a Frenchman full of wit and elegance. A literary conscience was missing in this unheard of array of talents, any one of which would suffice to make a writer famous.

No one delved into truth with such sagacity nor felt such vital admiration for beauty, but a religious dedication to these two sentiments was missing. The fickleness of his imagination, the impulse of this or that momentary passion, and his occasional contemplation of self, deprived his opinions of all stability. A skillful critic on the one hand, a concerned judge on the other, rashly pronouncing misguided sentences. Lacking a strict grounding in steadfast principles, not fully aware of the terms of the fame whose love devoured him, spoiled by precocious acclaim, exasperated by unfair criticism intended just to humiliate him, and sustained by a degree of public favor that was continuously fed by his philosophy, he ignored the voice of conscience. He depicted not faithful portrayals but brilliant lies, rested his laurels on the seductions of his pen, and thought too much about his own century and not enough about posterity.

In short, he treated his own talent with fatal indulgence, never to be atoned. Had it not been for this, he might have left us nothing but masterpieces. What could not have been expected of such a man had he prevailed against himself, like an unyielding critic, and never compromised with his deep feeling for the beauty of nature and for the rules of art? 3/

M. Tissot examines each book of the Aeneid one by one, preceded or followed by the Latin text, from which he sometimes translates passages with uncommon success. His style is elegant and vigorous, his phrasing poetic and graceful, and his rendering of the poem as accurate as one can give in prose.

The prologue is a literary production beyond all praise. It is not just an embellishment but an instructive exordium that summarizes the excellent principles of this useful treatise. M. Tissot mentions himself there once, with the wholesome candor of an upright man, sure of himself and of his right to public esteem. The last paragraph ought to be quoted here:

Ay, rewarding Muses! Who can fail to feel how good and sweet you are? Were I not to have you, I shall never at least deny your delights. You have beautified the pleasures of my life and consoled my sorrows. Like the bees of Hybla, your honey has tempered the cup of absinthe given me more than once by fate and men. When writing part of this work, I was at death's door, you gave me strength to live and to overcome death, nor is that all. You nurtured my spirit and salvaged my imagination in the midst of bodily decay, your magic treatment gradually restored my health. I give you thanks for your goodness and take refuge on your breast like the weary traveler seeking port after the tempest. And you, illustrious translator of the Georgics, whose friendship does me such honor and whose selection caused me such care! Since your death, not one day passes that I fail to recall my debt to your memory. All my efforts are dedicated to the one who conferred them upon me. Accept in these studies the devoted offering of a pupil to his teacher.

Delille could receive no better tribute than a work which he in a way inspired, a work the purpose of which was to propagate the sound doctrines of a literature to which he devoted sixty years. The Studies on Virgil are equally suitable for a man of the world or a man of letters, for young people starting their studies in the arts or parents eager to examine and assess the progress of their children.

A unanimous concert of acclaim is already witness to the recognition given by enlightened sectors of the public to the learned professor and painstaking emulator of Quintilian. The similarity between the epochs in which both lived highlights his own. The former fought the doctrine of the Senecas, Lucans and Eustaces, who in their anxiety to explore new paths corrupted the art of men like Lucretius, Virgil, and Ovid. Now, when our literature is threatened with decadence, the lessons on this modern-day Quintilian shall guide the uncertain steps of the successors of the Racines, Voltaires, and Delilles.

NOTES

1. M. Tissot was Delille's handpicked successor to his chair in Latin poetry in the College de France (T).

2. "Le style est tout l'homme." P. F. Tissot, opus cit., p. clxxvi (A).

3. This long quotation is from the introduction to Tissot's work, originally titled Etudes sur Virgile (T).

JUDGMENT ON THE POETRY
OF JOSÉ MARÍA HEREDIA

Bello's commentary of the 1825 New York edition of Heredia's Poesías was first published in El Repertorio Americano, II, London, January 1827, pp. 34-35. He had announced this article earlier in El Repertorio Americano, I, London, October 1826, p. 320, in a brief note mentioning the "productions of a young man from Havana, which, aside from some slipshod language, displays a rich and vivid imagination, a tender heart, and other outstanding poetic qualities. We will devote a separate article to them in the next issue."

Bello again mentioned the literary work of Heredia in El Repertorio Americano, IV, August 1827, p. 306, in his criticism of a theatrical work by Jony, "The translator of this play is Mr. Heredia, who probably did not have the time to polish his translation. This is not on a par with his best work either in style or versification, but it does have passages revealing his full store of merit and talent. With a little more study and refinement he would compete with the best poets of our day in any language or any country."

We are pleased and proud to second the applause in Europe and America that has welcomed the poetical works of José María Heredia. They are replete with excellent strokes of imagination and sensitivity; in a word, he is a truly inspired poet. Instances of the intellectual precocity displayed by this young man are not common. To judge by the dates of his compositions and the information he himself offers in one of them, he is apparently twenty-three years old. Some of the compositions were printed in 1821, and one sounds like it was ready by 1818. This greatly increases our admiration for their beauty and style and should make us look indulgently on the shortcomings noticed here and there in his work.

One of Heredia's major appeals is his judgment in organizing his works, their coherence, and an occasional elegance of taste we would not have expected in such a young poet. Although he often imitates, there is normally a good deal of originality in his images and concepts.

We also note how successfully he conveys the impressions of the majesty of nature in the equatorial region, so worth contemplating, studying, and setting to verse. We see this especially in the compositions entitled <u>A mi caballo</u>, <u>Al Sol</u>, <u>A la noche</u>, and <u>Versos escritos en una tempestad.</u> Virtually all of them display a wealthy vein of talent. His portrayals are generally sombre, with a predominantly melancholy sentiment at times bordering on misanthropy and somewhat reminiscent of the talent and style of Lord Byron.

He also follows the footsteps of Meléndez and other well-known Castilian poets of the times, though not always (nor should it be expected) with the maturity of judgment necessary in reading and imitating the moderns, from whom he unfortunately takes their affectation in archaisms, baroque constructions, and at times, their bombastic tone, filled with epithets and peculiar pompous endings. We would hope that if Mr. Heredia publishes a new edition of his works, he will purge these defects and some irrelevant words and phrases, and return to the anvil with some of his verses in which the prosody is not exactly correct.

The poems in this collection are of different types and styles, yet we find the most beauty and originality in those on American themes or composed to express feelings evoked by actual scenes and occurrences. The last of the group just mentioned is among that number, and we reproduce it in full as a sample of the merits of our young poet and of the errors he sometimes makes.

VERSOS ESCRITOS EN UNA TEMPESTAD

Huracán, huracán, venir te siento;
y en tu soplo abrasado,
respiro entusiasmado
del Señor de los aires el aliento.
En alas de los vientos suspendido
vedle rodar por el espacio inmenso,
silencioso, tremendo, irresistible,
como una eternidad. La tierra en calma
funesta, abrasadora,
contempla con pavor su faz terrible.
Al toro contemplad... La tierra escarban
de un insufrible ardor sus pies heridos;
la armada frente al cielo levantando,
y en la hinchada nariz fuego aspirando,
llama la tempestad con sus bramidos.
¡Qué nubes! ¡qué furor!... El sol temblando
vela en triste vapor su faz gloriosa,
y entre sus negras sombras sólo vierte
luz fúnebre y sombría,
que ni es noche ni día,
y al mundo tiñe de color de muerte.
Los pajarillos callan y se esconden,
mientras el fiero huracán viene volando;
y en los lejanos montes retumbando,
le oyen los bosques, y a su voz responden.
Ya llega... ¿no le veis?... ¡Cuál desenvuelve
su manto aterrador y majestuoso!
¡Gigante de los aires, te saludo!
Ved cómo en confusión vuelan en torno
las orlas de su parda vestidura.
¡Cómo en el horizonte

sus brazos furibundos ya se enarcan,
y tendidos abarcan
cuanto alcanzo a mirar de monte a monte!
¡Oscuridad universal! su soplo
levanta en torbellinos
el polvo de los campos agitado.
¡Oid...! Retumba en las nubes despeñado
el carro del Señor; y de sus ruedas
brota el rayo veloz, se precipita,
hiere, y aterra al delincuente suelo,
y en su lívida luz inunda el cielo.
¡Qué rumor!... ¡Es la lluvia!... Enfurecida
cae a torrentes, y oscurece el mundo;
y todo es confusión y horror profundo.
Cielos, colinas, nubes, caro bosque,
¿dónde estáis? ¿dónde estáis? os busco en vano;
desaparecisteis... La tormenta umbría
en los aires revuelve un oceano
que todo lo sepulta...
Al fin, mundo fatal, nos separamos;
el huracán y yo solos estamos.
¡Sublime tempestad! ¡Cómo en tu seno,
de tu solemne inspiración henchido,
al mundo vil y miserable olvido,
y alzo la frente de delicia lleno!
¿Dó está el alma cobarde
que teme tu rugir?... Yo en ti me elevo
al trono del Señor; oigo en las nubes
el eco de su voz; siento a la tierra
escucharle y temblar; ardiente lloro
desciende por mis pálidas mejillas;
y a su alta majestad tiemblo y le adoro.

These verses contain courageous strokes and in order for them to offer the pure pleasure of poetry at its most beautiful, we miss only the precision that comes with age and study.

The following poem is another work in which we find Mr. Heredia on a nobler and loftier plane:

FRAGMENTOS DESCRIPTIVOS DE UN POEMA MEJICANO

¡Oh! ¡cuán bella es la tierra que habitaban
los aztecas valientes! En su seno,
en una estrecha zona concentrados,
con asombro veréis todos los climas
que hay desde el polo al Ecuador. Sus campos
cubren, a par de las doradas mieses,
las cañas deliciosas. El naranjo,
y la piña, y el plátano sonante,
hijos del suelo equinoccial, se mezclan
a la frondosa vid, al pino agreste,
y de minerva al árbol majestuoso.
Nieve eterna corona las cabezas
de Iztaccihual purísimo, Orizaba
y Popocatépetl; pero el invierno

nunca aplicó su destructora mano
a los fértiles campos, donde ledo
los mira el indio en púrpura ligera
y oro teñirse, a los postreros rayos
del sol en occidente, que al alzarse,
sobre eterna verdura y nieve eterna
a torrentes vertió su luz dorada,
y vio a naturaleza conmovida...
a su dulce calor hervir en vida
....
Era la tarde. La ligera brisa
sus alas en silencio ya plegaba,
y entre la yerba y árboles dormía,
mientras el ancho sol su disco hundía
detrás de Iztaccihual. La nieve eterna,
cual disuelta en mar de oro, semejaba
temblar en torno dél; un arco inmenso
que del empíreo en el cenit finaba,
como el pórtico espléndido del cielo,
de luz vestido y centellante gloria,
de sus últimos rayos recibía
los colores riquísimos; su brillo
desfalleciendo fue; la blanca luna
y dos o tres estrellas solitarias
en el cielo desierto se veían.
¡Crepúsculo feliz! Hora más bella
que la alma noche o el brillante día,
¡cuánto es dulce tu paz al alma mía!
Hallábame sentado de Cholula
en la antigua pirámide. Tendido
el llano inmenso que a mis pies yacía,
mis ojos a espaciarse convidaba.
¡Qué silencio! ¡qué paz! ¡Oh! ¿quién diría
que, en medio de estos campos, reina alzada
la bárbara opresión, y que esta tierra
brota mieses tan ricas, abonada
con sangre de hombres?...
Bajó la noche en tanto. De la esfera
el leve azul, oscuro y más oscuro
se fue tornando. La ligera sombra
de las nubes serenas, que volaban
por el espacio en alas de la brisa,
fue ya visible en el tendido llano.
Iztaccihual purísimo volvía
de los trémulos rayos de la luna
el plateado fulgor, mientras en oriente,
bien como chispas de oro, retemblaban
mil estrellas y mil....
Al paso que la luna declinaba,
y al ocaso por grados descendía,
poco a poco la sombra se extendía
del Popocatépetl, que semejaba
un nocturno fantasma. El arco oscuro
a mí llegó, cubrióme, y avanzando
fue mayor, y mayor, hasta que al cabo
en sombra universal veló la tierra.

Volví los ojos al volcán sublime,
que, velado en vapores transparentes,
sus inmensos contornos dibujaba

de occidente en el cielo.
¡Gigante de Anahuac! ¡oh! ¿cómo el vuelo
de las edades rápidas no imprime
ninguna huella en tu nevada frente?
Corre el tiempo feroz, arrebatando
años y siglos, como el norte fiero
precipita ante sí la muchedumbre
de las olas del mar. Pueblos y reyes
viste hervir a tus pies, que combatían
cual hora combatimos, y llamaban
eternas sus ciudades, y creían
fatigar a la tierra con su gloria.
Fueron: de ellos no resta ni memoria.
¿Y tú eterno serás? Tal vez un día
de tus bases profundas desquiciado
caerás, y al Anahuac tus vastas ruinas
abrumarán; levantaránse en ellas
otras generaciones, y orgullosas
que fuiste negarán....
           ¿Quién afirmarme
podrá que aqueste mundo que habitamos
no es el cadáver pálido y deforme
de otro mundo que fue?...

The eight-syllable ballad that follows, dedicated to his father, is an admirably simple expression of filial affection.

A MI PADRE, EN SUS DIAS

Ya tu familia gozosa
se prepara, amado padre,
a solemnizar la fiesta
de tus felices natales.
Yo, el primero de tus hijos,
también primero en lo amante,
hoy lo mucho que te debo
con algo quiero pagarte.
¡Oh! ¡cuán gozoso confieso
que tú de todos los padres
has sido para conmigo
el modelo inimitable!
Tomaste a cargo tuyo
el cuidado de educarme,
y nunca a manos ajenas
mi tierna infancia fiaste.
Amor a todos los hombres,
temor a Dios me inspiraste,
odio a la atroz tiranía
y a las intrigas infames.
Oye, pues, los tiernos votos
que por ti Fileno hace,
y que de su labio humilde
hasta el Eterno se parten.
Por largos años, el cielo
para la dicha te guarde
de la esposa que te adora
y de tus hijos amantes.

Puedas mirar tus bisnietos
poco a poco levantarse,
como los bellos retoños
en que un viejo árbol renace,
cuando al impulso del tiempo
la frente orgullosa abate.
Que en torno tuyo los veas
triscar y regocijarse,
y que, entre amor y respeto
dudosos y vacilantes,
halaguen con labio tierno
tu cabeza respetable.
Deja que los opresores
osen faccioso llamarte,
que el odio de los perversos
da a la virtud más realce.
En vano blanco te hicieran
de sus intrigas cobardes
unos reptiles oscuros
sedientos de oro y de sangre.
¡Hombres odiosos!... Empero
tu alta virtud depuraste,
cual oro al crisol descubre
sus finísimos quilates.
A mis ojos te engrandecen
esos honrosos pesares;
y si fueras más dichoso,
me fueras menos amable.
De la mísera Caracas
oye al pueblo cual te aplaude,
llamándote con ternura
su defensor y su padre.
Vive, pues, en paz serena;
jamás la calumnia infame
con hálito pestilente
de tu honor el brillo empañe.
Déte, en medio de tus hijos,
salud su bálsamo suave;
y bríndete amor risueño
las caricias conyugales.

This composition stimulates our esteem for Mr. Heredia's sensitivity and our admiration for his talent. It also seems fair, even though at the expense of a degression, to take this opportunity to render to the memory of his father the respect and gratitude due him by everyone in the Americas for his conduct in singularly difficult circumstances.

Heredia's father belonged to one of the first families of Santo Domingo. He emigrated from there, as we understand, at the time of the colony's cession to France and settled in Cuba, where our young poet was born. Raised to the post of magistrate, he served the regency of the audiencia of Caracas when it was under Monteverde and Boves. In performing his obligations, one hardly knows what was most outstanding: his honor and loyalty to the government whose cause he mistakenly followed; his integrity and firmness in making the voice of the law heard (albeit unsuccessfully) or his humanity towards the people of Venezuela, treated by the ruling tyrants and their satellites with outrageous cruelty, rapacity and insult.

Heredia as regent was relentless in his efforts to placate the fury of a military which brutally trampled on laws and treaties, and to instill in the people the hope, which he clearly had, that the new Spanish constitution would put an end to such a horrendous state of affairs. Spurned and vilipended and drawn to his death by force of affliction and disappointment, he achieved nothing except one more proof for the people in America of how illusory those hopes were.

Returning to young Heredia, we would hope he had written more things in this simple, natural style which he imbues with such gentleness, or more compositions devoted to innocent family affections, and less of the erotic gender which are in pernicious overabundance in the language.

Some of his shortcomings are due to his age, others (mostly errors in prosody) can be traced to the land where he was born and raised; a third group can be attributed to imitation of bad example. The latter include outdated words and endings which some believe make a style more lofty, but actually (unless used sparingly and properly) make it affected and pedantic. Archaisms may sometimes be tolerated and even produce a good effect when dealing with matters of unusual gravity. But loosing them everywhere and needlessly discarding phrases that bear the stamp of everyday use, the only ones our soul relates to its feelings and having the power to rekindle them, is a reprehensible evil.

Even though we see this done by such men as Jovellanos and Meléndez, we would have it banished from poetry and made part of the curse good taste declared long ago against the trappings of modern-day Gongorism. We fail to see the outdated words that so delighted Meléndez and Cienfuegos in the verse of Rioja, Lope de Vega, and the Argensolas. Add to this how bad these imitations of antiquity look in works that are otherwise below par for the language.

One of the worst archaisms is the use of the verb inflection fuera, amara, temiera, as a pluperfect indicative. The confusion this may and does at times cause because of the different uses already assigned this verb form by the Castilian conjugation would be enough to condemn it. But today's poets, especially Meléndez, not content with use in the past, have employed it in a sense we believe it never had. The writers of the past only used this form in the indicative as a pluperfect tense. Meléndez and through his example, Mr. Heredia, give it the additional force of other past tenses. Besides its subjunctive and conditional meanings, the tense amara thus becomes a simple past, imperfect or pluperfect indicative. If this is not a real corruption, we are at a loss to know what is.

Another place where the style of modern poetry apparently deviates from the rules of strict taste, is in describing tactile objects with metaphysical epithets. In poetry, a waist should not be called elegant, flesh morbid, a landscape picturesque, and a volcano or waterfall sublime. Expressions like these, true barbarisms in the idiom of the muses, belong to the philosopher who analyzes and classifies the impressions caused by the contemplation of objects, not to the poet whose business it is to portray them.

As a safeguard against these evils and others much more excusable in Mr. Heredia than in the writers he imitates, we recommend the Castilian classics (too much neglected in our circles) and the great models of antiquity. The former will correct his diction and make him spurn outdated words, the latter will polish his taste and teach him to keep a rein on the imagination, which never loses sight of nature and never exaggerates it nor does it violence.

We flatter ourselves that Mr. Heredia will attribute the freedom of this censure only to our desire to see him publish finished works worthy of such an outstanding talent as the one he possesses. As far as his resolution to give up verse and not even amend those already written, expressed in a note to Los placeres de la melancolía, we would loudly protest this poetic suicide if we thought Mr. Heredia were capable of carrying it out. But the muses are not so easily banished from a once captive heart which nature molded to experience and express her beauty.

LEYENDAS ESPAÑOLAS,
BY JOSÉ JOAQUÍN DE MORA

This study was first published in El Araucano, no. 535, Santiago, November 27, 1840, and included in Bello's Opúsculos literarios y críticos, Santiago, 1850, pp. 31-39. It is a commentary on the edition of Mora's Spanish Legends published in London in 1840.

Bello had published two previous notes on the literary work of Mora, the first in El Repertorio Americano, October 1826, p. 320, on the Cuadro de la historia de los árabes (London, 1826), in which he said, "These pictures of Arab history have great historical interest. They are beautiful in design and coloring. Very few modern works can compete with their ease, grace and elegance of style."

The second note, on the Meditaciones poéticas (London, 1826), appeared in El Repertorio Americano, April 1827, pp. 312-313, as follows: "This is a short collection of twelve excellently designed and engraved plates which should be regarded as the heart of the work. The text is merely a poetic illustration of philosophical-religious themes portrayed with notable inventiveness in their allegories and in very vividly expressed images and profound thought. The meditations are inspired in a work by the English poet Blair, entitled The Sepulchre. They are not a mere translation but a well executed imitation suited to Castilian poetry with well conceived changes helpful to the intended reader, in keeping with the best Castilian poets. This was Mr. Mora's everpresent purpose and one he developed successfully even in the many original thoughts brought into the work."

This is a collection of poetry that does credit to the flourishing, well attuned pen of its author, who has attemped a genre of narrative compositions apparently new to Castilian. In their alternatingly vigorous and festive style, the long digressions constantly weaving in and out of the narrative (not the part where the poet's vivid imagination glitters least), and the assurance and ease of versification, they resemble Lord Byron's Byppo and Don Juan. The poetry in Leyendas almost always flows like a full stream, gently transparent, unfaltering and plain, without the purely adroit, difficult meters that are a sign of pretense and exertion. Missing too is the endless rhythmical symmetry that eventually becomes monotonous.

Everything is grace, ease and assurance. Think not for a minute there is little wealth of poetic elegance in this natural, serene, and plain way of speaking, which avoids any hint of epic loftiness and gracefully descends to the tone of an everyday conversation. Mora's beauty is of a different order, yet no less effective than that of a more serious genre in stirring the imagination. Judging by its effect on us, his style has a peculiar appeal not found in the emphatic majesty some thought inseparable from epic poetry.

The descriptions (which abound in these Legends) are particularly successful, for example, the following one from the beginning of La judía:

> Solo está el bosque. Sin testigo mueve
> sus linfas el raudal, de espuma leve
> salpicando las flores de su orilla,
> y el techo que le forma la varilla
>   del mimbre y del aromo.
> Sola en la cumbre del celeste domo
> plácidamente el argenteo disco
> la luna ostenta; y el pelado risco
> con varios tintes sus vislumbres quiebra,
> ora en blanquizca masa o sutil hebra,
> ora en grupos de nácar. El reflejo
> celestial, en su copa, el roble añejo
>   de forma extraña viste;
> y con pendiente rama el sauce triste
> en móviles figuras la convierte.
> Con esplendor más fuerte,
> la luminosa inundación dilata
> sus anchas olas de bruñida plata
> por el llano vecino desde donde,
> bajo florida rama que la esconde,
> susurra y juega en armoniosa risa,
> cargada de placer y olor la brisa;
> y al mover de sus alas, se difunde
> la exquisita fragancia, y leve cunde
> por la callada esfera. En lejanía
> vaporosa levanta oscura frente
>   noble castillo ingente
> masa de enormes piedras, que algún día,
> día de un siglo excelso, aunque remoto,
> retumbó con el bíblico alboroto,
> y oyó de alegre fiesta el alto grito;
> y en el opuesto lado, cual sañudo
> gigante, sus colosos de granito
> levanta el monte, cuyo aspecto rudo
> disfrazan con diáfana cortina
>   la luna y la neblina.

The eight-syllable compositions almost never depart from the tone of our beloved ballads. Few of the latter have verses that are more fluid, gentle and graceful than these from the couplet of Pedro Niño:

Cuando don Juan, el infante
de Portugal, en quien brilla
grande valor, fe constante,
nombre y honor sin mancilla,
con escuadrón arrogante
vino de paz a Castilla,
donde con pompa esmerada
don Enrique le dio entrada;
    Consigo trajo una estrella
que eclipsaba a la más pura:
doña Beatriz, su hija bella,
flor de gracia y de hermosura;
mas tan rebelde doncella,
que el padre en vano procura
darle un ilustre marido,
de los mil que la han pedido.

    Porque de Aragón y Francia,
Navarra y otras naciones,
a jurarle fe y constancia
vienen potentes barones.
Mas ella, con arrogancia,
contesta en breves razones,
insensible y altanera,
que en vano espera el que espera.

    En Valladolid convoca
don Enrique a la grandeza,
a quien el empeño toca
de lucir gala y riqueza;
y la emulación provoca
su vanidad, cuando empieza
a ostentarse en galanteos,
y en saraos, y en torneos.

    Pasan alegres los días;
gastan profusos tesoros
en ruidosas cacerías,
bailes y fiestas de toros,
y en valientes correrías
de cristianos y de moros,
copiando al vivo los lances
de historias y de romances.

    Llega en tanto un caballero
portugués, a quien la fama,
como invencible guerrero,
sin par en la lid proclama.
Fatal es siempre su acero
al que en combate lo llama;
y por brioso y robusto
a un gigante diera susto.

    Y el renombre de Castilla
su vanidad tanto hiere,
que con toda la cuadrilla
justar a caballo quiere.
Sin mal odio y sin rencilla,
salga al campo el que saliere,
a los más fuertes y activos
hará perder los estribos.

Admiten los castellanos
con venia de Enrique, el reto;
y se aperciben ufanos
a salir de aquel aprieto,
y reciben de albas manos,
besándolas con respeto,
bandas de varios colores,
prendas de tiernos amores.

Siéntase en la galería,
que ornan ricos tafetanes,
la vistosa compañía
de damas y de galanes.
Al resonar la armonía
del clarín, los alazanes
tascan briosos los frenos,
de ardor generoso llenos.

In the jousts that follow, Pedro Niño had the glory of unseating the Portuguese champion. The infanta takes a liking to Pedro Niño and he, in love, writes her this note:

-"Lo que al alma aprisionada"
(le dice) "ofreceros toca,
los sostendrá con la espada,
con la pluma y con la boca;
buena fama bien ganada,
pecho firme como roca,
y honra pura como armiño:
vuestro esclavo -Pedro Niño".
. . . .
Pasó la noche dispierta,
pensando que fuera ultraje,
tan inesperada oferta,
de su nombre y su linaje.
Por la mañana a la puerta
viendo de servicio al paje,
le diz: -"Menino discreto,
cúmpleme hablarte en secreto".

The infanta asks who Pedro Niño is and he responds:

"Pedro Niño es el guerrero
más audaz que vió Castilla,
pues nunca emprendió su acero
contienda sin decidilla.
A Enrique en combate fiero
ganó su fuerte cuchilla
gloria que hoy al mundo espanta".
-"Prosigue", dijo la infanta.

-"Delante de Pontevedra,
a un jayán que allí vivía,
fuerte y duro como piedra,
temerario desafía.
Mas nada su pecho arredra;
y aunque doncel todavía,
con nunca vista fiereza
le partió en dos la cabeza.

"En las ilustres arenas
donde floreció Cartago,
por las huestes agarenas
sembró el terror y el estrago.
Las empinadas almenas
se rendían al amago
de su espada; y la fortuna
postró de la media-luna.

"Cuando las anchas riberas
del Guadalquivir maltrata,
y villas y sementeras
el atrevido pirata,
Niño con fuertes galeras
lo acomete y desbarata,
y el imperio de las alas,
dio a las armas españolas.
. . . .

"La voz de Francia extendida
de hazañas tan superiores,
el rey francés lo convida,
y bienes le da y honores".
-"Buen menino, por tu vida,
refiéreme sus amores",
(así interrumpe la infanta)
"con la señora almiranta".
. . . .

-"Y después de ese mensaje,
¿vio a quien tanto lo enamora?"
pregunta Beatriz y el paje
le contesta: -"Sí, señora.
Hízole tierno homenaje,
pero lo demás se ignora".
La infanta, con ceño oscuro,
dijo -"Ya me lo figuro".

-"Mas ayer con gran respeto"
(presto el paje le replica),
"en un mensaje secreto
su intención le significa:
que a más elevado objeto
sus afectos sacrifica,
y que perdone lanela,
si por otra se desvela".

Entre risueña y airada,
diz la infanta: -"Buen menino,
tu plática bien fraguada
muestra tu ingenio ladino;
mas te aprovecha de nada:
que he de ser de acero fino
contra amorosos extremos".
Y el paje dice: -"Veremos".

The entire legend, one of the best in the collection, is written
that way. One of the things our readers have probably noted is how
the poet manages to insert into his language certain phrases that

precisely because they are in the most colloquial tone, are characteristically expressive. Such phrases are most often found (as was to be expected) in the sarcastic, comic passages of the legend (not few in number). We will limit ourselves to two or three cited below which were chosen from the many examples that could be cited from Don Opas. That perverse prelate was losing sleep in plotting a rebellion to topple Rodrigo from the throne and place the race of Witiza there instead.

> Viendo cuán vanos eran sus conatos,
> dijo Don Opas entre sí: -"Paciencia;
> ya que lo quieren estos insensatos,
> consúmanse en brutal indiferencia.
> Cubran mi mesa suculentos platos;
> brillen en casa el lujo y la opulencia;
> manténganse los sacos de oro llenos,
> y haya buena salud; del mal el menos".

Don Julián, his nephew the count, informs him of certain dealings with the Moors and inquires whether he might tuta conscientia join the infidels to revenge the mortal insult he received from the monarch:

> -"Sólo falta que ilustres mi ignorancia
> y calmes los escrúpulos que abrigo.
> ¿Es lícito tratar sin repugnancia
> al enemigo de la fe, de amigo?
> ¿Habrá quién luego absuelva mi arrogancia,
> si, porque se le antoja a don Rodrigo
> dar rienda a su apetito con la Cava,
> en sangre goda mi baldón se lava?"

> -"¡Que tenga yo un sobrino tan salvaje!"
> clamó don Opas, dando un golpe recio.
> ....
> Toma la pluma y fragua una respuesta,
> digna de aquella singular consulta.
> -"¿Qué ignominia", decía al conde, "es ésta
> que tu imaginación crea y abulta?"
> ....
> "¡Una corona te seduce! Tonto,
> una corona es un joyel liviano
> que el aliento deslustra: no más pronto
> disipa airado viento el humo vano.

> Yo más arriba mi ambición remonto.
> ¿Qué sirve un cetro en impotente mano,
> si vive el que lo empuña en ansia eterna?
> Mejor es gobernar al que gobierna.

> "Con ese moro amable que te estrecha,
> toda dificultad la astucia zanje.
> Sus ofertas benignas aprovecha;
> liga tu agudo acero al corvo alfanje.
> Renuncio a tu amistad, si en esta fecha,
> puesto al frente de intrépida falange,
> con ella a nuestra España no galopas.
> Toledo y Mayo veintitrés -Don Opas".

The octaves reproduced below are a good example of how successfully the poet handles the language and of his digressions in the style of Byron. The poet compares the Middle Ages to the centuries of the modern day:

No habrá protocolos ni gacetas,
máquinas de sofisma y de patraña,
que, con frases pomposas y discretas,
convierten en blandura lo que es saña;
ni en narcóticas rimas los poetas
daban a la política artimaña,
barniz de convulsiva fraseología,
que desde media legua huele a logia.

El crimen era crimen, pero franco,
y decía a las claras: -"Esto quiero".
No aspiraba a tornar lo negro en blanco,
ni quitaba a su víctima el sombrero,
ni al amarrar a un mísero en el banco,
lo halagaba con tono lisonjero;
ni decía el poder al sacerdocio:
-"Partiremos el lucro del negocio".

Juzgábase una causa en la palestra,
cuerpo a cuerpo: sistema aborrecido,
en que el fallo pendía de la diestra,
y pagaba las costas el vencido.
Mas hoy la ilustración ¿cómo se muestra?
¿En esto hemos ganado, o bien perdido?
El influjo, cual antes la pelea,
¿no dicta los oráculos de Astrea?

Llámese fuerza, o bien llámese influjo,
¡qué importa lo que diga el diccionario,
si bajo el grave peso yo me estrujo,
cuando estrujar debiera al adversario!
Que ganen la belleza, el oro, el lujo,
al favor de vascuence formulario,
o el tajo y el revés de estoque y daga,
¿al fin no es la justicia quien la paga?

Y a propósito, ¡qué ruin pobreza
la del célebre idioma castellano!
Justicia es la verdad y la pureza,
y justicia es un juez y un escribano.
Y así cuando me oprima con fiereza
fallo vendido por proterva mano,
diré correctamente y sin malicia:
¡qué cosa tan injusta es la justicia!

Y para ser justicia en el sentido
metafórico, absurdo, de que trato,
¿se requiere tal vez ser buen marido,
ciudadano provecto, hombre sensato?
No, señor; nada de eso se ha pedido.
¿Filósofo tal vez, o literato,
en quien profundo estudio deje impreso
lo que es injusto o justo? —Nada de eso.

¿No se exige del juez cumplida ciencia
del ser mental? ¿del hondo mecanismo,
cuya acción modifica la conciencia,
y la convierte en templo o en abismo?
¡Qué! ¿No ha de conocer la íntima esencia
del vicio y la virtud, para que él mismo
no quede entre los límites suspenso
de la virtud y el vicio? —Ni por pienso.

    ¿Pues quién me va a juzgar? Un mozalbete,
que en seis años de oscura algarabía,
logró cubrirse el cráneo de un bonete,
símbolo de precoz sabiduría.
Con esta iniciación, y algún librete,
que más le ofusca el seso todavía,
no ha menester más tiempo ni trabajo;
bien puede echar sentencias a destajo.
. . . .
    Así la espada de Damocles pende,
y amenaza invisible fama, vida,
familia y bienestar; así se extiende
doquiera la asechanza, apercibida
por incógnita mano, que sorprende
en su sueño al honrado; y de la herida
siente el dolor, y atormentado muere,
sin ver el filo agudo que lo hiere.

    Lejos del conde y de Tarif estamos,
y dando sin querer enorme brinco,
del año setecientos diez, pasamos
al de mil ochocientos treinta y cinco.
Con andar más de prisa ¿qué logramos?
¿qué vamos a ganar si con ahinco
perseguimos la historia paso a paso,
para hallarnos al fin con un fracaso?

LA ARAUCANA,
BY ALONSO DE ERCILLA Y ZÚÑIGA

This study was first published in El Araucano, no. 545, Santiago, February 5, 1841, and later reprinted in the Anales de la Universidad de Chile, vol. XXI, July 1862, pp. 3-11. The bibliography of this work lists an edition in book form entitled La Araucana, juicio por Andrés Bello, Mexico (Tip. de V. G. Torres, Calle de San Juan de Letrán 3), 1862, 200 pp. Actually, Bello's article appears on pp. 3-25 only of the book, but the fact that the latter was given the title of the article caused the bibliographic error.

Before letters were invented, or before writing at least became common, all human knowledge was entrusted to poetry. History, genealogies, laws, religion, traditions, and moral utterances were all consigned to meter, which fixed ideas in a poetic context and made them easier to retain and communicate.

Earliest history was in verse. Heroic deeds, military expeditions and all momentous events were recited in verse, not to entertain the public by mixing factual truth with myths (this came after), but for the very same reason later historians and chroniclers wrote in prose. The earliest epics or narrative poems were history in verse, recited to transmit important events from generation to generation in order to perpetuate them in the memory of the people.

In that early age of civilization, ignorance, superstition, and a love for the supernatural doubtless twisted historical truth, infesting it with one overlapping concoction after another, until eventually a cumulus of cosmogonic, mythological and heroic fables was developed under which the history of nations is found buried when traced to its source.

The Greek rhapsodists, the Germanic skalds, the Breton bards, the French trouveurs, and the old Castilian romanceros, belonged to the class of poet historians whose original intention was merely to set history to verse; who then padded it with miraculous tales and popular tradition, accepted implicitly and for the most part believed; and who, by embellishments of their own invention, gradually and unwittingly created a new genre, fictitious history. Hence, the fictitious epic succeeded the epic as history, borrowing its materials from actual happenings and extolling famous heroes, yet mingling fact with fiction and no longer expecting to capture men's faith but instead to bewitch their imagination.

Many compositions from the period of the epic as history are preserved in the modern languages. What are the devout poems of Gonzalo de Berceo, for instance, but biographies and tales of miracles, candorously told by the poet and welcomed with implicit faith by his credulous contemporaries?

We do not mean that once this division took place, history, more or less contaminated by apocryphal traditions, no longer provided material for verse. Spain is proof to the contrary. There the custom of putting real or the even more appealing reputedly real events into couplet form endured for a long time, right down to our own day, although with a subject matter that has changed greatly. The old collections of ballads extolled the glories of the nation, the triumphs of the Christian kings of the Peninsula over the Arabs, the deeds of Bernardo del Carpio, the fabulous adventures of the house of Lara, and the deeds both real and alleged of Fernán González, Ruy Díaz, and other famous leaders, sometimes rounded out with the stuff of ancient, sacred and profane history. But in later times, the pens of plebian poets and the voices of the blind were more often moved by the courage, prowess and unhappy endings of brigands, smugglers and bullfighters in all their notoriety.

It was in the thirteenth century that the Castilians cultivated the epic as history most successfully. Very few compositions of this type born in the fourteenth and fifteenth centuries contain the slightest trace of poetry. One should not confuse them, as some critics beyond the Pyrenees have done, with some of the seventeenth century narrative ballads imitating the language of the poets of old, which are finished works equally rich in inventiveness and elegance of style.1/

There is another kind of old Spanish ballads that are narrative but not historic in intention. These extol the combats and amorous adventures of often wholly legendary foreign personnages. The ballads of Galvain, Launcelot of the Lake, and other knights of the Round Table, viz., the fabulous court of Arthur, king of Brittany (called Artus by the poets); or those about Roland, Oliver, Baldwin, the marquis of Mantua, Richard of Normandy, Guy of Burgundy, and the other paladins of Charlemagne, belonged to this class. All of them are merely faded, abbreviated copies of the ballads composed in France and England in the eleventh century. The place where the inventive talent of the Spanish first stood out was in the tales of chivalry.

Once people learned to read, they no longer had to rely on the itinerant jongleurs and minstrels who traveled from castle to castle and place to place reciting accounts of battle, romance and enchantments to the tune of the rote and the vihuela at banquets, fairs and local religious celebrations. The fictitious tales, in a form meant for reading, not recitations, began to make their appearance in prose not later than 1300, according to our belief. At least, prose ballads are known to have been commonplace in France during the fourteenth century, still dealing for the most part with such familiar themes as Alexander of Macedonia, King Arthur and the Round Table, Tristan and Isolde, Launcelot of the Lake, and Charlemagne and his twelve peers.

Once this new form of fictitious epic or tale began, it soon spread to new and usually wholly imaginary personnages. This was when Amadis, Belianis and Palmerin with all their reincarnations and the tumult of errant knights entered the scene. Their adventures were the pastime all over Europe in the fifteenth and sixteenth centuries. The Spaniards were particularly avid readers and creators of this type of tale until the immortal hero from the Mancha placed it in ridicule and consigned it to oblivion forever.

The prose form of the epic inevitably gained ground as the cultivation of letters, particularly the elemental skills of reading and writing, spread in the modern era. As long as the art of representing words with visible signs was totally unknown or accessible only to a few, meter was necessary so that traditions and ideas could be memorized and transmitted from one period to another. As intellectual culture spread, the advantage of poetic forms lessened.

A more refined taste imposed strict rules on rhythm and demanded more polished work of the poets. Epic poetry became less necessary and more demanding, for both reasons, fictitious tales in prose became more widespread. Written to entertain the public, they multiplied and took on infinite variety, deriving their materials from fables, alegories, adventures of chivalry from a pastorale world no less idealistic than errant knighthood, and from prevailing customs. Every social class and every scene from life were represented, from the court to the village, from the salons of the wealthy to the huts of the poor, and even the least savory nooks of crime.

These descriptions of society, called <u>novels</u> in Castilian (although at first this name was given only to short tales such as the <u>Exemplary Novels</u> by Cervantes), are the favorite epic of modern times and represent in today's society what the rhapsodists were in Homer's time and the rhymed ballads in the Middle Ages. There is a fictitious tale which is peculiar to each social epoch, each cultural change, each new intellectual development. In our time it is the novel.

The fondness for positive reality is such that even the versified epic has had to resort to it, leaving behind its fairies and magicians, its islands and enchanted gardens, in order to portray settings, manners and people whose originals actually have or might have existed. The depiction of nature and morals is what typifies the most popular fiction of today, whether in prose or verse.

The epics of the Greeks and the romantics and the tales of the Orient amused us by their miracles wrought by supernatural agencies. Yet, whether because the latter are spent or such things bore us more quickly, or because in reading the literature of distant ages and countries we tacitly adopt the principles, tastes and concerns that influenced their writing while letting the rest be governed by our own beliefs and usual feelings, the fact is that we now expect another sort of actors and settings in European fiction. That is, characters within our reach, action that is contrived, and incidents that are not unnatural or improbable. Anyone who includes the workings of the <u>Jerusalem liberata</u> in an epic poem today would certainly risk displeasing his readers.

One should not conclude, therefore, that the field for the epic is narrower than before. Just the opposite. There have never been so many eminently poetic themes at its disposal. Human society seen in the light of historic change and the different stages of history posed in the waves of religious and political revolution, are an endless mine of materials for the novelist and the poet. Lord Byron and Walter Scott showed how moral traits can be influenced by factionalism and sectarianism, and the profound interest social upheaval can give everyday life.

How many new creative resources poets have found in the spectacle of the physical world now that the earth, explored to its uttermost reaches, has revealed endless local tones as background for the human drama of real life. Add the advances in the arts, the prodigies of industry and the secrets of nature uncovered by science, and then let it be said whether having discarded magic and supernatural beings, we do not possess a wealth of epic and poetic materials that are more varied, more plentiful and better in quality than those used by Ariosto and Tasso.

Navigation and wars have been powerful movers of fiction for centuries. Yet Lord Byron has shown that modern travel and feats of arms are as adaptable to the epic as they were earlier, that enthusiasm for them can be created without translating Homer, and that war as waged today--the battles, sieges and assaults of our times--are themes that lend themselves to poetic tones as brilliant as the struggles of the Greeks and Trojans and the plunder and ruin of Ilium.

> "Nec minimum meruere decus vestigia graeca
> Ausi deserere et celebrare domestica facta."

The metrical ballad reached its peak in the sixteenth century with Ariosto's immortal poem. This was followed by a period of decline and total disappearance among the ruins of errant knighthood, which saw its final days in the seventeenth century. The Spanish prototype of the Italian-style metrical ballad is Bishop Valbuena's Bernardo, a work praised by one literary party much more than it deserved and consequently belittled by another with an equal degree of exaggeration and injustice.

One must confess that in this long poem a few bold strokes, wealth of color, many adventures and ingenious episodes, pretty comparisons and successful verses hardly compensate for the intolerable prolixity of its descriptions and tales, its inappropriate and foolish language of love, and the sacrifice of reason to rhyme, which far from being Valbuena's slave, as one Spanish critic claimed, orders him about like a tyrant, tugs him violently hither and yon, and is the principal cause of his clumsy, winding narrative style.

The metrical ballad left the scene and opened the way to the classical epic as represented by Tasso. Cultivated rather successfully all over Europe down to our time, it proliferated particularly in Spain though generally in an ill-starred manner. The Austriada, the Monserrate, and the Araucana are reputed to be the best poems in this genre written in Castilian. Hardly anyone reads the first two anymore, except professional men of letters. The third might be considered an intermediate species, more historical and positive as far as its deeds are concerned yet closer to the ballad stylewise in its simple, down-to-earth tone.

Even taking the Araucana into account, if we were to abide by the opinion of some Spanish and foreign critics we would have to say that Castilian has little to brag about. But we have always thought this judgment too severe. Ercilla's poem is read and enjoyed not only in Spain and Spanish America, but also in foreign countries. This entitles us to protest the precipitate decision of Voltaire and even the begrudging praise of Boutterweck.

To our knowledge, 2/ Martínez de la Rosa was the first to judge the Araucana with insight. He generally does justice to its foremost qualities but was sometimes misled by his own inflexible literary principles.3/ We disagree with his view concerning "the poor selection of subject matter." We are unwilling to concur that in order to be worthy of an epic poem an enterprise must be <u>grandiose</u> in the meaning given this word by critics of the classical school.

We do not think the interest with which an epic is read is measured by the number of square leagues covered or the number of leaders and nations involved. Any action that can arouse vivid emotions and maintain suspense enjoyably is worthy of epic poetry, or, to avoid quibbling over words, can be the subject of an interesting narration in verse. Is the subject of the <u>Odyssey</u>, perchance, more grandiose than the one chosen by Ercilla? Is not the <u>Odyssey</u> an excellent epic poem? What does the subject matter itself of the <u>Iliad</u>, stripped of its Homerian splendor actually come down to? What is so important and grandiose about the undertaking of a minor kind of Micenas leading other minor kings of Greece who held under siege for ten years the small city of Illium, the head of a small district whose very obscure choreography has been and still is the subject of so many sterile scholarly debates? Any grandeur, splendor and magnificence in the <u>Iliad</u> is entirely due to Homer.

From another point of view, the subject matter of the <u>Araucana</u> might seem to be a poor selection. Writing about deeds in which he himself intervened, the deeds of his companions in arms with which everyone was familiar, Ercilla was obliged to stick somewhat slavishly to the truth. His contemporaries would not have tolerated any injection of the showy phantasmagoria used by Tasso to embellish the times of the first Crusade, and by Valbuena, the legend of Bernardo del Carpio.

Proper, effective use of miracles, which sixteenth century taste did not find objectionable, even then required a subject matter centuries old and mysteriously obscured by the passage of time, which predisposes the imaginations to accept prodigious events unbegrudgingly: <u>Datur</u> <u>haec</u> <u>venia</u> <u>antiquitati</u> <u>ut</u> <u>miscendo</u> <u>humana</u> <u>divinis</u> <u>primordia</u> <u>urbium</u> <u>augustiora</u> <u>faciat</u>.

Hence, the fictitious episode of the wizzard is one of the least appealing parts of the <u>Araucana</u>. Once it is agreed that the subject matter of the poem, especially the deeds committed by the Spaniards, had to be treated so as not to deviate from historical truth, was Ercilla wrong in making this selection? It clearly would not allow for the artifice found in <u>Jerusalem</u> or <u>Bernardo</u>. But is this the only recourse art has in order to hold the attention? Customs and people copied from life, not with the severity of history but with the color and minute fictions that are the essence of graphic art, and in which Ercilla could use his imagination freely without incurring the wrath of his readers or deviating from the historian's fidelity to truth, much more than Tito Livio did in the annals of the early centuries of Rome. A portrayal done this way, we say, could be developed without betraying the nature of the ancient epic and in a way more suited to the philosophic era that was dawning in Europe.

Our century no longer recognized the conventional laws which would have forced artists to follow in the footsteps of Greek and Latin poetry. The vain efforts made after Tasso's time to compose epics in the mold of Homer and of Aristotelian rules proved it was time to change direction. Ercilla had the first inspiration of this kind, and if he can be blamed for anything, it is his failure to consistently abide by it.

In order to judge Ercilla, one must remember that his protagonist was Caupolicán and that the ideas most to his taste were those of Araucanian heroism. Unlike Virgil, Ercilla did not set out to praise the national pride of his countrymen. The predominant sentiment in the Araucana is of a more noble sort: love of humanity, the pursuit of justice, a generous admiration for patriotism, and the bravery of those who were conquered. Unsparing in his praise of the courage and steadfastness of the Spaniards, he censures their greed and cruelty. Was it more worthy of the poet to flatter his country than to give it a moral lesson?

The trait that sets the Araucana apart from all epic poems is the presence of the poet as one of its actors, a man who unprepossessingly relates what he felt in the midst of deeds he himself witnessed, demonstrating, together with the military and chivalresque honor of his nation, honest and pure sentiments that were not those of the soldiers, nor of Spain, nor of his century.

Although Ercilla had less cause to complain of his countrymen as a poet than as a soldier, the Spaniards still fail to give his work its full due. Posterity, however, is beginning to do it justice. We will not take the time to list its other qualities and beauty, first because Martínez de la Rosa has vindicated the poet of Caupolicán and, second, because we must assume the people of Chile are familiar with the Araucana, their own Aeneid, which was composed in Chile, the only modern nation whose founding has been immortalized in an epic poem.

Before we leave the Araucana, something should be said about Ercilla's tone and style. These, together with his partiality toward the Indians, were an important factor in Spain's disregard of the Araucana for so long a period of time. Ercilla's style is plain, moderate and natural. It has no sonority, rhetoric, archaisms or clever transpositions. Nothing could be more fluid, terse, and transparent.

The words in his descriptions are always the right ones. His personnages, when they speak, do so in the ordinary language normally used to express their feelings. Despite this, the narration is lively and the harangues eloquent, comparable to and, at times, surpassing Homer. For the former, Ercilla's model was Ariosto, and although doubtless inferior in that rarest of all qualities in a work of art, artlessness filled with grace, as far as his execution is concerned (which is what we are discussing), the Araucana still holds a respectable place among the epics of modern times and may be the first of them all after Ariosto and Tasso.

The epic poem tolerates a variety of tones and the poet is free to select the one best suited to his talent and subject matter. What a difference there is between Homer and Virgil in the historical mythological epic. In the epic of chivalry the contrast between the unrestrained, frolicsome, festive and at times jesting manner of Ariosto, and the somber tempo, measured movements and contrived symmetry of Tasso is even greater. Ercilla chose the style best adapted to his narrative talents. Anyone striving for individuality as he did, shuns the sonorous loftiness scornful of the minute details that are so right when properly chosen for making poetic scenes warm and lively.

But this moderate, familiar tone in Ercilla, which admittedly becomes faint and trivial at times, could not help but detract from his poem in the eyes of the Spaniards during an age of eloquence and bombastic grandeur that followed the more wholesome, purer taste of poets like Garcilaso and Fray Luis de León. The Spaniards set aside the simple, expressive naturalness of their earlier poetry to take on, in nearly every work of a non-humorous vein, an air of majesty that shuns any contact with the idiomatic, familiar phrases so closely linked with the emotions and so effective in evoking them.

Except for lyric ballads and a few scenes from theatrical comedy, eighteenth century Castilian poetry rarely has passages that speak the language of the human spirit. There is enthusiasm and warmth, but naturalness is not its predominant quality. The style of serious poetry became too artificial, with its very elegance and loftiness depriving it of much of the facility and spontaneity it once had. Seldom was it successful in expressing human emotions with vigor and purity.

Castilian managed to represent Corneille and Pope with a fair degree of truth, but how could the finest passages from Shakespeare's tragedies or Byron's poems be translated into this language? We are happy to see the privileges of nature and the freedom of genious vindicated at last. A new era is dawning in Castilian letters. Writers of great talent, humanizing poetry and forcing it down from its stilts, are working to restore its earlier candor and innocent grace. Nothing can compensate for their absence.

NOTES

1. Sismondi, Litterature du Midi de l'Europe, chapter 24. The author of the Tableau de la Literatura (In Volume 24 of Courtin's Encyclopedia) and several others, made this mistake (A).

2. Since this article was written, we have seen the entry in the Biographic Universelle on Ercilla. Its author, M. Bocous, seems to be intelligent and fair in his assessment of La araucana (A).

3. In the prologue to his Poesías (1836) he professes a more relaxed and tolerant literary creed than in the Arte poética (A).

ROMANCES HISTÓRICOS,
BY ÁNGEL SAAVEDRA, DUQUE DE RIVAS

This article appeared in El Araucano, no. 595, Santiago, January 14, 1842, and was later included by Bello in his Opúsculos literarios, pp. 67-71. It is no doubt a commentary on the 1841 edition of the Romances históricos printed by Vicente Lalama in Madrid.

Angel Saavedra has taken it upon himself to restore a genre that has fallen into disuse. The eight-syllable historic ballad, banished from learned poetry, had become the property of the common people. With very few exceptions was heard only in the songs of the blind and in churlish couplets celebrating the misdeeds of bandits and smugglers, the heroes of the Spanish commoners, in an epoch when despotism had undermined the law and frontal assaults on authority had acquired a certain air of virtue and nobility.

With the meter of perhaps the only Castilian productions able to rival those of Greece in originality, fecundity, and purity of taste corrupted by this association, its restoration in brief, serious narrative compositions and in historic or traditional reminiscenses --that is, in the legends, composed in that meter alone in the past-- was thought impossible, notwithstanding a few efforts that had been made in that direction.

The prejudice against the eight-syllable ballad reached such a point that Hermosilla in the Arte de hablar had no hesitancy in saying that "even though Apollo himself wrote in it, he could not get rid of its meter, form, rhythm, air, sing-song cadence, nor change nor extend its periods as epic poems and heroic odes sometimes require." It was thus banned from narrative poems or any kind of serious poetry at all.

Angel Saavedra has questioned this ban in the Prologue to his Romances históricos and refuted Hermosilla's statement categorically with unimpeachable reasons. What is more, he has given the lie to that statement with these very Romances, in which legend redons its primitive dress and assonated eight-syllable verse once again performs with the naturalness, energy and variety of old.

This is not the first time the Duque de Rivas has virtually proven the adverse decision of the Arte de hablar to be unjustified. Earlier, in El moro expósito he had vindicated the assonant

178

hendecasyllable from the derision of the poems and critics of the era of Jovellanos and Meléndez in his beautiful ballads published at the end of that poem. With no less success, he let it be known that eight-syllable verse in assonance still retained its rights to short compositions recounting a fictitious event, or where traditions of the past were consigned and embellished. Later, Zorrilla also tried this genre, and his ballads hold a distinguished place among his best productions.

The successful undertakings of this same sort that make up the present publication would dismiss any remaining doubts that might exist. In it the reader will find a number of scenes that are perfectly developed and placed, with those special traits that depict custom and the physical and moral environment of centuries and countries where the poet seeks to transport us. All this is done in an easy natural manner that seemed could never be restored to serious Castilian poetry and will still be looked upon disdainfully by those whose taste was formed in the school of Herrera, Rioja and Moratín alone.

The entire work is sustained by a versification which, though it lacks the ease and melody of seventeenth century eight-syllable ballads, is generally smooth and harmonious. The greater interest of the subject matter offsets this, the action is almost always grandiose, impassioned and progresive, consistent with the philosophic spirit of the author's nineteenth century readers.

In our judgment, the descriptive talents of Angel Saavedra, already renowned for his earlier writings, are the principal asset of the Romances históricos. But in his revival of former legend, he endows it with entirely new qualities. There is a great difference between the descriptive taste of the poets of old and contemporary tastes adopted by the Duque de Rivas. Inanimate material objects were dealt with only in brief but timely and telling strokes, scattered here and there in Greek and Roman poetry and in Castilian poetry in the centuries that preceded our own. Poets never lost sight of their personnages and so absorbed did they become in depicting their feelings that they took little note of the scene around them. They saw landscape and decor with the same eye as their protagonists and paid no attention to them except as they had something to say about the action and the vital interest behind the drama.

Unless we are mistaken, this was the true nature of the descriptive style in those times, their depictions were all movement and feeling. Conversely, our contemporaries portray vast scenes in which a somewhat detailed analysis develops form, color and combinations of light and shadow. The action occupies as little room as human figures do in the portrayal of landscapes.

A good example of this is Lamartine's Jocelyn. The poet does more than portray; he explains, interprets and comments. He attaches a mysterious meaning to whatever is felt by his senses and develops the reflections stirred by physical perceptions in a contemplative mind. The poetry of our contemporaries is teeming with aspiration and presentiments, theory and delirium, philosophy and mysticism. It is the faithful echo of an essentially speculative age.

This pensive, philosophic bent appears even in the scenes found in these ballads, despite their narrow dimensions. The descriptions are not just detailed and specific but feeling and reflective. We would give a petty idea of their worth then if we were to call them a mere revival of old Spanish legend. Angel Saavedra has amended the latter to advantage, giving it the character and forms peculiar to the age in which we live as the past inventors of the ballad would no doubt have done had they flourished in our time.

C. Law

PRINCIPLES OF INTERNATIONAL LAW

Prologue to the First Edition, 1832

My main purpose in publishing these Principles is to further the study of an important part of the law of nations not sufficiently covered in the best works that exist in Spanish because of new developments in international jurisprudence which the authors of those works were unfamiliar with or because their object, in considering the topic from a purely speculative and abstract viewpoint, was not so much to explain internationally recognized positive laws as to investigate the general principles on which these laws must be based in order to protect the common welfare.

The discussions surrounding the mutual claims of belligerents and neutrals in the European and American wars of the past eighty years have settled not a few controversial issues, particularly bearing on maritime commerce, by setting the limits of each party's rights and jurisdiction and developing precise rules of procedure and adjudication in the prize courts. This new doctrine was scattered throughout voluminous digest of judicial proceedings collected in Europe and the United States. Unless I am mistaken, it appeared for the first time on a regular, systematic basis in A Treatise on the Laws of Commerce and Manufactures and the Contracts Relating Thereto, by Joseph Chitty, Esq., published in London in 1824. This work is a complete summary of British mercantile law; its first chapters contain an enlightened exposition of the law of nations today as it affects navigation and commerce.

Later, Judge James Kent published his Commentaries on American Law in New York. The first part is an excellent compendium of the universal law of nations as interpreted and practiced today. Although the American author in matters common to both works does little more than reproduce and even copy the English work word for word, his book has the advantage of covering all parts of the law of nations (whereas Chitty limits himself exclusively to commerce) and of pinpointing areas in which the interpretation of international law by the American government and judiciary is inconsistent with the principles of Great Britain and other governments.

These two works are the ones used most consistently as my guide in the additions I have made to the general doctrine of the writers of the eighteenth century. I have also availed myself of another American work, the Diplomatic Code by Elliot, which has an instructive though too concise summary of the most interesting court decisions in the United States on cases involving international law. I have also consulted the maritime ordinances of France promulgated by Louis XIV, with their later amendments, and have indicated the major differences governing French practice in different periods of time. Finally, in a desire to draw together in a single body all the necessary elemental notions, I have inserted in the third part of these Principles an extract from Baron Martens' Diplomatic Manual in which I hope all the substance of this useful manual on modern diplomacy will be found summarized in a few pages.

Continuing what I have taken from these sources with the doctrine of Vattel, narrowed down to a few elements that might be useful to students of jurisprudence, and availing myself of the works of other men of letters when I thought this would be helpful, I have attempted to provide my young countrymen with a summarized yet comprehensive outline of the current status of international law.

I have not hesitated to borrow literally from the authors I follow, though condensing their texts and attempting to preserve consistency and uniformity of idea and language. The sources of passages used as authorities and supporting references are cited to indicate where the subjects covered can be consulted and studied more thoroughly. When I occasionally deviate form the views of those who acted as my own guide, I stated the reasons for doing so. I am brief in dealing with matters satisfactorily explained in the works of Vattel, Martens, and others already translated into Castilian, and give only a synopsis of what I thought worth memorizing.

But on matters containing something new, I felt it my duty to be more detailed and to go into the history of the international institutions or practices mentioned, testing their existence and explaining the justification for efforts to sustain or challenge them. According to this plan, which I thought best for my young readers, the length of the explanations is not so much related to the importance of each subject as it is to the difficulty of finding it in books that are not easily accessible and in a language just beginning to be understood here.

I would hope this book might somehow match the generosity of its sponsor, the government of Chile, and the latter's customary zeal for the promotion of scholarship. I would be satisfied if, despite the shortcomings which I by no means attempt to conceal, this book were of some use to the youth of the new American nations in the cultivation of a science previously ignored with impunity and now of the utmost importance for the protection and vindication of our national rights. Should this at least encourage others more talented than I and with more time and materials at their disposal, I would feel flattered that I have not worked in vain.

Prologue to the Second Edition

Santiago, July 1844

The indulgence with which these Principles were received, the use made of them now and in the past in several educational institutions in Spanish-America, and the few copies of the first edition still available in Chile, despite frequent reprintings in America and Europe, have moved me to republish them in revised form with a further and clearer exposition of some chapters, in an attempt to make this work more worthy in every way of its favorable response and the generosity with which the government of Chile has again and again contributed to its publication.

For this new work I was able to consult many books earlier known to us in name only that are now available in the libraries of the courts and high government offices thanks to the concern of the government for the propagation of knowledge. The number of references has been expanded, not to display a learning I do not possess but to indicate to our young people which sources they should turn to, when, in the course of their studies in letters or the professions, they wish to support their views or examine a matter more thoroughly. These references could easily have been expanded further by copying those found in the footnotes of other elemental books, but I have almost always restricted them to works consulted by myself.

I am convinced that in the practical implementation of this science, theoretical deductions are worth much less than positive rules sanctioned by the behavior of civilized people and strong governments, and on decisions of the courts made in accordance with international law. This conviction, used as my guide in the first edition, inspired virtually all the augmented sections, illustrations and notes with which I set out to improve the present edition.

Prologue to the Third Edition, 1864

With earlier editions of this book used as texts in secondary and higher education in Chile now out of print, the present edition was undertaken at the behest of the dean of the School of Law and Political Science. It had been made doubly necessary by the changes that have taken place in international law in recent years.

For this task I had writings available that enabled me to expand and improve upon the doctrines published earlier, to the extent my strength allowed, and to report on the serious international issues that have recently unsettled the political world and foretell a new era, in which greater reference will be made to the over-riding interests of commerce, the incessant promoter of civilization and public prosperity.

Consistent with the practice followed from the start, I should mention the works principally used to give this compilation its present form, not merely to validate its tenets but also to bring them to the attention of students and followers of this important branch of law, particularly those called upon to argue and analyze points of law in the courts and legislative chambers, so they can refer to them in search of fuller, more profound and perhaps more accurate notions than this book contains.

I call this a compilation because in all justice I can hope for no other label than that of a mere compiler, except to the extent that I was forced to select from among varying or conflicting precepts and to justify that selection.

The American writer Henry Wheaton, mourned by a science indebted to him for his fine works as an elemental writer, accomplished collector of legal decisions, and historian of international law, has been my constant teacher and guide no less in this edition than in the earlier ones. His Elements, 1/ published in French under his direction with notable additions (Paris, April 15, 1847), has been reprinted several times in America and Europe; the second Leipzig edition (1852) is the one referred to by me. His History of the Law of Nations was first known to me in the Spanish translation made by the Paraguayan (sic) minister Carlos Calvo, who not too long ago defended his country's cause in the London court with such skill and dedication. We are indebted to him for the continuation of the history to the present time, published in his Spanish version of the work (Besanzon, 1861). 2/

Other auxiliary references were:

Le droit international public de l'Europe by A. G. Heffter, councilor of the supreme court and professor at the University of Berlin, translated into French by Jules Bergson (Paris, 1857). This is an excellent manual in which understanding and impartiality go hand in hand.

Inquiries in International Law by James Reddic (second edition, enlarged, London, 1851).

Elementos de derecho público internacional de España by Antonio Riquelme (Madrid, 1849). Vol. 2, entitled Apéndice, is a collection of official documents, frequent applications of which can be made in the South American republics.

Des droits et des devoirs des nations neutres en temps de guerre maritime by L. B. Hautefeuille (second edition, Paris, 1859), a vigorous defense of neutral immunities.

Commentaries upon International Law by Robert Phillimore, member of the British parliament and Her Majesty's barrister in the Admiralty court (London, 1854, 1856, 1857, and 1861). A magistral work abounding in diplomatic erudition; of all the British writers, perhaps none is more outstanding for his sense of moderation and justice. Volume 4 is devoted exclusively to private international law.

Other authorities consulted are noted in their proper place.

I would finally express my gratitude to the government, which on this occasion, as before, assumed the cost of printing the work with a generous subscription.

NOTES

1. Henry Wheaton, Elements of International Law: With a Sketch of the History of the Science, Philadelphia, 1836 (T).

2. Historia de los progresos del derecho de gentes, en Europa y en América, desde la paz de Westfalia hasta nuestros días translated and enlarged by Carlos Calvo, Besanzon, 1861 (T).

CIVIL CODE OF THE REPUBLIC OF CHILE

The Civil Code of Chile is one of the major works executed by Bello in that country. It represents an effort that lasted for over fifteen years. During that time he was the soul of the commission responsible for writing the several drafts of the code, all later printed. The final version, of which the Foreword is a part, was completed in 1855. The President of Chile and the Minister of Justice used that Foreword when they referred the draft Civil Code to the Congress on September 22, 1855. Bello's authorship of this preamble to the Code is beyond doubt. It was first published in El Araucano, no. 1655, Santiago, November 24, 1855.

See Pedro Lira Urquieta's prologue on the Civil Code in Bello's Obras completas, vol. XII, Caracas, 1955.

Foreword

Many of the most civilized nations today have felt the need to codify their laws. It might be said that this is one of society's periodic needs. No matter how complete and perfect a body of legislation is assumed to be, changes in custom, the very progress of civilization, political vicissitudes, the immigration of new ideas (precursors of new institutions), scientific discovery and its application to art and everyday life, and abuses stemming from bad faith (ever alert for reasons to evade the law) constantly stimulate the passage of new measures interpreting the old ones, or expanding, modifying and repealing them. Until finally the confusing mass of different, incoherent and contradictory parts of the law must be rewritten to make them consistent and harmonious and to relate them to the prevailing ways of society.

Attempts of this sort made over the past decade, and their generally successful results, encouraged us to undertake this task, with the advantage that we could avail ourselves of studies done in other scientifically enlightened nations with long experience in this area. We began this work, as you know, years ago. When it was finally finished, I submitted the draft for examination to a commission of magistrates and jurists who set to work on it with unparalleled zeal and assiduity.

This was not a matter of copying any of the modern codes to the letter. We had to take advantage of them mindful at the same time of the circumstances peculiar to Chile. To the extent that the latter posed no real obstacle, there was no hesitation in introducing useful innovations. The most important and transcendental ones are sketched briefly below.

Following the example of virtually every modern code, custom no longer has the force of law.

Time is an element of such great consequence in legal relations and has caused such differences in court decisions and in the doctrine of jurists that it was considered essential to set uniform, apparently meticulous standards in order to determine the exact moment when rights and obligations on which time has a bearing originate and end.

As in most modern codes, absolute rules or, in other words, uncontestable assumptions concerning the birth and death of an individual have been developed. Our laws contain no full, exact provisions on the assumption of death when a person has been absent for a long time, called <u>disappearance</u> in this draft, thus distinguishing two legal states of quite different types. An attempt has been made to fill this void in our laws by following the legislation of other nations, albeit with substantial differences. Generally, the time of provisional ownership of the assets of a missing person has been shortened. Provisional ownership is an impediment to the circulation and growth of assets and should last no longer than necessary to reasonably protect any private rights that may be inconsistent with the general interests of society.

Long distance communications have become enormously faster and easier in our time. The probability that a person about whom his family or business circles have had no word for some time has either died or willfully severed the bonds with his former place of residence has grown at the same rate. Granted that legal assumptions may be fallible under special conditions, some attempt has been made to provide for exceptional cases.

Reciprocal bonds of marriage are a matter left, in this draft, entirely up to the honor and conscience of each party. No civil obligation derives therefrom. Ecclesiastical authority retains the right to decide on the validity of a marriage; the same impediments to marriage are recognized as those decreed by the Catholic Church. A marriage valid in the eyes of the Church is also valid as far as civil law is concerned. The temporal power, however, would not violate its reasonable bounds should it deny the civil effects of a marriage deemed harmful to society and the home, even though ecclesiastical authority has sanctioned it with other considerations in mind and has waived its usual rules because of special circumstances.

In preserving marital authority, the code attempts to curb its abuses, the status of women has been improved in many respects. The privileges of the dowry are eliminated. The traditional classification of dowry and paraphernal assets is dropped in favor of the trend in Spanish jurisprudence. The mortgage lien of married women follows the path of similar liens; in this draft it is abandoned, thus finally accomplishing the trend the law has taken since 1845. In recompense, the separation of assets beneficial to women has been developed and expanded, the inequities of the civil effects of divorce have been narrowed, community assets have been regularized, and effective guarantees given for preservation of a wife's real property managed by her husband.

Filiation is legitimate, natural or simply illegitimate. As to illigitimate children conceived in true or putative marriage, there are no substantial differences between the present draft and the provisions stipulated in other bodies of law, including our own. Children legitimized by marriage after conception (the only type of legalization allowed herein) are covered by procedures that combine the standards of Roman Law, Canon Law and the French Civil Code. Under Roman Law, a man who married his concubine was required to grant a writ in order to legitimize his children by her, not to validate a marriage entered into by consent alone but so there would be a record that the concubine had become his legitimate wife and which of their children, if any, were being legalized. This is the doctrine of the most enlightened interpreters of Roman Law.

Accordingly, legalization was a voluntary act on the part of the parents and covered only those children of the concubine so stipulated by the father. Legalization was also voluntary on the part of the children; without their consent they could not become alieni juris nor be associated with a father of possibly poor repute and immoral ways. These two principles, legitimacy granted by public instrument, legitimacy voluntarily granted and accepted, have been abided by in the draft except for two instances: a child conceived before but born after marriage, and a natural child (that is, an illegitimate child who has been previously recognized formally and voluntarily by the father or the mother) are both legitimized ipso jure by the subsequent marriage.

Status as a legitimate child is one of the most important titles created by civil law. How then can this matter be left to the mercy of oral evidence, so easily contrivable if not in the lifetime of the parents at least after their death? Can the law delve into those clandestine associations and allow them to constitute per se a presumption of paternity which is rightfully the privilege of matrimony? Is a dubious carnal relationship, where there are no guarantees of the fidelity of a woman who has degraded herself, to be the principle of legitimacy, without corroboration of the father? And assuming the latter thinks the illegitimate offspring is his own, should he be forced to legitimize a son or daughter of immoral ways, and to choose between not marrying the woman or bringing into his home a source of immorality and depravity? Should a son be forced to become a party to another's debasement and place the administration of his property into the hands of a man of immoral conduct? Canon Law in this area relaxed the principles of Roman Law but temporal authority must prescribe the conditions necessary for the enjoyment of civil rights.

The code of the Partidas 1/ confers legitimacy ipso jure, but only on the concubine's child, the natural child. The present draft concurs with the Partidas on this point. It is a necessary consequence of the aforementioned principle that legitimacy must be formally notified and accepted. The French Code and other contemporary codes have been followed, but with less severity, as to the time of its conferral. The initial objections made to drawing up an instrument in which the parties make their own weakness a matter of record were not thought to be very compelling.

This is a sacrifice required by society, the just expiation of guilt. The conferral says nothing not revealed much more eloquently by the presence of the legalized children in the paternal family. An authentic act was deemed highly necessary to protect the reciprocal rights and obligations of the legalized children and those conferring legitimacy from any future claim. The existence of preconstituted documents is an object provided for in other areas of civil law as the best way to avoid and resolve disputes.

Voluntary recognition of children conceived outside matrimony, who assume the legal title of natural children and acquire important rights, has also been subjected to similar formalities. Illegitimate children not voluntarily recognized by either parent are only given the right to demand maintenance. For this purpose, no other proof is accepted than acknowledgment of them by the father, evidently a harsh condition but one justified by the experience of every country, not excepting Chile. The French Code and other codes today have been still more strict in absolutely forbidding inquiries on paternity. Only rarely has investigation of maternity by ordinary means been banned, although very serious grounds exist for making the father and mother equal on this point, which an eminent jurist, the chairman of the commission that drafted the Spanish Civil Code, justified with a great deal of common sense, truth and reason.

On reaching majority, which has been set at twenty five years of age, a son is emancipated by operation of law. In our society, this would only improve his condition, for, as you know, there is no limit under Roman and Spanish Law to that state of dependency based on age alone. Several contemporary codes have shortened the duration of parental authority much more than we have. But, while it did not seem appropriate to copy them on this point, the latter has been made much less restrictive and onerous, thus providing an effective stimulus for study and work in the early years of life.

Any property a son may acquire in the performance of an occupation, trade, or any employment whatever is exempted from the usufruct the laws grant the father over his property. In this sense, the latter is granted true, quasi-independent personality, which of course extends to emancipated minors as long as they are under guardianship. The different types of guardians have been precisely defined, as well as reasons for disqualification or exemption from exercising these responsibilities, and their administrative powers, duties, emoluments, and responsibilities.

As far as ownership, use and enjoyment of property is concerned, major innovations have been introduced that will have beneficial results. In the draft submitted herewith, the delivery of real property ownership from one party to another and of the other real rights constituted therein, except easements, should be done by means of registration in an official registry similar to the one now covering mortgages and <u>censos</u> 2/. This involves in fact a new merger of the mortgage regime and the association of two inter-connecting or mutually inclusive objects by placing mortgages in full public view and making the status of landed fortunes a matter of public record.

With regard to the former, it might be said that nothing more has been done than to implement the provisions of the laws of October 31, 1845, and October 25, 1854, and to call the order of things developed by the latter by their real name. By virtue of Article 15 of the law of October 25, 1854, special mortgages had preference over legal mortgages of any date, which, prevailing over one another according to their effective date, have preference only over unsecured credits. Ever since a legal mortgage in Chile failed to keep a debtor from alienating part of his assets and could not be pursued through third party holders, it actually ceased being collateral and, therefore, was no longer a mortgage. The only thing that, to a certain extent, justified the name, was the fact of competing with special mortgages. Once this prerogative was removed by the aforementioned Article 15, the name was totally inappropriate. The proper thing seemed to be to do away with it. In this draft there is no other mortgage than the one formerly called a <u>special</u> mortgage, now simply a <u>mortgage</u>. Otherwise, the position of persons with a legal mortgage is exactly the same as stipulated under the law of October 25.

As far as making landed fortunes a matter of public record, the most simple criterion was to make registration of all sales of real estate compulsory, including hereditary transfers, adjudications, and the constitution of all real rights thereon. Appurtenant easements were exempted as of insufficient importance.

The transfer and conveyance of ownership, the constitution of all real rights except easements, requires delivery of the property and the only relevant form of delivery is registration in the official registry. As long as this is not done, a contract may be perfect, may originate obligations and rights among the parties, but it does not transfer ownership, it does not transfer any real rights, nor does it exist as regards third parties. Registration is the act that grants true and effective possesion; as long as this has not been discharged, the person who has not registered his deed does not own the property, he is a mere holder.

Since the official registry is open to all, there can be no more public, more solemn, more incontestable possession than registration. Under some legal systems, registration is a guarantee both of possession and of the existence of the property itself, but to go that far registration by all property owners, usufructuaries, users of real property, would have had to be compulsory, once the existence and value of their deeds was justified. Obviously, this would only have been possible by means of judgments sparking many troublesome legal proceedings with frequent contested, costly and lengthy trials.

By limiting official registration to a mere act of handing over the property, the possession conferred thereby leaves intact the rights of the real owner, which can only be liquidated by prescription. But, inasmuch as acts between parties who are living as well as hereditary transfers, are subject to registration, all the mentioned assets, except those belonging to juridical persons, will therefore be registered and free from attack within a certain number of years. Registration would then be an unimpeachable title of ownership, thus providing the result that others were anxious to achieve without necessary recourse to adverse measures that would cause serious turmoil in all landed property.

The benefits to be derived from this state of affairs are evident: manifest, incontestable possession of real estate, quickly leading to the time when registration, possession and property would be identical terms; landed property throughout the republic a matter of public record in a framework that would instantaneously depict, so to speak, its changes, encumbrances and successive divisions; solidly based mortgages, land credit strengthened and capable of being mobilized. The institution I have just mentioned approximates what existed in several states of Germany in the past, which other civilized nations currently expect to imitate. Its good effects have been amply demonstrated by experience.

As to possession, the intention was to adopt a less cumbersome and less ambiguous nomenclature than the one presently existing. All possession is essentially characterized by the reality or appearance of ownership. The possessor of an estate is none other than the person who considers it his own, either because it is materially in his possession or in the possession of someone else who acknowledges him as its owner. But there are several real rights; a person not the owner may have a right of usufruct, use, settlement, an inheritance, collateral or mortgage right, or an easement right. The usufructuary does not own the fructuary thing, that is, he does not have real or ostensible ownership thereof; he only possesses the usufruct over it, which is a real right and one susceptible to possession. But the lessor of a property possesses nothing, he has nothing more than his own personal effort to keep the rights conferred upon by him by his contract.

A person with property in the name of another is no more than the representative of the true owner, nor is he granted more than simple tenancy. Thus, the terms civil possession and natural possession are absent in the draft submitted herewith; the words possession and tenancy are always opposing terms, possession is in one's own name, tenancy in that of another. But possession may be regular or irregular, the former acquired without force or surreptitious means, with just title and in good faith, the latter meets none of these prerequisites. All possession is backed by law, but only regular possession places the possessor on the path of acquisitive prescription. This is the system followed in this project: definitions place precise limits on each of the two types of possession, with each preserving the generic character that consists in the granting of a real right.

Among the various categories of ownership, particular attention has been given to that which limits ownership to a condition that once verified causes it to pass to someone else, who acquires it indissolubly and absolutely. Usufruct and fiduciary ownership, property which upon the fulfillment of a certain condition lapses in one person to be born in another, are two contrasting juridical states: in the one, termination must occur, in the other, it may occur. The former assumes two co-existing current rights; the latter, one alone, for it assumes the exercise of a right which is no more than an expectation that can vanish and leave no trace of its existence. This is how a trust is constituted, on which the draft contains little or nothing that is original, but an attempt has at least been made to describe these two legal states so as to avoid confusion between them, provide clear norms for interpetation of the provisions whereby they are established, and enumerate their several special effects.

Though eliminated in several modern codes, appointment of a fiduciary heir is retained in this draft, thereby recognizing an emanation of property rights which any property owner seems entitled to so he can impose the limitations and conditions he pleases. But full recognition of this principle would be inconsistent with the interest of society by preventing the movement of assets or curtailing incentives for their maintenance and improvement, for which the strongest encouragement is the expectation of enjoying them perpetually without restriction or liability and being able to transfer them freely among the living and after one's death. Hence, allowance is made for a trust, but testamentary substitutions, even when not perpetual, are banned except in the form of a ground rent, on which everything legally relevant to succession has been covered. In the ground rent itself, the several special kinds that are harmful and adverse have been weakened.

A fundamental standard of this draft is the prohibition of two or more usufructs or testamentary trusts. Both are deterrents to the movement of property and lessen incentives to maintain and improve assets, which is what give industry vitality and momentum. Another rule having the same purpose limits the duration of suspensive and resolutory conditions, generally deemed null and void if not met within thirty years.

In the matter of easements, the French Civil Code has been followed step by step. The Civil Code of Cerdena has been used for legal easements covering water supplies. I believe this is the only one known which sanctioned the same principle as our decree of November 18, 1819, under which much land has been diverted to agriculture that seemed doomed by nature to perpetual sterility. But on this and all matters concerning the use and benefits of water, the draft, like the code used as its guide, does little more than lay the foundation. The details are left to special ordinances, which would probably not be the same for different localities.

Intestate succession is the area where this draft deviates most from what now exists. The right of representation is excluded except as it pertains to legitimate heirs of the deceased. These in turn are limited to both legitimate and natural children or siblings. The representation descends to all degrees thereof and is not affected by an absence on the part of the deceased of any right to transfer. Non-participation in the inheritance for any cause whatever is sufficient.

The fate of the surviving spouse and natural children has been significantly improved. A surviving spouse with inadequate means of support is assured a not insignificant share of the estate of the deceased, as provided for under present law, except that widowers are placed on the same par as widows. If this ever occurred in the past, it was only by force of an unjustifiable interpretation of Roman and Spanish law. In addition to this forced allotment, which has precedence even over testamentary provisions and is determined by the legitime of the legitimate children, if any, the spouse is legally entitled to a share of the intestate succession if there are no legitimate descendants and to the entire succession if there are no ascendants relative, legitimate siblings or natural children of the deceased. The spouse and natural children collectively enjoy equal rights in an intestate succession.

The inability of people to succeed one another whose reputation has been blemished by a harmful and punishable union does not affect the innocent offspring of this relationship. Collateral heirs have only sixth degree rights to intestate succession.

With regard to legitimes and any supplemental amounts consigned to one child, half of what the legitimaries or forced heirs would have been entitled to in an intestate succession, represents the part of the estate set aside as their legitime. This can be increased considerably but cannot be reduced or encumbered in any way. If the deceased has no legitimate descendants to succeed him personally or representatively, anyone can freely dispose of half his state. Otherwise, he can legally distribute no more than one-fourth of his assets with absolute freedom; the remaining quarter must be invested on behalf of at least one legitimate descendant to be chosen by him. Finally, each person is empowered during his lifetime to use his assets as he sees fit. Only in extreme cases does the law intervene to charge the excess of what was distributed among the living to the one-half or one-fourth free by disposable share or, if necessary, revoke it.

Thus, property rights are thought to be reconciled with the obligation to provide for the welfare of the offspring or persons to whom the deceased is indebted. Other restrictions have been omitted which would insure legitimes and safeguard against any inequitable distribution of assets parents may be induced to make because of favoritism, even when none of the legitimaries is really defrauded.

More reliance has been placed on the judgment of parents and on natural sentiments than on the law. When the former are misguided or absent, the voice of the latter is powerless and its prescriptions very easily evaded. The reach of the law is very limited. What good would the law be in matters of wills and donations against habitual dissipation, against the luxury of ostentation which jeopardizes family fortunes, or against the gambling table? This draft is restricted to controlling the excesses of an unwise liberality. Although not the most dangerous threat to the just expectations of the legitimaries, it is the only area accessible to civil law without violating its reasonable limits, trespassing on domestic affairs, or decreeing inquisitorial measures difficult to implement and in the final resort ineffective.

In the determination of hereditary shares in the event the provisions of a will involve numerical problems, the standards of Roman Law and the code of the Partidas have been substantially followed with, I believe, just one exception. The fact that the draft rules are expressed in mathematical formulae may be surprising. Alfonso X gave no explicit norms; a judge must deduce them from the examples given, a generalization more appropriate to the law than to men. With this need acknowledged, only two means were possible: a phraseology vaguely indicative of the mathematical procedure, or strict formulae that would lead to a resolution of each problem via the shortest path possible. The latter appeared to be less open to inaccuracy and error, and since arithmetic today is a part of elementary instruction everywhere, the terms peculiar to it must be assumed to be understood by everyone with even the most commonplace education.

With regard to contracts and quasi-contracts, you will find very little not based on current legislation, or less frequently, on the authority of a contemporary code, particularly the French Code, or on the doctrine of a prominent jurist. The peculiarities of prevailing practice in this country appeared to demand special provisions and have been kept very much in mind in some contracts, such as leases. A change of ownership of real property is not perfected except by a public instrument nor is it consummated except by registration in the official registry, which, as I said earlier, is the one and only way in which this type of asset can be handed over. The French Code as explained by its commentators has been closely followed on the cancellation and rescission of contracts and other voluntary acts constituting rights for the holder.

The greatest innovation on this point is the removal of the prerogative held by minors and other natural and juridical persons associated with them to gain full restitution against acts and agreements to which they are a party. This prerogative was considered very detrimental to credit and contrary to the real interest of the very persons holding the prerogative. As noted by a contemporary jurist, this prerogative makes it possible to break contracts, invalidate all obligations, and declare legitimate rights null and void. "This restitution," he adds, "is an endless source of unjust controversy and an easy pretext for making a mockery of the good faith of contracts."

All the restrictions leveled on this privilege have failed to correct its most serious drawback. It invalidates agreements undertaken in full compliance with the law, makes ownership uncertain and stands in the way of transactions with orphans, who generally have no less need than other men to enter into agreements in order to protect and develop their interests. The provision in the French, Sicilian, and Sardinian codes, among others, are much more just and advantageous to the wards themselves. Under these codes, a contract entered into without the consent of a guardian is not null and void ipso jure although it can be rescinded.

However, a contract entered into in full compliance with the law is subject to the same conditions as those entered into by adults. The jurist Jaubert said, in explaining the reasons for this provision: "It is indispensable in order to fully protect the rights of those dealing with minors in observance of legal formalities. Were it not needed, this precaution would at least be useful because of the deep-rooted reservations felt against wards, and the justified belief that there is no guaranteee in making agreements with them."

Under the title On Proof of Obligations, the presence of a deed covering an object worth more than a given amount is made compulsory, but much broader provision is made for allowance of other types of proof than in some legal systems, particularly France and Portugal, where a limitation on evidence provided by witnesses has existed for a long time and been beneficial. Needless to say, the most legitimate rights can easily be challenged and overthrown by means of sworn affidavits. The existence of an infamous class of men who earn a living by making false statements under oath is well known in towns in the interior. From this viewpoint, the solutions in this draft will seem somewhat tepid, but wary of making transactions more difficult, we thought it best to wait until the use of deeds is generalized everywhere and the admissibility of verbal evidence can be narrowed without difficulty.

The several kinds of ground rents (except annuities for life) have been reduced to one alone and made subject to identical rules and regulations, one of which makes the annuity divisible with the real property involved. Under another concerning a contract based on real property the value of which considerably exceeds the amounts charged, the ground rent can be reduced to a predetermined share and the remainder exempted from all liability.

At the same time, the interests of the annuitants have also been taken into account by placing a limitation on divisions, which if continued indefinitely would make collection of the rent too cumbersome and costly and within a few generations would convert the ground rent into an infinite number of imperceptible fragments. Should this succeed in discouraging the assessment of ground rents, a great good would be achieved. The problems involved in the other contracts are not found in short-term contracts for life. Hence, these are the only ones on which no redemptions, reductions or divisions are admissible under the terms of this draft.

In partnership agreements, it was thought best to follow the example of nations whose extensive trade has taught them the true demands of credit. The members of a general partnership under this draft are responsible for the total liabilities entered into on its behalf. At the same time, an attempt has been made to place the partnership under strict rules and regulations as far as its management is concerned, and as far as the mutual obligations of the partners and of the latter vis-a-vis third parties are concerned. The same specific norms and clarity have been sought in contracts of agency, public works contracts, and bonding.

Antichresis is included among the licit conventions. Innocent per se, useful in borrowing, and at times qualified, it can now exist openly under the sanction of law. Generally speaking, the code of the Partidas and the French Civil Code have been the two guiding lights kept most in mind. When they differ with one another, what seemed to be best and most adaptable was chosen. The arrangement for rating credits has been significantly simplified, with the promotion of credit the prevailing consideration.

Concurrent creditors have been divided into five classes: those with a general prerogative; those with a prerogative over chattels; mortgage holders; minors, married women, and others whose assets are managed by legal representatives, and unsecured creditors. Several general and specific prerogatives have been eliminated, including any devolving on real property. Needless to say, neither general conventional mortgages nor scriptorian credits are restored herein as preferential credits. The work set afoot under the laws of 1845 and 1854 has been completed.

Innovations no less advantageous to the security of assets and credit will be found under the title <u>Concerning</u> <u>Prescription</u>. The prescription covering thirty continuous years applies to all credits, all privileges, all real actions. Any personal obligation that has not been called in the same period of time is cancelled. But this exception should always be claimed by a person hoping to benefit therefrom, judges cannot furnish it.

I shall conclude with a few general observations. In this draft, public and private instruments (which a recognized contemporary jurist has called <u>preconstituted</u> <u>proof</u>), become compulsory for certain acts and agreements for which they are not legally required today. This includes the legalization of offspring by subsequent marriage and recognition of natural children, already mentioned; the distinction of guardianship or trusteeship in all instances, whether a wife assumes the administration of a partnership or whether it is recovered by the husband; acceptance or repudiation of an inheritance.

The drawing of an official inventory for a father who administers the assets of a son and marries a second time is prescribed; an inventory of hereditary assets is also specified whenever an heir refuses liability for them except to the extent of the value of his own share in the inheritance. A public or private deed is required for any conventional obligation in excess of a certain amount. Any change in ownership and any constitution of real rights over real property is subject to an official public instrument, without which no civil obligations should be derived even between the parties themselves. Credits with fourth-degree preference in a bankruptcy proceeding have no real right unless they are a matter of record, except damage suits charging mismanagement by legal representatives.

The usefulness of this type of proof is evident in order to guard against disputes and witnesses, in order to protect the interests of minors and other privileged persons without detriment to the credit in which they themselves and everyone else are concerned, and to undo frauds being plotted in the shadow of their privileges.

As to the plan and method followed in this code, I would note that it could have been made less voluminous by omitting the examples generally accompanying the abstract norms or corollaries derived therefrom, unnecessary for lawyers and judges. But in my opinion the opposite practice, imitating Alfonso X and the <u>Partidas</u>, was justified. The examples demonstrate the true meaning and spirit of a law in its application. The corollaries demonstrate what is involved therein which might escape less observant eyes. Brevity was felt to be a secondary consideration.

The draft as submitted for your examination has been fully discussed and modified by a select and dedicated commission worthy of your trust. Discussion of an urgently needed work of this type in the legislative chambers would delay its passage forever, nor could the legislature give the code the unity, concert and harmony that are its indispensable features. I do not pretend that it is perfect in these respects, none has been in the past. But I do not hesitate to voice my opinion that, once this draft is approved, many difficulties that now make the administration of civil justice cumbersome will vanish; many suits will be clipped at their roots, and trust and respect for the judiciary will grow as the consistency of its decisions with legal precepts becomes more evident. Practice will no doubt reveal faults in the implementation of such a difficult task, but the legislature can easily amend them on sound grounds as other countries have done, including France, which has the most famous code of all, one that has been a model for many others.

An additional matter still remains, a transition law to facilitate observance of the code. That the law should not become effective retroactively is a principle sanctioned by the code itself and is as evident as it is fair. But the application of this principle is no easy matter. Many cases may come up in which the enforcement of such a rule would stir controversy, just as in every country where one body of law has been replaced by another. Mere expectations must be distinguished from acquired rights, form from substance.

I believe what I have said is sufficient to recommend to your wisdom and patriotism passage of this draft Civil Code, which I hereby propose to you in conformity with the Council of State

NOTE

1. The fourteenth century Partidas of Alfonso X were the earliest Spanish codes and heavily influenced the evolution of Hispanic Law (T).

D. Higher Education

ADDRESS DELIVERED AT THE OPENING OF THE UNIVERSITY OF CHILE, SEPTEMBER 17, 1843

Address delivered at the opening of the University of Chile on September 17, 1853. Published in El Araucano, October 1843, this is one of the fundamental expressions of Bello's thought and has been reprinted many times. It was reprinted in Chile and Venezuela in observance of the one-hundredth anniversary of the University of Chile (1842-1942). See Key Ayala, Santiago; Discurso pronunciado en la Universidad de Caracas con motivo del centenario de la Universidad de Chile, Caracas, 1942; V. Tosta, Sentido democrático y republicano del pensamiento educativo de Andrés Bello, Caracas, and Luis Beltrán Prieto, Bello, educador, Caracas, several editions.

Gentlemen,

The Council of the University has asked me to express on its behalf our deep gratitude for the honor and trust bestowed on us by the government. I should also express the recognition of the University for the kind remarks made by the minister with regard to its members. As for myself, I am but too well aware that these honors and trust are owed much less to my own powers and ability than to my longstanding concern (this is the only quality I can claim unpresumptuously), for the diffusion of learning and sound principles, and to my devotion to certain areas of study that I have never interrupted or abandoned in the midst of other grave tasks.

I feel the weight of this trust, realize the extent of the obligations it imposes, and understand the magnitude of the effort it demands. Such responsibility would be overwhelming for a single individual, for another kind of mind more qualified than my own might be. But I am encouraged by the cooperation of my distinguished colleagues on the Council and the entire university body.

The law (to my good fortune) has ordained that the direction of studies be a common endeavor. With the assistance of the Council and the enlightened and patriotic efforts of the various university schools; under the auspices of the government, under the influence of freedom, the driving force behind Chile's institutions, I can legitimately expect the watershed of science and talent already available to the university to grow and spread rapidly, to the benefit of religion, morals, material interests and freedom itself.

The University, gentlemen, would not deserve a place among our institutions if (as dim echos of past oratory proclaim) the cultivation of science and letters were considered morally or politically dangerous. Morality (inseparable in my view from religion) is the very lifeblood of society, and freedom the stimulus that makes its institutions sound and flourishing. Whatever is harmful to morality interferes with the orderly yet free development of the individual and collective faculties of man. And, furthermore, whatever causes them to be squandered, must be denied a part in the nation's organization by an enlightened government.

But in these times, in Chile, in this gathering which I regard as a solemn tribute to the importance of education; in this gathering which by a meaningful coincidence is the first anniversary of the independence of Chile, I do not feel called upon to defend science and letters against the paralogisms of the philosopher of Geneva nor against the reservations of the fainthearted who would gladly quell any stirrings of reason forever and render more harm to the very causes they advocate than the abuses attributable to enlightenment. Not to refute what has been refuted time and again but to show the correlation between what the minister of Education has just said and the underlying spirit of the University, I shall add a few general ideas to those you have already stated, sir, concerning the moral and political influence of letters and science, the office of literary bodies, and the special tasks reserved for our university faculties in this present moment of Chile's history.

All truths touch on one another, from those that govern the path of the planets in space and the wondrous agencies on which movement and life in the universe depend, transform the structure of plants and animals and the inorganic mass under our feet, govern the intimate life of the soul in the mysterious theater of the consciousness, to those that delineate the actions and reactions of political forces, sustain the immovable foundations of morality, set the conditions for the development of trade, and promote and give direction to the arts. Progress in one line attracts progress in all others, all are connected and propel one another forward. I naturally include in the term "progress in all lines" that which is most important to human happiness, progress in the moral and political realm.

What accounts for the progress of civilization, this yearning for social betterment, the thirst for freedom? To find out, we must compare Europe and America with the empires of Asia where the iron sceptre of despotism weighs on necks first bent by ignorance, or the hordes of Africa where man scarcely superior to the beasts is, like them, an article of traffic for his own brothers. When Europe was enslaved, who struck the first sparks of civil liberty if not men of letters? Was it not the intellectual heritage of Greece and Rome, reclaimed by the human spirit after a long epoch of darkness? It was there where this vast political movement began that restored so many enslaved races, spreading everywhere, steadily expedited by the press and letters, moving at an uneven pace—some places quickly, others slowly—in all places essential and inevitable, until the day will come that it will remove all obstacles and cover the surface of the globe.

All truths touch upon one another, an assertion I extend to religious dogma, to theological truth. People who imagine there may be a hidden antipathy between religion and letters are slandering one of them, I know not which. Conversely, it is my belief that there is and must be a close alliance between positive revelation and universal revelation which speaks to all men in the book of nature. Misguided minds that misuse their knowledge to impugn dogma prove nothing other than the very condition of all things human. If human reason is frail, if it stumbles and falls, substantial nourishment and solid supports are all the more necessary.

The curiosity and daring that challenges the secrets of nature and the enigmas of the future cannot be smothered without also rendering the mind incapable of all that is great and inaccessible, all that is beautiful, generous, sublime and holy, without poisoning the sources of morality, without making religion itself ugly and vile. I have said that all truths touch on one another. Yet this statement is not enough. All human faculties make up a system in which there can be no regularity and harmony without the presence of each member. A single fiber, so to speak, of the human soul cannot become paralyzed without crippling all the rest.

Aside from this social worth, this instrumental importance, the coating of amenity and polish given human society which must be counted among its benefits, science and letters have an intrinsic merit of their own to the degree that they augment the pleasure and enjoyment of people who cultivate and love them. A pleasure inaccessible to the senses, pure pleasure in which the soul says not:
...Medio de fonte leporun
surgit amari aliquid, quod in ipsis floribus angit
(Lucrecio)

Science and literature are their own recompense for the hours devoted to them. I do not mean the fame that comes from great scientific discoveries or the aura of immortality that crowns the works of genius. Such expectations are reserved for few. I speak of the rather exalted and intense pleasures common to all ranks of letters. For the mind, as for all human faculties, activity per se is enjoyment. A Scotch philosopher, Thomas Brown, said that it saves us from the inertia we would otherwise give in to, to our own detriment and that of society.

Each avenue science opens to an educated mind is beguiling; each new countenance discovered in the ideal type of beauty makes a human heart tremble. A learned mind, withdrawn in meditation, hears the thousand voices of nature's chorus; a thousand fanciful visions flutter around the solitary lamp that lights his vigils. For him alone, nature reveals itself on an immense scale and creation arrays herself in all her magnificence. But science and letters, while providing great exercise for the mind and the imagination, also enhance man's moral character, weakening the power of sensual seduction and ridding the vicissitudes of fortune of most of their terror. Second only to the humble, contented resignation of a religious soul, they are the best preparation for the hour of misfortune. They bring comfort to the sick, the exile, the prisoner and the condemned.

On the eve before he drank the hemlock, Socrates illumined his cell with the most sublime speculations left us by the Greeks on the

future of the human race; Dante composed his <u>Divine Comedy</u> in exile;
Lavoisier asked the hangman to delay his execution so he could
finish an important study; Chenier, instants before his death,
scribbled his final verses, left unfinished so he could walk to the
gallows:

> Comme un dernier rayon, comme un dernier zephire
> anime la fin d'un beau jour,
> au pied de l'echafaud j'essaie encor ma lyre

Such are the recompenses and solaces of letters. I personally
have partaken of their benefits and joys. They were a bright ray in
the morning of my life that remains with me still, like a flower in
the midst of ruins. They have been my succour in long wanderings,
directing my steps to this land of peace and liberty, this adopted
country that has given me such benevolent hospitality.

Another viewpoint exists in which we may find ourselves faced
with specious concerns. Are universities and literary societies
appropriate instruments for the propagation of learning? I can
hardly conceive of such a question in an age which is <u>par excellence</u>
one of association and representation, when societies for
agriculture, commerce, the trades, and charity multiply everywhere,
in the age of representative government. Europe and the United
States of America, our model in so many ways, will provide the
response to that query.

If the propagation of learning is one of their most important
conditions--otherwise letters would provide but a few bright spots
in the midst of dense shadow--the literary societies, which are
mainly responsible for speedy literary communication, are of the
utmost use to enlightenment and humanity. Hardly does a new truth
emanate from a person's thought than it becomes the property of the
whole republic of letters with scholars in Germany, France, and the
United States assessing its value, consequences, and applications.
In this propagation of learning, academies and the universities act
as additional repositories where all scientific advancement steadily
accumulates and flows outward from these centers to the several
levels of society. The University of Chile has been established
with this specific purpose in mind. If it is faithful to its
reorganizing legislation and the expectations of the government, it
will be a body eminently devoted to the expansion and propagation of
knowledge.

Others advocate that the momentum given instruction should be
the first concern of primary education. I, of course, regard
universal education, the education of the people, as one of the most
important goals to which the government might turn its attention,
one of its highest priorities, an urgent, primary need, the basis
for all sound progress, the indispensible foundation of republican
institutions.

But for that very reason, I believe there is an urgent need to
promote instruction in literature and science. The elemental
learning demanded by the working classes (the majority of mankind)
has become generalized only where science and letters have
flourished first. I am not saying that the cultivation of letters
and science is automatically followed by elementary education on a
broader scale, although science and letters do indeed have a natural
tendency to spread when unimpeded by artificial causes. What I am

saying is that the former is an indispensable condition for the latter, that the latter cannot take place, notwithstanding all official efforts, unless the former exists in an appropriate way.

The diffusion of learning presupposes one or more hearths from which light emerges and spreads, gradually probes into the intermediate spaces and ultimately reaches the outermost edges. Generalized education entails a great number of properly trained teachers, and their aptitude as its ultimate handlers represents per se rather distant emanations of the major repositories of scientific and literary learning. Good teachers, good books, good methods, good teaching guidance are necessarily the work of a very advanced intellectual culture. Literary and scientific instruction is the source from which elementary education is nourished and strengthened, similar to how the wealth of a well-organized society's most privileged class is the wellspring for the subsistence of the working classes and the welfare of the people. But in reorganizing the University, the law did not rely just on the natural tendency of knowledge to spread and multiply.

Printing in our time gives knowledge a power and mobility previously unknown. The law has thus linked the two types of education and given one section of the university the specific task of overseeing elementary instruction, observing its progress, furthering its propagation, and contributing to its advancement. The promotion of the religious and moral instruction of the people is a duty each member of the university assumes by virtue of his connection with the institution.

The law reorganizing the old university, to accommodate it to the present state of civilization and needs of Chile, sets forth the major objectives the university should pursue. The Minister has already mentioned the considerations that presided over the reorganization of the university, the goals the legislators had in mind, and the expectations it is called upon to fulfill. In the wake of his development of these ideas, I can do no more than make an idle commentary on his address. I will at any rate add a few brief observations which I feel are important.

The promotion of ecclesiastical science, aimed at training priests and ultimately providing the towns of Chile with competent religious and moral instruction, is the university's first and foremost objectives. There is still another angle from which attention to the cause of morality and religion should be focused. While ecclesiastical studies are important for the performance of a priest's ministry, it is also important for every student of science and letters to be trained in a knowledge of dogma and the annals of the Christian faith. Their role as an integral part of general education, indispensible for every profession and for everyone who hopes to hold a place in society above the common man needs no proof.

A vast field is opened to the school of law and political science, the one most susceptible to practical applications. You have listened as it was said that practical utility, positive results, the betterment of society are what the government most expects of the university. We as heirs of the laws of Spain must purge them of the blemishes left from the influence of despotism, clarify incoherencies that tarnish a work so many centuries in the making, representing so many alternating interests, so much opposing inspiration. We must again make our legislation consistent with republican institutions.

There can be no greater or loftier purpose than the development and strengthening of our organic laws, the honest and rapid administration of justice, the safeguarding of our rights, the integrity of commercial transactions, and domestic peace. I dare say the university shall not endorse the view that considers the study of Roman Law to be useless and harmful; rather, I believe the university shall give it fresh vitality and place it on firmer fundations. Doubtless, the study of Roman Law shall be regarded by the university as the best apprenticeship in judicial and forensic logic. Let us listen to the testimony of L'Herminier, a man who surely cannot be labeled partial to old-fashioned doctrines, a man who may have gone to the other extreme in his enthusiasm for democracy and freedom of the people: "Science places its seal on law; logic sets forth the principles, formulates the axioms, deduces the consequences, and derives endless possibilities from the idea of what is just. From this perspective Roman Law has no equal; some of its principles may be challenged, but its method, logic and icientific system have made and kept it superior to all other law. Its texts are a masterpiece of juridical style, its method that of geometry strictly applied to moral thinking." Earlier, Liebniz had said, "In jurisprudentia regnant romanid. Dixi saepius post scripta geometrarum nihil extrare quod vi ac subtilitate cum romanorum jurisconsultorum scriptis comparari possit: tantum nervi inest, tantum profunditatis."

The university is also to examine the specific nature of Chilean society from the economic angle, where problems are posed of no lesser scope nor of less uncertain solution. The university shall examine, help develop and discover in Chile's statistics a statement of our material interests. In this and every branch of study, the university program is wholly Chilean in nature; any borrowings from Europe shall be made for application in Chile. All the avenues planned for investigation by its faculty or for study by its students converge at one focal point: The fatherland.

Following the same plan, medicine is to investigate the effects on man caused by the climate, customs and food of Chile; issue standards for private and public health; engage tirelessly in a search for the causes of disease; and insofar as possible disseminate knowledge on simple methods for preserving and restoring health. It is needless at this time to list the positive, scarcely considered benefits of the material and physical sciences and their applications to a new-born industry which has but a few rude methods, no well understood procedures, no machines, and none of the most common utensils, or their applications to a land criss-crossed with ore beds, a fertile soil, and plant resources rich in nutritious substances.

But in encouraging practical applications, I am far from advocating that the university follow the wretched motto of "cui bono?" or fail to appreciate the value of a knowledge of nature fully. The former because proper direction of practice means the mind must reach out to understand the culminating points of science and learn its general formulae. The university is not to confuse practical applications with the manipulations of a blind empiricism. As stated earlier, the cultivation of a contemplative intelligence, which prods the physical and moral universe to unravel its secrets, is _per_ _se_ a positive result and one of the utmost importance. Here, to avoid repetition, I will copy the words of an English friend, Nicholas Anott, who said:

> The thought that people learned in general laws may have their attention divided and hardly have time to learn anything well has been a matter of some concern. The opposite, however, is true. General knowledge makes for specific knowledge that is clearer and more precise. The theorems of philosophy are keys that open up the most appealing gardens the mind can imagine; they are a magic wand that uncovers the face of the universe and reveals infinite objects that ignorance fails to see. A man learned in the laws of nature is, so to speak, surrounded by familiar beings and friends, whereas, unlearned men wander in a strange and hostile land. One who can use the general laws to read in the book of nature finds in the universe a sublime story that talks to him of God and occupies his mind worthily for the rest of his days.

And now, gentlemen, I go on to the department of literature, which in a special and foremost way has the ability to polish manners. Literature refines language, making it a faithful, beautiful and clear vehicle for ideas. Through the study of ancient and modern languages, it puts us in contact with antiquity and the freest, most cultured and civilized nations of our time. Makes us hear (not through the imperfect medium of translations, which are inevitably unfaithful) the sounds of foreign wisdom and eloquence in lively, sonorous and vibrant tones; through the contemplation of ideal beauty and its reflection in words of genius, purifies taste and reconciles imagination and reason. By initiating the mind in severe studies, necessary aids to literature and a necessary prelude to all science and every occupation in life, literature is the foremost discipline for an intellectual and moral human being to follow, expounding the eternal laws of the mind in order to direct and make its step firmer, and touching the innermost depths of the heart to keep it from harmful aberrations, to set the rights and duties of man on firm ground.

To enumerate these different subjects, gentlemen, would be to represent the program of the university in philosophy and the humanities. One, the study of the Spanish language, I regard as of the utmost importance. I shall never advocate a rigid purism that censures innovation in matters of language. Quite the contrary, I believe the many new ideas that come into general circulation from literature everyday require new words to represent them. Would we find a dictionary of Cervantes and Fray Luis de Granada--there is no need to go back so far--in a dictionary of Iriarte and Moratín, adequate means or lucid signs for expressing the notions common to the average man, to say what society thinks? New institutions, new laws, new customs; changing ways and materials all around us, yet old words, old phraseology!

Besides being wrong, because it would conflict with the basic purpose of language, the clear, easy transmission of thought, such a pretension would also be impossible. But language can be expanded, enriched and accommodated to every demand of society, even fashion (which exercises and unimpeachable authority over literature), without adultering it, corrupting its constructions or doing violence to its native peculiarities. Is the language of Chateaubriand and Villemain different from that of Pascal and Racine? Does not the language of the former reflect the social thought of France today, so different from that of France under Louis XIV? Furthermore, suppose we tolerate this sort of culteranism, suppose we give carte blanche to every neologism. America would soon recreate the jumble of languages and dialects and slang, the Babylonic chaos of the Middle Ages, and ten nations would lose one of their strongest bonds of brotherhood, one of their finest tools of communication and commerce.

The university shall promote the study both of foreign languages and foreign literatures. Yet I do not know whether I am mistaken. Those who hold the opinion that we should accept the synthetic results of European enlightenment without looking at their credentials and examining it ourselves will find little support in the University. I respect other ideas and reserve only the right to dispute them. But it would admittedly be just as inappropriate, in order to stimulate the mind and train it to think for itself, to abide by the moral and political conclusions of Herder, for example, without first studying ancient and modern history, as it would be to adopt Euclid's theories without the prior intellectual work of testing them.

I regard Herder, gentlemen, as one of the writers who has performed the greatest service to mankind. He gave history dignity by reinstating the plan of divine providence and man's vocation here on earth. But Herder himself did not set out to substitute factual knowledge but rather to illustrate and explain it, nor can his doctrine be assessed without prior studies in history.

Replacing them with deductions and formulae would give youth a skeleton instead of a vivid portrayal of society, a collection of aphorisms instead of a moving, instructive anecdotal panorama of institutions, manners, revolutions, great nations and great men. It would deprive moralists and statesmen of deep convictions only borne of factual knowledge; it would deprive human experience of the wholesome power of its lessons, precisely in an age most susceptible to lasting impressions; it would deprive poets of an endless source of images and colors.

What I say of history must also be applied to other branches of knowledge. This means long but enjoyable periods of study. Nothing makes education more tedious than abstractions, and nothing is easier or more interesting than a process that uses the storehouse of memory and also exercises the understanding and heightens the imagination. Reasoning should generate theorems, and examples leave lessons deeply engraved on the memory.

How could I, gentlemen, just in passing, not allude to the most bewitching of literary vocations, the essence of literature, the Corinthian column, so to speak, of a cultured society? How could I, particularly, fail to allude to the sudden appearance on our horizon of talented young poets? In all sincerity their verses have faults, things that a disciplined, strict reason rejects. But correction is a product of study and maturity not to be expected of those caught in a moment of poetic and patriotic emotion, embarked in this new arena with a resolve to prove that this divine fire also burns in the souls of Chileans, though absent by an unjust prejudice. Brilliant examples not limited to the sex which has cultivated letters almost exclusively here in the past.

I do not know whether my own partiality towards the attempts of young minds misleads me. I say what I feel. I find in these works unquestionable marks of talent and in some of them true poetic genius. In some I see an original and fertile imagination, successfully bold expressions and (what evidently comes only with long practice) a harmonious, flowing versification that purposely seeks difficulties in order to struggle with them and brightly succeed in this perilous trial.

In encouraging our young poets, the University should perhaps tell them: "If you would have your name reach beyond the narrow confines of the Andes and the Pacific, if you would have posterity read your works, study diligently, beginning with your native tongue. Do yet more: Deal with themes worthy of your country and of posterity. Leave behind the vapid tones of Anacreonte and Sappho; poetry in the nineteenth century has a more lofty mission. Let humanity's great concerns inspire you. Let your works beat with moral feeling. Let each of you say as you take up your pen: "Priest of the Muses, my song is for pure and innocent souls,
> Musarum sacerdos,
> virginibus puerisque canto.
> (Horace)

How many lofty themes our young republic has ready for you'! Celebrate its great days, weave garlands for its heroes, enshrine the shroud of our country's martyrs. The University shall remind young people of the advice given by a great master of our time, Goethe, "Art must rule the imagination and turn it into poetry."

In hearing the word art, although taken from the lips of Goethe himself, some people will class me among the partisans of the conventional rules who usurped its name for a long time. I solemnly protest such an affirmation and do not believe my record justifies it. I do not find art in the sterile precepts of a school, in the inexorable unities, in the wall of bronze raised between style and genre, in the fetters placed on poets in the name of Aristotle and Horace, attributing to them what they never thought themselves.

But I do believe there is a basic art in the impalpable, ethereal relations of ideal beauty, accessible to the penetrating gaze of a properly educated genius. I believe there is an art that guides the imagination, that without art the imagination aborts sphinxes, monstrous enigmatic creations, instead of encarnating the ideal of beauty. This is my literary creed. Liberty in all things. Yet I see not liberty but licentious debauchery in the orgies of the imagination. Freedom as the counterpart of a slavish docility that accepts everything unquestioningly, and of a chaotic license that rebels against authority and reason and against the noblest and purest insticts of the human heart, shall doubtless be the theme of the University in all of its sections.

I shall not try your patience any longer. The subject matter is far-ranging, all I could do was try to cover it lightly. I regret not having occupied the attention of this distinguished audience more worthily and thank you for your indulgent attention.

E. Philosophy

PHILOSOPHY OF UNDERSTANDING
Introduction

Bello published only a small part of the
Philosophy of Understanding under the title of Theory
of Understanding in El Crepúsculo, Santiago, issues
1-10, from June 1843 to February 1844. The rest of the
work remained unpublished until after his death. When
the government of Chile approved the edition of his
complete works in 1872, efforts began on collecting his
known unpublished works.

Miguel Luis Amunátegui relates the problem
experienced in preparing the first volume on the
Philosophy of Understanding in an 1878 report to the
Congress, published in Santiago at the time by the
Imprenta Nacional. Juan Escobar Palma, a teacher at
the National Institute, was placed in charge of its
preparation using manuscripts supplied by relatives of
Bello to the commission appointed by the Council of the
University of Chile. The Philosophy of Understanding
was published in 1881 as the first volume in the Obras
completas. I reproduce the introduction, or first
chapter, of the work.

For Bello's ideas on philosophy, see the
preliminary studies to the two modern editions of the
Philosophy of Understanding, by José Gaos, Mexico,
Fondo de Cultura Económica, 1948, and Juan David García
Bacca, Caracas, 1951 (Obras completas, vol. III). Also
Walter Hanish Espidola, "Tres dimensiones del
pensamiento de Bello: Religión, filosofía, historia,"
Historia, Santiago, IV, 1965, and Leopoldo Zea, "La
filosofía de Andrés Bello," Cuadernos Americanos, VII,
no. 6, Mexico, 1948.

I. Notion and division of philosophy. Mental psychology and
logic or philosophy of understanding. Moral psychology and ethics
or moral philosophy. II. The human spirit is the true object of
philosophy: Its definition. III. Faculty and act: Phenomena of
consciousness. Unity and individuality. General division of the
spiritual faculties: Understanding and will.

I

The object of philosophy is knowledge of the human spirit and proper guidance of its acts.

Our spirit is known to us only by the affections it experiences and the acts it performs. About its innermost nature we know nothing.

There are two kinds of affections and acts. Through the former the mind learns, investigates truth and ascertains its possession. Through the latter it desires happiness and works to attain and keep it.

Every affection and every act presupposes a special power of faculty: If we feel, we are able to feel, if we judge, we have the capacity to judge. Accordingly, the soul has two kinds of powers or faculties: Through the one we learn, through the other we desire. The former as a whole is called mind, understanding, intelligence; the latter as a whole, will, mind, understanding, intelligence.

Insofar as its object is to know the faculties and operations of the understanding, philosophy is called mental or intellectual psychology. Insofar as it provides rules for the proper direction of these faculties and operations, it is called logic. Insofar as its object is to learn about the faculties and acts of the will, it is called moral psychology. Insofar as it provides rules for the proper direction of our voluntary acts, we give it the name of ethics.

The philosophy of understanding consists of mental psychology and logic. Moral philosophy consists of moral psychology and ethics. 1/

II

The human spirit is a being that is conscious of its acts and can to a certain extent control them at its will. What difference there is with other beings of the same nature, that is, endowed with consciousness and will, is to us an insoluble question. Anything we are conscious of exists in the spirit, or properly speaking, is the spirit itself, which acts or feels in a particular way at a given time. We have no consciousness of what actually occurs in the mind, nor can we have.

When, according to our usual expression, we feel pain somewhere in our body, the pain we are aware of exists in the mind and it is the mind itself that experiences a particular change perceived within itself immediately and directly. The spiritual change is accompanied by certain phenomena circumscribed to the body, especially the nervous system; phenomena that may involve mechanical, physical, chemical, electrical or any other type of mutation. But we do not perceive these phenomena immediately, have no consciousness of them, nor do we acquire a knowledge of them until much later and even then imperfectly, by means of investigations and observations performed by the sight, touch, and the other senses, which help us study material things in the only way possible. As we will see later, this is indirect and symbolic.

We use the words spirit and soul synonymously. With them we designate our self, our own spirit and the human spirit in general to which by analogy we attribute the nature and quality of our own self.

III

Faculty and acts are correlative words that explain one another. Any action or passion of the soul, any action performed by the soul upon itself or another being, and any effect produced in it by its own or another's action is an act of the soul. The fact that we call an act in the soul what is often the effect of an action by one's self or another should not seem strange. In the seemingly most passive changes that take place in our spirit there is always something active that differentiates them from the absolute inertia of matter.

We are not always conscious of each act of the soul because many are so fleeting and rapid that they go unnoticed. But at least the consciousness is what first provides a knowledge of <u>all</u> the different types of acts to which our soul is susceptible. It is not reasonable to acknowledge the reality of any spiritual act of which we have <u>never</u> been conscious.

<u>Faculty</u> is merely the capacity to perform an act. Accordingly, we have as many different intellectual faculties as there are acts the human spirit is capable of performing. The nature of a faculty is fully embodied in the nature of the act because the potential for the act is all there is to the faculty.

We must not regard the spiritual faculties as particular parts of the soul. The soul as a whole, the <u>self</u>, is present in every one of its acts. The soul that feels is the same one that remembers, judges, reasons, desires, fears, loves, and hates. No matter how carefully it contemplates itself, its changes cannot be attributed to different portions or parts of itself. The consciousness is the clearest testimony of the simplicity or indivisibility of the soul and its constant identity with itself in all its acts.

In order to classify the spiritual faculties accurately, we must first acquire a knowledge of them. For now, we can only presuppose the most obvious and most generally known division. We attribute to the <u>understanding</u> the faculties we use to examine objects and to investigate truth, that is, what really happens within our soul or outside. We attribute to the <u>will</u> certain acts by means of which we pursue objects that provide us with welfare or pleasure, or we alienate ourselves from objectives that cause us annoyance or pain.

Entering into an examination of the faculties of the understanding, we shall begin by the one we use most constantly and which intervenes in all the others.

NOTE

1. Metaphysics or the science of the basic truths which in part is Ontology (the science of being or that deals with existence in its generality), including Pneumatology (which deals with the spirits), and Theodicy (which by means of reason inquires into the existence and attributes of Divinity), will not be special sections in this book. These subjects are closely related to mental psychology and logic, for the analysis of our intellectual acts gives us the basis and primary expression of all these notions, and the theory of judgment and reason leads us naturally to a knowledge of the principles or basic truths that serve as a guide for the understanding in its investigation of all other truths. I have thus dissolved metaphysics into mental psychology and logic, leaving for an appendix what seemed less closely related to the science of human understanding (A).

FUNDAMENTAL PHILOSOPHY,
BY JAMES BALMES

Bello's work on Balmes' Fundamental Philosophy was first published in three articles in El Araucano, no. 917, March 3, 1848; no. 918, March 10, 1848, and no. 924, April 21, 1848. The first two works revised by Bello and included in his Opúsculos literarios y críticos, pp. 182-194.

I have merged the three articles (parts I, II and III of his work on Balmes) into a single article; the one later published by Miguel Luis Amunátegui, copied directly from Bello's unpublished manuscripts, in the introduction to his edition of the Obras completas, vol. VIII, Santiago de Chile, makes up parts IV, V, and VI of the present Anthology.

See the study by Miguel Batllori, S.J., "Bello y Balmes," Revista Nacional de Cultura, no. 105, Caracas, July-August 1954, pp. 101-106.

Why is Philosophy, the science of the innermost sense with its supposedly infallible perceptions the most uncertain and fickle of all sciences, the one most subject to contradiction? The physical sciences possess a body of truths that have survived the test of time and produce new truths daily with amazing ease. Yet, why is it so hard for us to claim there is any certain, unimpeachable principle in psychology and metaphysics, fields in which systems overlap and succeed one another in a war waged to the death and the history of which is nothing but endless combat and ruin? Most noteworthy is the faith of each philosophical school in its own speculations and the confidence with which they all resort to the testimony of consciousness. What, then, is consciousness, that innermost sense assumed to be incapable of deceiving us?

In my opinion, the cause lies in the fact that the soul sometimes confuses the mirages of the imagination with true facts of its own on which the testimony of consciousness is unassailable. Let us take, for example, the term general idea, the theory of which has been an area of sharp controversy between philosophical sects since the time of Plato. According to some, there is nothing general in the general idea except the name. Its images are all separate yet variable because of their membership as part of the gender. Conversely, others look upon the general idea as an intellectual concept in which individuals disappear, leaving only a prototype that retains merely those forms and qualities common to all the individual parts. If the former are wrong, it must clearly be because the imagination causes them to confuse general concepts with the individual images accidentally associated with them. If the latter are wrong, to what can it be attributed other than the fact that they imagine they see in the understanding what in reality is not there?

This does not happen in the physical sciences. The mirages of the imagination vanish under the light of observations and experiments subject to examination by the corporeal senses that can be repeated, combined, modified a hundred ways, take note of every circumstance and detail, and be tested by mathematical criterion.

However this may be, it is undeniably very difficult so to purge the testimony of consciousness in psychological perceptions that we can be certain there is no imagination present in them anywhere. The result is a species of logic we believe has not been dealt with specifically in the past despite the fact that there is scarcely any subject in the art of investigating truth that deserves closer examination.

In his _Fundamental Philosophy_, James Balmes, a deservedly popular writer and perhaps the wisest and most profound thinker in Spain today, presents a new system in which not a few of the major issues of psychology and ethics are resolved in a very luminous, original way. The author's arguments against systems opposed to his own take up a great part of the work. Although we feel Balmes is not always the victor in this controversy, there are points on which he combats his adversaries persuasively. We do not presume to act as judges and speak only of our own impressions. We do, however, believe that even the humblest citizen in the republic of letters can explain his opinions, whatever they may be, and discuss those of others with the courtesy owed to all and the respect due wisdom and talent.

Mr. Balmes begins by what many may think is entirely unnecessary. Do we know anything at all? Have we any basis for believing there is any certainty, anything absolutely true in human knowledge? Can I be sure of my own existence, of the existence of other spirits and the material universe? Raising difficulties and doubts of this type, Balmes says,

> may arouse suspicion that such investigations offer nothing solid to the mind and serve only to feed the vanity of a sophist. I am far from believing that philosophers ought to be regarded as legitimate representatives of human reason.
>
> But when the whole body of philosophers dispute, humanity itself may be said to dispute. Every fact affecting the human race merits a thorough examination.... There should be no contradiction between reason and common sense, yet such a contradiction there would be if we should, in the name of common sense, condemn what concerns the most enlightened mind. What is grave and significant, that which makes a thinking man medidate, is often the result not of a dispute nor of the arguments adduced therein, but of the mere existence of the conflict _per se_. The latter may have little importance but what it points to may be of great consequence.

215

All philosophical questions are in some manner involved in that of certainty. When we have completely developed this, we have examined under one aspect or another all that human reason can conceive about God, man and the universe. At first sight it may perhaps seem to be the simple foundation of the scientific edifice, but in this foundation, if we carefully examine it, we shall see the whole edifice represented. It is a plane whereon is projected, visibly and in fair perspective, the whole body that it must support....

In descending to the depths to which these questions lead us, the understanding grows dim and the heart is awed with a religious fear. A moment ago we were contemplating the edifice of human knowledge and took pride in seeing its colossal dimensions, its beautiful forms, its fine and bold construction. We enter it and are led through deep caverns and, as if by enchantment, the foundation seems to crumble, to evaporate, and this superb edifice ends up floating in the air....

Whatever tends to raise man to lofty contemplation in the sanctuary of his soul contributes to his aggrandizement. For it separates him from natural objects, reminds him of his noble origin, and proclaims to him his high destiny. In a materialistic and sensual age, when everything appears aimed at not developing the powers of the spirit, except as they administer to the ones of the body, it is well to renew these great issues in which the mind roams free over the unbounded realms of space.

Only intellect can examine itself. A stone does not know when it falls; lightening calcinates and pulverizes without realizing its power; a flower knows nothing of its beauty, and animal follows his instincts without asking why. Man alone, a fragile organization appearing for a moment on earth before returning to dust, harbors a spirit that after embracing the world, longs to understand his own nature and enters into himself as into a sanctuary where he is at once his own oracle and questioner. Who am I? What do I do? What do I think? Why do I think? How do I think? What phenomena do I myself experience? Why am I subject to them? What is their cause, their order of production, their relationship?

The spirit asks itself these questions--serious, difficult questions indeed, but noble and sublime--an unfailing truth that there is within us something superior to inner matter susceptible only of motion and a variety of form, that there is something which, by an inner, spontaneous activity rooted in our very nature, provides us with an image of that infinite activity that by a single act of will created the world from nothingness

We willingly accept these profound reflections of Balmes' as to all kinds of philosophical questions. We believe, however, restricting ourselves to the matter at hand, that any search for the reason behind the basic principles and the logical justification for our reliance on them, is an attempt to involve ourselves in a sphere that is beyond the possible reach of human faculties.

Our understanding is forced either to believe there is certainty, and that there is a means to attain it and to acquire a knowledge of truth 1/, or else not think at all, not believe in anything, including our own existence. Investigating whether there is certainty and what basis there is for it and how we acquire it, is ipso facto to take for granted the primary truths and general rules of logic, without which it is absolutely impossible to take a single step in this investigation and any other.

Is there certainty? Are we certain of anything? Balmes says that "common sense responds affirmatively to this question." But if the authority of common sense is unimpeachable in this matter, why not in all others?

The matter involves laying down a supreme principle from which all others and all human knowledge may logically be derived. But what guarantee does a principle, an evident truth, provide us, no matter what it is, that other principles, other truths of the same type do not? If this guarantee consists in its being immediately evident (and none other is possible), the evidence is a legitimate justification for certainty in all kinds of matters. Whow would we deduce the other principles from the first one? Doubtless by following the general rules of logic. But if we rely on these rules on this issue, aren't we thus acknowledging the truth of everything involved in them?

No reasoning is possible, no matter how simple it may be, if we fail to take for granted that something cannot be and not be at the same time; that, in drawing the conclusion, I am the same person who laid down the premises; that memory, which plays an indispensable role in the series of judgments interrelated by reasoning, does not trick us. Fichte confesses that in his search for a single absolute truth from which all knowledge is derived, as if from a primary source, placed on a sacred summit, he tacitly acknowledges the rules of logic, the rules that govern the mind when it reasons, when it thinks, and that this process clearly goes in a circle, an inevitable circle.

"And assuming," he says, "that it is inevitable, and that we acknowledge this openly, the establishment of the most exalted principle presupposes our reliance on all laws of general logic." But if the circle is inevitable in some matters, this does not mean that one can reason in circles. This would make it impossible for us to arrive at a knowledge of truth. What would we say about a geometrician who in determining the surface of a parallelogram knew the surface of each triangle into which it was divided by the diagonal and then determined the surface of each of the latter by means of the surface of the former? Saying that reasoning in a circle is inevitable in a given subject, is the same as saying that authentic reasoning in that particular matter is impossible. Anyone who openly acknowledges the former must resign himself to acknowledging the latter.

Balmes' thoughts on Fichte's system seem very sensible. We shall present a brief extract of them:

"Everyone," according to Fichte, "admits the propositon A is A, or A equals A. This proposition is absolutely correct and no one could consider disputing it. By acknowledging it, we claim the right to suppose something absolutely. In affirming the preceding proposition, we do not suppose that A is or that there is an A but rather that <u>if</u> A is, A is thus, i.e., A is A. Between the conditional <u>if</u> of the first proposition and the affirmative <u>thus</u> of the latter, there is a necessary connection, and it is this necessary connection between both which is supposed absolutely and without other foundation. I call this necessary connection provisionally X.

"All this show of analysis," the author of <u>Fundamental Philosophy</u> observes,

amounts only to what every student of logic knows, that in every proposition the copula, or the verb <u>to be</u>, denotes not the existence of the subject but its relation to the predicate. There was no need of so many words, nor of such affected efforts of understanding, to say such a simple thing, and much less so dealing with an identical proposition. But let us be patient and continue to listen to the German philosopher.

Is there an A or not? Nothing has yet been decided thereon. The question then occurs: Under what condition is A?

X, as far as it is concerned, is in and by the self, because it is the self who judges in the above proposition, and indeed judges by X as by a law. Consequently, X is given to the self, and by it established absolutely and without other foundation must therefore be given to the self by the self.

Balmes next wonders what all this Sanscrit means. <u>2/</u>

Here it is in everyday language. In identical or equivalent propositions there is a connection which the mind knows, judges, and according to which it decides upon the rest. This relation is given to our mind. Identical propositions need no proof in order to obtain assent. All this is very true, very clear, and very simple. But when Fichte adds that this relation must be given to the self by the self, he asserts what he does not nor can he know.

Who told him that objective truths come to us from ourselves? Is one of the principal philosophical questions such as that of the origin of truth to be so easily solved with a stroke of the pen? Has he perchance defined his self or given any idea of it? Either his words mean nothing or they mean this: I judge of a relation, this judgment is in me; this relation, as known and abstracted from its real existence, is in me. All of which may be reduced to what Descartes said more simply and naturally: "I think, therefore, I am."

Had the German philosopher confined his forms, little calculated as they are to illustrate science, to what we have thus far examined, their greatest inconvenience would have been to weary both the author and his readers. But unfortunately this mysterious self, which makes its appearance at the very vestibule of science and which, in the eyes of sound reason, can only be what it was to Descartes--the human mind, knowing its existence by its own thought--goes on dilating in Fichte's hands like a gigantic spectre which, beginning at a single point, ends by hiding its head in the heavens and sinking its feet in the abyss.

That self, absolute subject, is then a being which exists simply because it supposed itself. It is a being which creates its own self, absorbs everything, is everything, and is revealed in the human mind as in one of the infinite phases of its infinite existence.

This species of metaphysics is what the German philosophers proudly call transcendental science, from whose elevated height they scarcely deign turn their eyes to what they disdainfully call empiricism, i.e., the truth we know only from observation and experience, and the principles engraved with indelible characters on the human mind.

II

Book I, chapter 26 of the Fundamental Philosophy (Volume 1, pp. 172 et seq.)3/ has a few things, among the many that demonstrate Balmes' exalted intellect, which we perhaps would be inclined to disagree with.

"Does all human knowledge come down to the simple perception of identity and could its general formula be A is A or a thing is itself? Some philosophers of note say yes, others no. I think there is some confusion of ideas here on the state of the question rather than its substance." It is not easy to understand what is the so-called state of the question as opposed to the substance. If we were to say that there is more unanimity than is first apparent on the substance of the question and that the difference of opinion derives more from the variety of aspects the matter takes than from any real opposition, we might perhaps be expressing ourselves more clearly and accurately.

Clear and exact ideas of what judgment is," Balmes continues,

and of the relation affirmed or denied by it, will greatly facilitate the accurate solution of the question. In every judgment there is perception of identity or nonidentity, accordingly as it is affirmative or negative.

The verb is does not express the union but rather the identity of the predicate with the object; and when coupled with the negation not, it simply expresses nonidentity, notwithstanding union or separation. This is so true and exact that in things really united no affirmative judgment is possible because they have no identity. We must then in such cases, if it would be enabled to make an affirmation, express the predicate concretely, i.e., in some sense involving the idea of the subject itself in it.

The same quality affirmed concretely cannot be affirmed abstractly, but must be denied. Thus we may say man is rational, but not man is rationality; a body is extensive, but not a body is extension; paper is white, but not paper is whiteness. Why is this so? Is it that rationality is not in man, extension is not united to body, nor whiteness to paper? Certainly not, but if rationality be in man, extension in body, whiteness in paper, we have only not to perceive identity between the predicates and subjects to render affirmation impossible. On the contrary, despite the union we have negation. Thus, we may say man is not rationality, a body is not extension, paper is not whiteness.

I have stated that in order to salvage the expression of identity we used the concrete instead of the abstract term and involved in the former the idea of the subject. It cannot be said that paper is whiteness, but it may be said that paper is white. For this last proposition means that paper is a white thing, i.e., we make the general idea of a thing, or the idea of a modifiable subject, enter into the predicate white concretely, and this subject is identical with the paper modified by whiteness.

This exposition of the proposition does not seem to present its true innermost nature. What do we mean when we say a lily is white? The answer is so obvious as to be trivial. Clearly, the person voicing this proposition is only trying to state the particular sensation a lily has on the soul, i.e., an effect of the lily, a quality that consists in affecting the soul in a certain way, in short, a causal relationship. This is the relationship that one is attempting to express directly and what occurs in the mind of both speaker and listeners.

We must distinguish between the substance of the proposition externally, its outer surface so to speak, which pertains to language rather than to understanding. Through language we have classified all objects and these classifications are always founded on relations of similarity. When I want to express a quality I perceive in something, I have no way of doing it other than attributing it to the class of things that resemble it in that particular quality.

Thus, in order to explain the sensations the specific color of the lily produces on the sight, I attribute it to the class of things that resemble one another in that color. Saying that a lily is white is the same as saying that a lily is similar to the class of things that are usually called white, and is so similar that it has the same general name. But this relation of similarity is not truly the object of the judgment I intend to state but the way in which I am compelled to state it because of how language is formed. Those who believed that affirmative propositions always involve expressing a relation of similarity were to a certain extent right, but their claim does not concern the innermost substance of the judgment but rather its exterior, verbal form.

The relation, which is the immediate object of the judgment, can be many and varied. There is no relation conceived by means of a judgment that cannot be the direct object of this intellectual faculty, the same that the proposition is merely the faculty of conceiving relationships by affirming them or denying them. When I say that spring follows summer, the relation which is the direct object of the judgment, is one of sequence. And when I say that nine is more than seven, the direct object is that specific relation stated by means of the words more or less; comparing nine with seven, I judge that the former is more and the second less.

But the external verbal form of these judgments is always a relationship of similarity. To say that one thing comes after another or is greater than another is to attribute it to the class of things that are similar to it in this relative quality involving time or size because later and larger are general names, names of classifications founded on a relation of similarity. The relation of similarity, like everything else, can sometimes be the direct object, the substance of the judgment.

When I say that a camelia is like a rose, the similarity between these two flowers is the direct object of the judgment. In order to state this, I use the predicate like or similar, by means of which I infer that the relation perceived is like that perceived between so-called similar objects. The similarity between the two flowers is the substance of the judgment; the similarity of the relation perceived with the other relations of its kind, is its external, verbal form.

Let us stop a moment on this relationship of similarity, which is the external form of every judgment. Saying that a lily is white is attributing it to the kind of things given this title, stating therefore the identity of the lily with a part of the objects included in that class. The relationship of similarity thus leads in the external form of the proposition to the relation of identity, but only externally, because substantively neither identity nor similarity are involved except when these relations are direct objects, as in these propositions: the arc of a circle is a curve in which all points are equally distant from another point; a camelia is like as rose.

Let us not be thought that this distinction in judgment and in the proposition stating it, the substance and the external form, is a sterile theory. Perhaps at another time we will be able to go into how important this distinction in the theory of reasoning is.

It is not then entirely accurate to say that a judgment is a perception of identity or nonidentity of the predicate with the subject. The judgment has an infinitely broader field. When the intellect says that two objects are or are not related to one another, what is this but judging? Thus, judgment is essentially the perception or conception of some relation or nonrelation between the objects the mind is comparing or contemplating, so to speak, one next to another.

This is a highly diverse relationship, which when transferred into language (when we actually communicate our ideas to others or in a way talk to ourselves just as we often do when we think) is stated by means of a relationship of similarity convertible into one of identity.

A natural inclination makes us attribute to the intellect what properly pertains to language. An inclination against which we must be alert and to which many errors that have prevailed in the philosophy of understanding must be charged. Balmes himself (if we may say so, while submitting our claim to the judgment of enlightened readers), seemed not to be sufficiently on guard against this sort of illusion.

The passage we copied gives us additional proof of this. If we cannot apply abstract predicates to concrete subjects, this is not because identity is not perceived, for it really is. No matter how many efforts the mind makes, reasonably and rationally they are all the same thing as far as it is concerned; the intellectual image awakened by the latter word is the same as that awakened by the former. Thus, there is identity and identity is perceived between man and rationality, between paper and whiteness. It is true that these propositions are shocking. Clearly we cannot say man is rationality or paper is whiteness. But, why not? Because of a law of the language, founded on the special role given to abstract nouns.

Abstract nouns involve a sort of fiction or metaphor, which consists in representing as part of something what is really the same thing from another aspect. When we say whiteness, we have a picture of this quality as a part of white beings, separate and distinct form the rest. We would say then that a body has whiteness or that there is whiteness in it, just as we would say that an animal has hands and feet or that a plant has thorns. This being the peculiar nature of abstract nouns, if we said that a body is whiteness, it would shock us just as much as if we said that an oak tree is an acorn.

This nature of the language has, so to speak, created a separate world composed of ficticious beings whose classification is parallel to that of real beings. Thus color is a gender that includes whiteness, greenness, etc., just as colored body is a gender that includes white body, green body, etc. Strictly speaking, between these two orders of beings, no identity or nonidentity can be conceived because no comparison is possible.

Let one not think that this fiction is an idle figure. Quite the contrary, we see therein one of the most marvelous instincts of the language. Without it, we could not express the true relationships of things with sufficient clarity and accuracy. For example, to say that virtue inspires love is to say that a virtuous man, because he is virtuous, and notwithstanding any circumstances that weaken or destroy the effect of this fact, is appealing.

Therefore, if we were to attempt to eliminate abstract nouns from a proposition and to express it in concrete words, we would often find ourselves in difficulty. We would have to use long and complicated paraphrases in order to explain confusedly what can be said briefly, exactly and luminously with abstract nouns. Thus, the abundance of abstract elements in a language can be regarded as an unequivocal indication of the degree of intellectual development reached by the people who speak that language.

Sensation, considered per se, is merely an internal affection, but it is almost always coupled with a more or less explicit judgment, more or less noted by the subject who feels and judges....

Mere sensation is not necessarily associated with the external object....

This correspondence between what is internal and what is external is behoven upon the judgment that accompanies sensation, not sensation itself....

Sensation, therefore, considered per se, affirms nothing, it is an effect produced in our soul.

No matter how developed and perfected we assume sensibility to be, it falls far short of the intellect.

The doctrine developed in the preceding propositions, imprinted in chapter 1 of book 2 of Balmes' work, is fundamental in psychology. If one has thought a little about the intellectual phenomena therein, it is impossible not to agree with them. The purpose of the following observations is merely to illustrate and expand them.

There are two orders of phenomena in the understanding that might be called primordial. One group pertains to consciousness, the other to sensibility. By means of the consciousness we retreat within ourselves, i.e., the soul upon the soul. Locke, therefore, called this reflection. For the same reason many have given it the name of innermost sense, which is only suitable metaphorically. By means of the consciousness, the soul acts in itself; through sensibility, external objects act on the soul, producing sensations.

Since sensation is not objective per se, the affections of the consciousness per se are not either. What makes both objective is the judgment that accompanies them. The judgment accompanying the affections of consciousness consists in attributing them to the self, the soul. A judgment involves perceiving a relation. The relation perceived in the acts of the consciousness is that of identity. The soul recognizes the affection, its particular state, and that it is the object of consciousness at a given time, like an affection or state of its own; it identifies this affection or state with itself; it sees itself in the particular modification being experienced. This is how it perceives its own modifications, a perception that really deserves the name because it is immediate and direct. The perceptions of the consciousness are true intuitions and using a precise nomenclature this name should be given to none other.

Let us pass now to sensation, which Balmes says is an internal event, an event of the soul, which per se does not relate to what is external, to bodies. How have sensations been objectivized? How has the soul, by means of sensations, gone on to acquire a knowledge of the corporeal universe? And what does that knowledge mean to us?

Sensation, as everyone knows, is produced in the soul as a result of a bodily action. The first thing that should necessarily be derived therefrom, and to a certain degree accompany it (because the sequence is so rapid that no intermediate time is perceivable), is the awareness, the intuition of sensation. The soul perceives in it a new state of its own and acknowledges it as its own. The soul is still turned in upon itself. There is no external objectivity whatsoever.

External objectivity begins only when the soul recognizes in a sensation the effect of an external cause. This does not mean that in the first stages of intelligence the idea of cause can be depicted in the mind with the same clariy and distinction as to us. But one law of the understanding, which we can regard as instinct, causes the soul when it experiences a sensation to come out of itself. It comes into contact with something mysterious that is not itself and endows it with its own sensation, which from that moment not only pertains to the soul as a means of existence thereof, but to something different, as a sign thereof, as a means of recognizing it and distinguishing it from other things, whose presence is reported by means of other sensations which represent it in turn.

This tendency of the understanding to objectivize sensation appears to be instinctive because it cannot be derived from experience. The soul attributes its sensations to external causes because it fails to see the cause for them within itself. It reasons according to the abstract principle that there is no cause without effect, but this reasoning is obscure and instinctive. The soul in the first stages of intelligence does not reason by laying down abstract principles and drawing conclusions, most men never do this. Abstract principles were originally instinctive tendencies and for most men are never anything else.

A peasant measuring two different lengths with a yardstick who finds they measure an equal number of sticks, calls them equal. He clearly reasons in accordance with the abstract principle that if two things are equal to a third they are equal to each other, although this principle in its abstract form does not occur to him. Strictly speaking, axioms are not premises of reasoning but formulas that stand for reasoning procedures which the mind performs by instinct. He thinks that if A and B are equal to C, A is equal to B. And reasoning this way asserts the general principle, albeit concretely. In this way he attributes sensations to external causes, because of an instinctive tendency to attribute anything new to a preceding fact and because the preceding fact is not its own.

This explanation is independent of any opinion on the existence or nature of matter. It is an unimpeachable fact that we have a tendency that makes us attribute sensations to external causes, i.e., outside the self, the specific application of an axiom to which we habitually match our reasoning in life: There is no effect without cause. That this tendency may or may not be a legitimate foundation of logic and what its true meaning may be, are questions on which the schools of thought are divided and on which the doctrine of Fundamental Philosophy is less than satisfactory. But whatever our thoughts on this may be, the preceding explanation remains.

224

We attribute sensations to external causes and make them signs of these causes; we thus perceive causes extrinsic to the self. External causes of sensation, matter, body, are expressions with the same meaning. This is still another order of perception; perceptions in which the object is represented by a spiritual phenomena which is not itself, but sensation; perceptions not intuitive, such as consciousness, but representative, and which through the means of representation of which we avail ourselves, which is sensation, can also be called sensitive. What the soul perceives directly therein are sensations; bodies do not in fact perceive them but depict them by means of sensations which become their signs.

We use the term signs, not images. There is no more similarity between a sensation and the physical quality represented thereby than between the letters and sounds of a language. There is, however, one aspect under which sensations represent the physical universe via imitation. The relations we perceive between sensations are images of the relations conceived by us between physical qualities. Groups of sensations represent groups of physical qualities, just as groups of letters represent groups of sounds. The composition of any one of these groups is an image of the composition of one of the latter. Resemblances between sensations not only represent but rather depict, so to speak, the resemblance between physical qualities and actions. The sequence of one sensation after another corresponds to the sequence of one physical quality and action, and another, the coexistence of each.

This is not to say that the depiction will always be faithful. On the contrary, it frequently tricks us. But we always proceed on the assumption that the mental relationships are a copy of the real relationships between physical qualities and actions. The way the order and similarity of letters in a perfect alphabet matches the order and similarity of their oral sounds.

We will return later with Balmes to the theory of representative or sensitive perceptions, but for now we shall only examine whether it is as difficult, as he believes it is, to draw a dividing line between what is sensible and what is intelligent.

We shall see that there is an arbitrary element in the classification of the minds, acts, and faculties, as in all other classifications. In all its acts and faculties, the mind is one and different. Separating acts and faculties into different kinds, according to their similarities and differences, is an operation that can lead to different results depending on the viewpoint of the observer.

Even so, with the propositions we copied at the beginning of this article accepted, we think the problem of the dividing line between sensibility and understanding, according to Balmes' own ideas, is fully and satisfactorily resolved. And we do not think he is consistent with his own principles when he feels he must resort to other considerations in order to resolve this problem.

Balmes distinguishes sensation from the judgments which almost always accompany it. But isn't judgment, according to Balmes himself, an operation of the understanding? The intellect starts, according to his own doctrine, in the very judgment that accompanies sensations. Can one hope for a neater dividing line?

To tell the truth, we conceive an intermediary phase between sensation and the objective reference that constitutes the judgment usually accompanying it. This intermediate phase is the intuitive perception made by the self of sensation, as it does of anything affecting it, and on which the consciousness is reflected. But this same reflex does not start out as a perception but becomes so through the judgment in which the self recognizes sensation an affection or state of its own. Thus, consciousness itself, without judgment, is a merely passive faculty; it affirms nothing, understands nothing; it is not a part of the intellect. Merely passive consciousness and sensibility, both terminate on the threshold of judgment and that is where the intellect begins.

Understanding, in its general meaning, involves all the faculties used by the mind in searching for the truth; in this sense, sensibility itself is a part of the intellect. When we distinguish what is sensible from what is intelligent, we give the latter a more limited scope to which we restrict ourselves when we consider judgment as the initial act of the understanding.

Judgment, as opposed to passive consciousness and mere sensibility, is also what is constituted by intellectual activity. In judging, the mind by comparing two objects, placing them next to each other, drawing therefrom a new object which is neither one of them, in other words a relationship between them, is eminently active, for it is productive and to a certain extent creative.

The activity of the mind has been made to consist of attention, which has been regarded as a special faculty, an outward effort of the soul, so to speak, as opposed to sensibility which seems to move inward. In a way, this would be consistent with actual sensitive perceptions in which the mind, when its attention is fixed on something, acts on the organ and stimulate the relevant sensations which we expect to dwell on to the exclusion of others insofar as possible. This, however, is not consistent with intuitive perception or acts of memory.

Perhaps it would be more accurate to consider attention not as a separate intellectual faculty but as a quality of intellectual acts, which consists in how forcefully and dynamically we perform them or experience them. The will frequently influences how strongly this is done, and then attention becomes voluntary and is accompanied by real activity of the mind but one properly pertaining to the will, not the understanding. Other times attention is accomplished, i.e., the images and conceptions of the understanding are made more vivid and dynamic with no assistance whatever from and frequently notwithstanding the will.

We cannot ignore sharp pain; the sensation of pain at that moment has a power that prevails over others and over remembered experience and imagination which would prevail in others and over remembered experience and imagination which would prevail in other circumstances. Out of many simultaneous sensations, the least familiar prevail and diminish the rest. Out of many simultaneous memories, the memories of those objects prevail that are associated with our predominant interest or passion. A seascape, for example, stimulates many ideas, some of which prevail, but not the same ones for different spectators. A physicist will perhaps remember the theory of the tides; a merchant, the vessel whose return he is expecting; a religious, contemplative soul, will think of the magnificience of the works of the Creator; a mother, in the absent child sailing on other oceans or living abroad. In each one a different idea prevails that diminishes the other and converts them into latent ideas.

The stronger an idea, the more the rest of the coexisting ideas are debilitated and diminished. One of them may be so vivid and so exciting that the consciousness may even fail to perceive present sensations. The mind appears to have unlimited amount of attention which is divided in different ways among coexisting ideas; any one of them cannot be stimulated and exalted without the others suffering proportionally.

IV

If anywhere the wise and profound author of the Fundamental Philosophy has not lived up to his potential, it is, in our judgment, in the relation of the internal world of sensations with the external world. Perhaps our little intelligence is to blame but, frankly speaking, Balmes' arguments against the idealistic system, which rejects or at least questions the existence of matter, seem totally unconvincing. The way he raises the question might lead one to think that he did not consider it from its real perspective.

"Can we infer the existence of an external world from the existence of that internal world resulting from the whole panorama of sensations?"

"Most men have no shadow of a doubt that there exists a real world, distinct from us, but in constant communication with us."

Balmes was right to a certain extent, but what is generally construed by reality of the external world or of physical nature must be clarified.

What is called real here is the regularity and consistency of the phenomena. We believe a tree really exists: 1. Because we see that everyone perceives it as we do; 2. Because we submit it to the study of several senses at the same time, mainly touch, and the testimony of each supports and confirms the rest; 3. Because repetition constantly provides the same results, and if not, if, for example, we note that a tree is missing a few branches or is missing from the place where it usually stands, we can account for these differences through certain accidents, either known or conjectured because of their consistency with the laws of nature. Laws independent of ourselves, to which our own and everyone else's sensations are subject. Briefly, we assume that our sensations are produced by causes not within but outside ourselves.

The reality of the physical world thus construed can only be rejected by a far-fetched skepticism that doubts everything; what the idealists deny as far as matter lies not in the existence of external causes, extrinsic, and independent of the self, but in the nature of these causes. The idealists acknowledge that there are external causes; the physical world for them is the whole of these causes, the thing is to know what they are like. Are they concrete beings, actual substances, such as our mind, although devoid of intelligence and sensibility? Or are they general laws that determine the chain of sensation and cause them to follow one another in the soul according to constant rules known everywhere, subject to experience and computation; laws that the Supreme Author of nature established and protects; laws not existing except in his sovereign will and which act on creative spirits immediately, not through the intermediary of other created substances without life and feeling?

Two rough images might be used in order to conceive of the question. Let's assume a huge machine made up of different orders of keys, each having under certain conditions different orders of sound; that the keys move by themselves, combining and coordinating movements according to constant laws, with the respective series and combinations of sounds emanating from this operation of the keys. Let us assume further that certain agents alien to the machine are able to move some of the keys, which in turn move others according to the same laws and within certain limits bring about changes in the natural operation of the machine, from which partial series and combinations of sound emanate.

This machine is an image of the physical world, as conceived by the materialists (including therein everyone who acknowledges the existence of matter, either reducing everything existing thereto or admitting other kinds of things); the keys are the bodies; the sounds the sensations; the foreing agents the soul by whose volition partial movements are impressed on the material world by means of which matter is made to serve their needs and communicate with other matter. The laws of physical nature are incarnated in real, substantial beings, which we call bodies or matter.

For the idealists, who might more properly be called spiritualists, this machine does not exist. The laws placed by the partisans of matter on the keys are placed directly on the sounds. For them there is no physical universe except in the laws originally imposed by the Creator on sensations, laws that directly produce the associations and sensations as a whole attested to by the consciousness, laws whose activity can to a certain extent be modified by the volitions of the soul with no intermediary whatsoever.

Reason without revelation has nothing that impels it to prefer the materialist system over the idealistic system or vice versa. Both are equally possible and both account equally for the phenomena. But the idealistic system is the simpler of the two; matter is an unnecessary assumption; the Supreme Being had no need of it for us to feel what we feel so that animal life with all its possible changes and vicissitudes could develop, so that civilized society with its science and art could exist, and so that the destiny of man, truth, virtue, would be exactly as they are. We say reason without revelation, for the Catholic dogma of trans-substantiation openly contradicts idealism. Thus the Protestant Berkeley, not content with the possibility of his system, went so far as to uphold its actual existence, and regarded it as a powerful argument against the doctrines of the Roman church.

Having established these considerations, we can continue with our examination. "It is self-evident," Balmes says, "that science which opposes necessity and contradicts a palpable need must be wrong. It merits not to be called philosophy if it struggles with a law to which all humanity, including the very philosopher who presumes to protest against it, is inevitably subject. All that can be said against this law may be as specious as you please, but it will only be a vain cavil, a cavil which if unanswerable by the frailty of understanding, nature herself will resist."

All this is very well taken against people who deny or doubt that our sensations must have causes and that the causes are not dependent on us, that we cannot avoid them, except within a very limited sphere and by availing ourselves of them as such. But nothing is effective against the rational idealistic system, which is not opposed to need nor does it contradict any palpable fact. What necessity do we have to assume that sensations are produced by other beings and not by general laws under certain conditions determining them?

The materialists, so to speak, presuppose two dramas. The one taking place in the senses is transferred from another which occurs outside their reach and about which we know nothing unless revealed to us by the first of the two dramas. But if the first is sufficient for the satisfaction of all our needs, under what conditions is the second one necessary? Is there an irresistable instinct which makes us imagine a nonself under each sensation existing as the self, which devoid of sensibility and understanding can scarcely be defined or conceived? Nature did not give us superfluous instincts, and none would be more so than one that showed man a metaphysical truth worth nothing to him.

Once again, idealism contradicts no palpable fact. We clearly notice external causes, i.e., we experience sensations of touch that have causes outside the soul that feels. There is no room for doubt here. The nature of these causes is open to doubt but human reason has no means of exploring it. Saying that idealism is at odds with a palpable fact is something ordinary people would say. In the ordinary concept, touch is the essence of matter. Telling a man that matter does not really exist would be like telling him that we have no sensation of touch; it would be denying a fact about which there is no possible doubt. But the idealists do not deny this, what they deny is beyond that. Thus the heart of the question between materialists and idealists is a metaphysical trifle that serves no purpose in life nor is it helpful at all in science. What matters there is to settle upon the idea at issue. Once this is done it will easily be perceived that the two schools are at odds on an incomprehensible issue, whose existence or nonexistence leads to nothing either theoretically or practically.

The great argument of Balmes is the difference between sensations recalled by memory and sensations here and now. The one is governed by the will but not the other. Balmes says,

I now experience that a picture is being represented to me; or, in plain language, I see a painting before me. Let us assume this a purely internal phenomenon and observe the conditions of its existence, abstracting however all external reality, that of my own body included, and that the organs whereby the sensation is, or seems to be, transmitted to me. Now I experience the sensation, now I do not. What has intervened? The sensation of a motion that has produced another sensation of sight and has destroyed the first; or passing from idea to real language, I have placed my hand between my eyes and the object. But, as long as the latter sensation lasts, why can not I reproduce the first? We see clearly that if external objects do exist, and my sensations are produced by them, my sensations then must be subject to the conditions which they impose upon them; but if they are only internal phenomena, there is no way of accounting for them.

The explanation is obvious. A volition has intervened; the volition has produced a change with a successive chain of sensations. Don't the idealists recognize that the volitions of the soul modify natural laws, altering the conditions of their activity and subordinating them within certain limits (clearly very narrow) to the will of man?

From this argument, Balmes concludes "that phenomena not dependent on our will but subject both as to their existence and their accidents to laws which we cannot change, are produced by beings distinct from ourselves." If by beings he means matter, this is not so. Balmes' premises do not allow for such a conclusion, for all those phenomena as to their existence and their accidents can be produced by general laws dictated by the Supreme Being, who, given certain conditions, produce at each point in space the internal phenomena conscious to the soul.

"The system of the idealists cannot stand," according to the author of Fundamental Philosophy,

>...without assuming that the connection and dependence of phenomena which we attribute to external objects exist only within ourselves, and that the causality attributed by us to external objects pertains only to our own acts.
>
>If I pull a cord in my office, a bell never fails to ring; or stated in idealist languages, the internal phenomenon formed by that group of sensations into which enters what we call the cord and pulling it, produces or involves that other one, which we call ringing a bell. Either from habit or some hidden law, that relation of two phenomena will exist, the never interrupted succession of which causes the illusion in us whereby we transfer to the real order what is purely imaginary. This is the least irrational explanation possible but a few observations will show how futile it is.

Before discussing Balmes' observations, let's stop here a moment. Idealists only regard as illusory or fantastic the same things the average man does. For them, the cord and the bell are real objects, using this word in the sense we explained earlier. The figure of a man seen by our eyes but which our hands cannot feel would be, as far as they and everyone else are concerned, a spectre, a ghost. They believe that present sensations are connected not by previous habits nor hidden laws but rather by general laws established by the Creator, many of which are known to us. This at least is the idealism of Berkeley, a philosopher who not only acknowledged the certainty of natural laws testified to by the senses but also himself helped illustrate a few of them relating to sight, for example. The idealism that confuses vigil with sleep and trusts not the senses is more of an absurd skepticism not worth refuting. But let's return to Fundamental Philosophy.

Balmes continues,

Today we pull the cord and, strangely enough, no bell rings. Why not? A causing phenomenon exists, for clearly the act called pulling the bell occurs within us, and yet we pull and pull again and the bell does not ring. Who has altered the succession of phenomena? Why did one phenomenon produce the other shortly before but not now? Nothing new has occurred within me; the first phenomenon was experienced just as clearly and vividly as before. Why then did not the second phenomenon appear? Why before did I experience the second whenever I wished by merely stimulating the first but not now? I performed an act of my will as efficiently as earlier, but why was my will ineffective?

This is a reasoning that collapses in the face of Berkeley's idealism, which considers the succession of sensations as independent of the will. In order for the sensations that we call pulling the cord to produce what we call ringing the bell, some connections are needed, and if one of them is missing, the first phenomenon fails to produce the second.

"Here it is to be observed," Balmes continues,

...that when I would account for the failure of the succession of these sensations which were always joined earlier, I can take recourse to many that are quite different ones, such as internal phenomena which as such have neither relation nor resemblance and can only have some connection as corresponding to external objects. When seeking the reason why the bell did not ring, in order to explain the cause of the change in the regular order of appearances, I may think of different causes which we for now may consider as mere appearances or internal phenomena. I may have the following sensations: a broken cord, a twisted cord, a broken bell, a bell that's been removed, a bell without a clapper. I can attribute the failure of sound to any one of these sensations but nothing could be more irrational than to attribute it to them if I consider them as mere internal facts, for as sensations they have no resemblance. I can only think rationally if I match each of these sensations with an external object, which per se suffices to interrupt the connection of the act of pulling the cord to the vibration of air produced by the sound.

There is nothing so weak as these arguments. In the same way that the external facts resemble each other, the corresponding sensations resemble each other. They all presuppose a necessary uninterrupted connection between what I call pulling the cord and what I call the air vibrating in the ears.

Balmes' reasonings are sufficient proof that our sensations have causes separate from the self, largely independent of the self.

They do not prove, as he presumes, that a body of matter exists outside ourselves which is submittted to necessary laws and that this matter is what produces sensations. Instead, there are necessary or rather constant laws to which our sensations are submitted mediately or immediately. We regard the idealistic system as a false hypothesis because it opposes Catholic dogma, although its fallacy cannot be demonstrated by reason alone.

V

Extension and space are a subject on which philosophers most differ. We find nothing in the Fundamental Philosophy to help reconcile them.

Balmes has extension consisting of multiplicity and continuity and judges it absolutely inseparable from the idea of body, propositions which we believe are accepted by all schools of philosophy. He observes with equal foundation that extension has the peculiarity of being perceived by different senses. Extension per se, and separate from any other quality, such as color or touch, cannot be perceived sensitively. In particular, he says, the perceptibility of extension entails no quality except disjunctively; both these qualities are indispensable and if either is missing, extension cannot be perceived.

"Extension in us is not a sensation but an idea," Balmes continues. This requires clarification. Resemblance in us is not a sensation but a particular relation between two or more affections, or between two or more sensations if bodies are involved. If idea means relation, physical resemblance in us is not a sensation but rather an idea, it pertains not merely to what is sensitive but to what is intelligent. The same is true of extension.

Extension is a relation or set of relations of a particular sort which consists in considering two or more material things as outside one another, so what we can sense them only individually; with the body reduced to a given point, a sensation of the effort entailed in order to pass the body over the things that are outside one another must intervene between every other sensation. The relation of extraposition, of outsideness, is thus the element of extension, just as the relation of sequence is the element of duration. We can conceive the former by conceiving of a set of tangible or visible points as being outside one another; we conceive of the latter as a series of spiritual affections that succeed one another.

The relation known as sequence is simple; it is impossible to break it down into components other than itself. Conversely, an analysis of the relation of extraposition indicates that this is not simple but complex. Let us suppose, for example, two tangible or visible points A, B. The extraposition between A and B consists in the fact that a sensation of effort succeeds the tactile or visual sensation of A, and the tactile or visual sensation of B follows the sensation of effort. All extension is a set of extrapositions perceived in this way, actually or potentially.

Conceiving extension in this way, we do not subscribe to its being a primary fact of our spirit, as Balmes presumed. All other relations would then be equally entitled to consideration as primary facts. It is produced by no sensation, no affection of the soul per se alone but is born of a set of sensations or of other affections that the soul compares and judges.

Let us look now at chapter VII of book III, which is one of those devoted to space.

Space is one of those profound mysteries which the natural order poses to man's weak understanding. The deeper he examines it, the more obscure it becomes. The mind finds itself engulfed in the shadows which we imagine exist beyond the bounds of the finite. It knows not whether what it beholds is illusion or reality. For a moment it seems to have found the truth and then discovers that it was embracing a shadow. It forms arguments which in any other matter would be conclusive but are not so here because they are in direct contradiction to others equally conclusive. We seem to have reached the limit placed by the Creator on the investigations of the mind, and in endeavoring to pass beyond that limit, the strength of the mind fails, its life is quenched like that of any other living being when it steps beyond the bounds of its own elements....

To descend into this bottomless abyss is not to spend time in futile discussion; even though we should not find what we seek, we obtain a very beneficial result in reaching the limits assigned to our intellect....

What then is space? Is it something real or only an idea? If an idea, is there any object in the external world corresponding to it? Is it pure illusion? Is the word space devoid of meaning?

If we do not know what space is, let us at least establish the meaning of the word and thus determine to some extent the state of the question. By space we understand the extension in which we imagine bodies to be placed, or the capacity to contain them, to which we attribute none of their qualities except extension.

Is space pure nothingness?...

I believe this opinion involves irreconcilable contradictions. To say extension-nothingness is a contradiction in terms; nevertheless, the opinion of these philosophers comes down to this.

We do not see that space regarded as pure nothingness, or extension-nothingness, involves any contradiction at all. Balmes' major argument that it does, is the scholastic axiom nibili nullae sunt proprietates; an axiom that must be limited to positive properties which in the material order all come down to positive actions of the objects performing reciprocally or on the soul.

What then is the extension of space? Is it perchance the extraposition of real, tangible or visible points? No. It is the

233

extraposition of imaginary points; an extraposition as imaginary as the points between which we conceive it. Imaginary points because they do not perform nor can we perceive of their performing any reciprocal action or any action on the soul, and between which we actually conceive relations such as we conceive between quantitites and figures, that do not exist, without therefore, conceding any objective reality to them nor to their conceived reciprocal relations.

The capacity we attribute to space of receiving bodies is what Balmes thought most incompatible with space-nothingness. But what is this capacity? The non-resistance of pure space to bodies, a quality as negative as absolute inertia, as intangibility, as invisibility. Here we find another proof of the illusions created by language. Because the word capacity involves no negative element it should not be deduced that the quality represented thereby is precisely positive. The capacity of flying is something positive because it is the power to perform a real action. The capacity of feeling is positive because it involves the potential for experiencing real affections. But the capacity to receive bodies, which is the inability to resist them, has nothing positive. If space were not able to receive bodies, it would resist them, it would necessarily perform a sort of action upon them; it would contain the force employed by those bodies to penetrate it, which would obviously contradict the idea of pure space, precisely because pure space is nothingness or <u>nihili nullae sunt proprietates</u>.

Someone will probably challenge me that space, having received bodies, subsists, and that nothingness, having received bodies, disappears. So one thing is not the same as the other. This argument lacks validity. Pure space is potential capacity, and space that is full, current capacity. Pure space is nothingness; space that is full is the same nothingness. If we subtract the bodies occupying it from the idea of full space, the residue is nothingness.

If this explanation should not seem entirely satisfactory, compare then the difficulties posed by any other explanation, by Balmes' idea, particularly the one from which he himself drew conclusions which in my judgment are further arguments <u>ad absurdum</u> against his own doctrine, as we will see later. For now let us continue with his application of the axiom <u>nihili nullae sunt proprietates</u> to the concept of space-nothingness.

"If everything in a room is reduced to nothing, it seems impossible for the walls to remain distant from one another. The idea of distance implies a medium between the objects involved, and nothing, being nothing, cannot be the medium required."

Yet who cannot see that the idea of a negative medium does not conflict with nothingness? The spell which the immense vitality of the language has on such a penetrating mind is truly amazing. He feels that <u>to act as the medium of nothing between two walls</u> is to attribute existence to nothingness, as if this meant anything else than do not act as a medium of anything, just as, when we say that nothing pleases a complainer, we do not mean that he likes nothing but that nothing pleases him. "If the interval is nothing," Balmes adds, "there is no distance," for using nothing as a foundation,

making nothing a property, is in his judgment an affirmation of the
possibility of being and not being at one and the same time. But
why seek a support on which to rest distance, which is no more than
a relationship between the two walls?

Another problem similar to the preceding one is that of motion
in space. "If space is nothing, motion is also nothing and,
therefore, nonexistent. Motion can neither exist nor be conceived
without a distance having been traversed, this is its very essence.
If distance is nothing, nothing is traversed, therefore, there is no
motion." Motion can exist and be conceived since bodies are at
different distances from one another, since the particular
relationship we call distance is different between them.

We will not follow Balmes in the discussion of the doctrine of
Descartes, Leibniz, Clarke, and Fenelon on space. Leibniz'
definition seems to be the best: space is a relation, an order, not
just of things existing but also of things possible as if they
actually existed.

Let us examine the explanations made by Balmes:

Analyzing how the idea of space originated, we find it is
merely the idea of extension taken in the abstract. If I hold
an orange before my eyes, I may by means of abstraction arrive
at the idea of a pure extension equal to that of the orange.
In order to do this I begin by dispensing with its color,
taste, smell, how soft or how hard it is, and all its
qualities which affect the senses. I then have left only an
extended being, and if I deprive it of its mobility, it is
reduced to a part of space equal to the size of the orange.

These same abstractions can clearly also be made in
relation to the universe, and the result will be the idea of
all the space that is in the universe.

Abstraction rises from the particular to the general.
From the idea of gold, by abstracting those properties which
constitute gold and attending only to those it possesses as
metal, I arrive at the much more general idea of metal, which
applies not just to gold but to all other metals. By this
abstraction I erase the boundary separating gold from other
metals and form an idea which extends to all, neither
specifying nor excluding any. If from the idea of metal I
abstract all that constitutes metal and attend only to what
constitutes mineral, I erase another boundary and arrive at a
still more general idea. Thus ascending the scale I pass
successively the idea of inorganic, body, substance, until I
come to a point where the idea extends to everything.

Thus, by successively erasing the boundaries that
distinguish and as it were separate objects, abstraction rises
to generalization. If we apply this doctrine to the
abstractions made upon bodies, we shall discover the reason
for the illimitability of the idea of space.

With all due respect for the Spanish philosopher, all this seems
to us to be more spacious than sound. The idea of gender includes

none of the characters of the species; it includes none in particular but includes them all disjunctively. Man in general is not European man, Asiatic man, American man, Negro, white, or Indian; but he is undoubtedly a man who belongs somewhere on earth and has a certain color. These disjunctive concepts necessarily enter into the idea of man in general. To dispense with color or country is not to exclude color or country but rather not to consider and establish them for the moment. This does not mean that we fail to see them vaguely, so to speak, in the distance.

The same is true with generalized extension. We dispense with the boundary but do not exclude the idea of boundary. If we exclude it, we necessarily conceive of infinite extension; doubtless this is what happens in the potential capacity we attribute to space.

It is not true that when we ask for the idea of extension in the abstract, yet terminated, we are asking for something that is contradictory. A given limit would undoubtedly take away the idea of generality from extension. But a vague limit, a limit which is not this, that, or the other, but which necessarily must be something, is absolutely necessary for generalized extension if we do not assume it is infinite.

Balmes summarizes his doctrine in the following propositions:

1. That space is nothing else than the extension of bodies.

2. That the idea of space is the idea of extension.

3. That the different parts conceived in space are the ideas of particular extensions, not having dispensed with their limits.

4. That the idea of infinite space is the idea of extension in general and, therefore, dispensing with all limit.

5. The indefinite space arises necessarily from an effort of the imagination in which the limits are destroyed by following the generalizing process of the understanding.

6. That where there is no body, there is no space.

7. That what is called distance is merely the interposition of a body.

8. That by removing every intermediary body, distance ceases; there is then contiguity and consequently absolute contact.

9. That if there were only two bodies in existence in the universe, it would be metaphysically possible for them to be distant from each other.

10. That a void of whatever kind is absolutely impossible.

236

We will not detain ourselves on the first five propositions because we have already said what we think about them. On the sixth, we note that if space, as our author believes, is the extension of the universe, it necessarily follows that where the universe ends, space ends; but space thus considered is not space as conceived by most men. Assuming the universe is finite, the existence of other bodies and other universes is possible beyond its limit. That possibility infers the capacity to receive bodies, the nonexistence of bodies; a quality which, as we already said, constitutes pure space which is no different from nothingness. By saying that there is no space beyond the limits of the universe is to say that everything is lacking there and that at the same time the lack of everything is missing, which is nothingness; this is obviously contradictory.

The seventh proposition gives us a confused and inacceptable idea of distance. The distance between two bodies is a particular relationship between them, which according to the way most men think, would subsist even though the rest of the universe were annihilated. The ninth proposition seems to us to be absurd and, as a conclusion of Balmes' system, is a powerful argument against his theory. We have the same thing to say about the tenth proposition. The idea of a void has nothing that conflicts with the understanding. Balmes did not see it that way because he gave too much extension to the aforementioned scholastic axiom.

We will not challenge Balmes' theory with the need for a predetermined void which, according to the corpuscular theory, is necessary for the movement of bodies in the universe. This theory is a hypothesis, and the phenomena of rarity and density, dilation and condensation might be absolutely accountable without it.

We know nothing about the innermost constitution of matter. Balmes himself was amazed at the conclusions reached from such a principle and suspected there was some error hidden therein. Those in chapter XIII are even more objectionable, if we may say so, to common sense. We believe that it is sufficient to present them in order for the principle incontestably derived therefrom to be appreciated: "If there were only one body it could not move because it would be moving in nothingness."

VI

The arguments made by Balmes against the idea of space-nothingness are major proof of the dominion scholastic habits can have over the loftiest minds. If everything in an empty room is reduced to nothingness, it seems, according to him, that the walls can no longer be distant from one another because distance is an interval. Nothingness can be no interval because nothingness has no qualities. If the interval is nothing there is no distance.

But the axiom nihili nullae sunt propritates does not prevent us from attributing negative predicates to nothingness. Surely no one will condemn these propositions as absurd: nothingness has no color, nothingness cannot be touched, nothingness can produce no effect.

Anyone saying that nothingness can make no resistance to bodies or motion, far from saying something absurd, would be expressing an obvious unimpeachable truth. The capacity we attribute to space-nothingness is merely the impossibility of resistance. The idea of distance between the walls of a room which we assume to be entirely void of matter is no more than the idea of necessary motion, so that anything mobile placed in the room can be carried from one wall to the opposite wall. Hence, saying that there can be no motion in nothingness because motion in nothingness is nothing, assuming that nihili nullae sunt proprietates, is it not a vain play on words?

The best way of demonstrating to what degree this axiom has misled Balmes is to present to the reader the corolaries he himself deduces from the idea which he thought most acceptable among those that might be formed of space.

"Where there is no body there is no space."

"What is called distance is nothing else than the interposition of bodies."

"When all intermediate bodies are removed there is no more distance; there is contiguity, and consequently absolute contact."

"Assuming two bodies alone existed in space, it would be metaphysically impossible for them to be distant from one another."

"A void of whatever kind is absolutely impossible."

"A body alone cannot move because movement necessarily involves distance and there is no distance when there is no more than one body."

"A body with projecting angles 4/ existing alone is absurd because its shape requires that distance AD be the distance from point A, the vertex of an angle, to point D, the vertex of another angle. This distance cannot exist because where there is no body there is no distance."

This is the situation of the universe, according to Balmes. Its final surface has no angles and infinite cavities, and this by virtue of a metaphysical need so that not even God himself could have made it any other way.

Balmes' own common sense could do no less than protest against such strange claims. "If the reader," he says, "asks me what I think about them and on the principle on which they are founded, I must ingenuously admit that although the principle seems to be true and its conclusions legitimate, the strangeness of some of them, nevertheless, makes me suspect that there is some hidden error in the principle or that the reasoning from which the conclusions are inferred has some defect not easily defined. So that I merely present a number of conjectures and reasons to support them rather than a well determined opinion." It seems to me that all of Balmes' dialectual structure collapses from the time it is acknowledged that the capacity of pure space means non-resistance, a quality nobody will challenge of nothingness.

1. Certainty should not be confused with truth. The latter represents the agreement of our intellectual concepts with the reality of things; the former is merely the ascent of the soul to truth or what appears to be truth (A).

2. We have simplified it somewhat to make it easier to understand. Even so, we think few will consider the term used by Balmes too harsh. The Sanscrit of the scholastics never reached such lengths (A).

3. Balmes, Fundamental Philosophy, translated by Henry F. Brownson, New York, 1896 (T).

4. Inverted angles in Balmes' words, but I think he meant projecting angles. Otherwise, I fail to understand his reasoning if it is applied to what are commonly called inverted angles, which move inward on plain surfaces or solids (A).

F. Journalism

"The Hispanic-American Republics," "Defamation," and "Copyrights," were published in El Araucano, Santiago, in 1836, 1839, and 1848, respectively. I have selected these three articles from Bello's voluminous work as a journalist, as representative of the lofty manner in which he addressed the reading public. On this subject, see Miguel Luis Amunátegui Reyes, Nuevos estudios sobre Andrés Bello, Santiago, 1902, which focuses particularly on analyzing Bello's work as a journalist and frequently transcribes articles from El Araucano, not included in the Obras completas.

Other works deserving of examination, are Ricardo Donoso, Desarrollo político y social de Chile desde la constitución de 1833, Santiago, 1942, especially nos. 24 et al; M. Silva Vildosola, "Andrés Bello en Chile," Cultura Venezolana, XII, 99, 1929, pp. 298-307; Federico Alvarez A., Labor periodística de Don Andrés Bello, Caracas, 1962; Héctor García Chuecos, "Recuerdos de Andrés Bello," El Universal, Caracas, December 28, 1938; Raúl Agudo Freytes, "Bello, periodista ejemplar," Revista Nacional de Cultura, no. 65, Caracas, 1947, pp. 47-53; José Ratto Ciarlo, El primer redactor y el primer colaborador en la prensa de Venezuela, Caracas, 1948; Alfonso Bulnes, "Don Andrés Bello y el periodismo," Boletín de la Academia Chilena de la Historia, Santiago, 1953; Raúl Silva Castro, Prensa y periodismo en Chile (1812-1956), Santiago, 1958, and Manuel Pérez Vila, "Andrés Bello, redactor de El Araucano," Revista Nacional de Cultura, Caracas, no. 101, November-December 1953.

THE HISPANIC-AMERICAN REPUBLICS

The idea of a large continent making its appearance on the political scene freed from its past masters and suddenly adding new members to the great society of nations, awakened the enthusiasm of idealists, misgivings on the part of freedom's enemies (who realized the distinctive nature of the institutions chosen by America), and the curiosity of statesmen. For Europe, only recently recovered from the crisis into which the French Revolution hurled all of its monarchies, the revolution in South America was a spectacle similar to, yet more grandiose, than the one it had gazed upon in North America shortly before the turmoil in Paris. The emancipation of the British colonies was but the birth of a great power emerging on this side of the Atlantic, and that of the Spanish colonies had to be regarded as its complement.

Such a momentous event in world history occupied the attention of every cabinet and the reflection of every thinker. Some believe that a considerable number of nations located on a vast continent that are identified with one another by institutions and origin and, with the exception of the United States, by custom and religion, will in time form a respectable body balancing European policy. As they grow in wealth and population and all the social wellbeing they should enjoy under the protection of law, some further think their example may provide an alternative to the principles of government in the Old World.

Even so, few have failed to foresee that to attain such a goal we would have to tread a rough, blood-spatreed path; that our inexperience in the science of government must necessarily cause frequent changes in our condition, and that until the vices and aftermath of the colonization were forgotten with the passage of generations, we could not see the first rays of prosperity.

Conversely, others denied there was any chance we could live our own lives under the protection of free institutions, which they considered generally inconsistent with every element that might go into the making of Spanish American governments. In their view, the principles of representation so successful in the United States, responsible for making the British settlements a single great nation whose power, industry, commerce and population are growing and growing, could not provide the same result in Spanish America.

The position of the British and Spanish colonies at the time of independence was essentially different. In the former, property was equally divided; in the latter, it was amassed in a few hands. The former were accustomed to exercising major political rights which the latter did not possess nor did they have any idea of their importance. The former could give liberal principles all theirpresent latitude; though emancipated from Europe, the latter had a large, influential class in their midst with which their interests conflicted. These are the major reasons used by the enemies of our independence to feign despair over the consolidation of our governments.

It is quite easy, as a matter of fact, given the state of advancement of the social sciences in our time, to make rather plausible constitutions, to ingeniously balance the powers of government, to proclaim guarantees and to uphold liberal principles. Yet, a thorough awareness of the type and needs of the people for whom legislation is intended; wariness of the seductive appeal of shining theories; careful, impartial heeding of the voice of experience; sacrifice of cherished opinions for the sake of the public good, are not the qualities most commonly found during the infancy of nations nor in the midst of crisis when a great political transition such as ours sets men's souls afire.

Institutions theoretically worthy of the greatest admiration because of their consistency with the principles set forth by well-known publicists, meet insurmountable obstacles. They may be the best ever known to political science yet, not like those fashioned by Solon for Athens, the ones best for a given nation. The science of legislation, studied little in our midst when we had no active part in governing our countries, could not flourish enough from the early days of independence for American legislators to use it reflectively, judiciously and properly, and to follow a better standard in developing the new constitutions than abstract principles and general rules.

These ideas are plausible but it would be worse than revolutionary frenzy itself for us to overestimate them. A timid, pusilanimous policy would dishonor American patriotism, and is surely inconsistent with the daring that put weapons in the hands of the patriots for the struggle against tyranny. Acknowledging the need to adjust governmental forms to localities, custom and national character should not make us think we are being denied life under free institutions, and guarantees that ensure liberty, the right of any human society worthy of the name.

In America, the state of unrest and uncertainty, which may have frightened the friends of humanity, is purely temporary. Despite the circumstances of our independence, it should be thought that time and experience would remedy mistakes, observation reveal the tendencies, custom and character of our peoples, and wisdom merge all these factors to shape therefrom the basis of our organization. Obstacles that seem insurmountable will gradually disappear; the governing principles, unaltered in substance, will necessarily be amended in their outer form so as to accommodate them to each nation's pecularities.

We shall have stable constitutions that safeguard freedom and independence, together with peace and order that will allow us to consolidate and grow. No matter how much the disparity between our own social conditions and some of the institutions prevailing in the free nations is exaggerated, can anything stranger be imagined than the United States itself, where freedom is the basis of the political system but where almost two million Negro slaves moan under the whip of their owners? Yet even so, that nation was formed and is flourishing.

In the meantime, there is nothing more natural than to withstand the cares that affect nations in their initial political effort. They will eventually be over and America will perform the role for which it is destined by its size, the variety of its natural resources and the many elements of prosperity it possesses.

During this period of transition, it is truly satisfying for the people of Chile to be living in a time of peace made possible by our institutions, the spirit of order that sets the national character apart, and the lessons of past calamities, which has spared us the scenes of horror that have afflicted other nations of the hemisphere. In Chile, the people's arms are the law; in the past, these weapons have been used only to maintain order and the most cherished social benefits. This consoling observation is all the more important as we fix our sights on the present circumstances and the nation's presidential elections.

The stormy unrest that usually accompanies these political crises has not occurred, hatred slumbers, passions do not dispute the terrain, circumspection and prudence accompany the exercise of the most important of political rights. To others, however, these same considerations are discouraging and perhaps despairing. They would have this event take place amidst popular tumult, be presided over by every sort of violence, and allow the most cherished guarantees and public order to be jeopardized. May these wishes never come true in Chile!

DEFAMATION

Nothing undermines liberty more than license, and nothing harms freedom of discussion and action so much as licentious attacks on individual reputations.

New to the enjoyment of the rights and guarantees of a popular government, we, not surprisingly, deviate in its application and exercise, and failing to distinguish between what the laws should allow and what they should prohibit, believe this restricts and interferes with their use when it merely does away with abuse. But then, what are all manner of laws but curbs on the most natural inclinations, the most unimpeachable rights in order to chart their course in a way that best suits the general good of society? Is perchance a person's good name a less cherished property than that of material goods? Or the blows against one's reputations those that cause less painful wounds? The legislator is compelled to safeguard against and repair these types of injury no less carefully than he does others. He would be neglecting his mission as badly by leaving good conduct and the respectability of his country's citizens open to the outrages of calumny, as if he left their life and goods at the mercy of thieves and assassins.

These are trivial truths which we would be embarrassed to dwell on if we were not aware how widely they are ignored and forgotten. Yet, since in this matter the example of free nations usually supports us better than deductions of abstracts principles, we shall mention a few here, taken from "Offences Affecting Reputation," included in the Penal Code of the State of Louisiana 1/ by Livingston. This code is considered the most liberal and philosophic one ever composed, and its author is a man held in the highest regard in the United States.

Defamation, if it imputes a crime, may be punishable by a fine of up to three thousand dollars and by imprisonment in close custody for one year. If the defamation is by libel, imprisonment in close custody always forms a part of the punishment.

Defamation may exist without necessarily imputing a crime. It is sufficient for an act or omission to be attributed to a person which, although not a crime, is of a nature to bring upon him the hatred of the public or lessen confidence in his integrity in social intercourse. Defamation is committed whenever the natural tendency of the words, signs or representations used is to bring upon the person to whom they refer the hatred, ridicule or contempt of the public.

It is not deemed an offense to express an opinion on the performance of officials in public office nor to examine their public conduct, criticize their writings or literary work in general. But the facts alleged must be true and if not proved truthful constitute defamation. Observations on the official acts of persons in public office and on the motives in performing them are permitted under the law even if the author should mistake the tendency or motive; but a false suggestion of such motives as would constitute a crime is defamation. If a person is imputed to be incompetent or dishonest in the performance of his station, profession, or trade, without proof of the allegations, this also constitutes defamation. All those who make, publish or circulate a libel are guilty of the offense of defamation, etc.

These are provisions that some may find excessively severe. But they leave all the freedom needed for discussion of public affairs, for reporting on the tendency of the acts under censure, for making the public aware of the incompetence or delinquency of public employees, for calling police attention to any frauds committed in the professions; in a word, for all useful purposes. How do disparagement and ridicule benefit society? And how can those who engage therein justify themselves in the eyes of their own conscience?

NOTE

1. Found in Livingston, Complete Works, II, New York, 1873, pp.100-111 (T).

COPYRIGHTS

The time has come for copyrights on original, revised or translated publications to receive the close attention of the government and legislature.

We have a law on this in Chile, our first undertaking in this difficult area. Its provisions are rather judicious and liberal; but in the present circumstances, they leave something to be desired. Delicate issues are raised by the rating of works published here and the rather broad privilege enjoyed by writers according to the originality and amount of effort involved in their works. We urge our colleagues' attention to this matter, which concerns them personally and is of no little concern to the development of our nascent literature. Our own thoughts on this will be dealt with in another article. For the moment, we will do no more than give an idea of the rules and regulations followed in other nations so we can examine what may be most applicable to Chile's present situation. Our information is drawn from a British review of the year 1841 and therefore, does not cover the legislative provisions passed at a later date in Europe and in the United States.

In England, following a long debate in which the country's foremost jurists aired contradictory opinions, the House of Lords declared in 1774 that the law did not recognize the perpetuity of a copyright. With the exception of two countries (Holland and Prussia) in which the principle of perpetuity was first allowed, then later abandoned. Protection for an author elsewhere in Europe rested on a patent or specific privilege. This system was later almost universally abolished.

The rules observed in England today are less advantageous to authors than those of virtually every other European nation. The privilege granted an author used to extend for 15 years counting from the time of publication and, if he was still living at the end of that period, was stretched out for another 15 years. Under the 1841 statute, ownership is absolute for 28 years. An author living beyond that time is given a renewed copyright that lasts for the remainder of his life.

In the United States, an author is protected for 28 years, at the end of which the privilege is renewed either in his own name, if he is still living, or in the name of his widow or descendant heirs. In Holland and Belgium, the author holds the copyright as long as he lives, The privilege passes to his heirs for the first 20 years after his death.

In Prussia, the former law recognized absolute ownership by an author as long as he lived and allowed it to be conveyed to his heirs by will. In the absence of an express bequest, the right to reprint the work passed to the public domain with the stipulation that any of the author's descendants would have a certain share of the profits from its sale. The current law (which dates from 1837) protects an author during his lifetime and extends protection to his heirs for 30 years after his death.

In the different states of Saxony and the rest of Protestant Germany, the privilege remains in effect as long as the author is living and for some time thereafter. The state of Saxony-Cobourg-Gotha follows the norm set by Prussia in its entirety. In others, the right of the heirs is for a term of twenty, ten, and six years. Furthermore, the general law of the Germanic Confederation recognizes absolute ownership by the author or his representative, in all territories subject to the league, for ten years after the time of publication.

Russia and Austria pose a great contrast. In Austria, the author's copyright lasts until his death, but his heirs have no rights other than that granted them under the law of the Germanic Confederation. In Russia, the author's family holds the copyright for twenty five years after his death. What is more, if the work is reprinted during the final five years of this period, the copyright remains in effect for another ten years. In practice, then, the family's copyright lasts for thirty five years.

In France, when the old cooperations and privileges were abolished in 1793, literary ownership was left unprotected. The resulting injustices and harm were so severe that the legislature issued a decree sanctioning ownership by the author of any scientific or artistic work, as long as he lived, and by his family, if any, for ten additional years.

Napoleon presided over a long debate in the Senate in 1810, which ended with ratification of the law of 1793, with some amendments, all beneficial to the rights of authorship. This law, still in force, provides that an author's widow or descendants, if any, enjoy ownership for twenty years. In their absence, his other heirs enjoy ownership for ten years; regulatory procedures provide for a subdivision of proceeds during these two periods in many instances. As often occurs with regulations, many more controversial cases have arisen than expected.

The result is that in England and every country where literary and scientific works are published, except the United States, an author has absolute ownership as long as he lives; that when American law differs from English law in this respect, it probably does so to the author's benefit. Both are undoubtedly much less beneficial to the latter than the law in any other highly civilized country, except Austria, that once powerful empire which has yet to contribute a single first-rate author to German literature.

The Napoleonic Code is much more favorable to authors than British law. Even so, repeated efforts have been made in the past twenty years to amend the code so as to improve the status of authors. The vote in the Chamber of Deputies to extend the privilege up to fifty years was lost in the upper house by only a small majority at a time when M. Guizot, one of the sponsors of the bill (also supported by M. Lamartine), was not a member of the government.

In the United States many publications rather skillfully demanded the law be amended to benefit either American or British authors, who in the past have derived no profit from the circulation of their works in the United States. Congress is expected to approve some action shortly, at least to expand the protection granted native American literature.

This was the status of affairs in 1841. Later, Austria changed its law. In an 1846 law, an extract of which appeared in El Mercurio, in Valparaíso, on August 26 of last year, ownership of any literary production or work of art was granted to its author or artist and their assignees. Equal ownership rights were given the translator of an original work unless there is a statement by the author in the introduction or on the title page that he must be included in the translation rights. In any event, a translation appearing within a year without the consent of the original author is regarded as an infringement.

Anyone reproducing a political address after its text has been issued to a publisher by its author is liable to charges of forgery. Performance of a new theatrical play or musical composition without the author's consent is liable to the same penalty. An author's copyright endures as long as he lives plus thirty years, and up to fifty years after his death for works published by a government-recognized scientific or artistic body. The privilege covering performance of a play or musical composition remains in effect only ten years after the death of the author.

Forgers are penalized with loss of all copies and of all implements used in printing the work, plus a fine or, in the event of insolvency, a number of days in prison proportional to the fine imposed. Authors in all states of the Germanic Confederation have the same protection under the law. The principle of reciprocity exists to cover works published in other nations.

II

Let us now see what principles copyrights should be based on here. First of all, we believe the privilege should not be identical for every kind of literary work. Common sense dictates that a mere translator is not entitled to the same compensation as a person who, although still translating someone else's ideas, must take them from a variety of sources, using many other authors as references, in order to turn them into a coherent and methodical body of doctrine. The authors of basic works, an effort which it is very important to stimulate here, usually fall into this category. There is, apparently, no need to undertake these works in Chile for we can reprint or translate foreign publications. But, for one thing, there are almost no teaching materials in which what has been adapted for a European school would not have to be changed and added to for use in our localities, institutions and circumstances.

The best example we can give of this is the material on Canon Law which the Bishop—elect of Ancud is publishing. Suppose it were a matter of a course in world history. There may be very sound reasons why an otherwise excellent work from abroad would not be acceptable everywhere. Its literal translation might be a great disservice to young scholars, whereas the careful deletion of dangerous or unsuitable ideas would make a good book available to students of history, better than any other one known for the particular purpose in hand.

Furthermore, the space each author of a world history text devotes to any one section, depends on the country where he is writing. A French historian dwells at greater length on France and skips over the events, people, and institutions of other nations. Spain and America would be given a secondary place by such an author. An American adapting the text must expand the scale of the original author in this area and lengthen the minute space devoted to matters of greatest interest to us. If a fundamental work on botany is involved, the plants indigenous to Europe will have to be replaced by those accessible to students in Chile. Nor is that all. A teacher who adapts a foreign work to make room for his own views, thus giving it a stamp of individuality, will do a better job teaching with that book. Everyone has his own peculiar view of things and communicates the thoughts he himself has fashioned and digested more easily because he explains them clearly, energetically, and convincingly. Anyone with experience in teaching knows how true this is.

Working with the ideas of someone else can be done in several ways and with varying degrees of intensity, which involves a greater or lesser degree of competence and learning. It would be desirable, though manifestly impossible for royalties, to be scaled in a like manner. This would mean legislators would have to devise a detailed classification of works. But even assuming they did it well, implementation would be extremely difficult.

We do believe, however, that some distinctions must in all fairness be made and suggest a division into three classes: mere translations, those in which a foreign work is adapted with a few significant changes, and those in which the doctrine of many books is reworked into a single one which has outstandingly original and useful qualities of form, method, and application to local conditions. The dividing line between these authors and authors of original works is somewhat difficult to trace, yet is occasionally obvious. A poem, a piece of oratory, a new system, the history of a country or epoch not dealt with earlier would be no cause for hesitation. In questionable cases, the panel of judges might well tip the balance towards the most favorable, liberal opinion.

The law of January 10, 1843, excellent in many ways, could have been better, in our opinion, if it had a rating system that recognizes the four [sic] classes of original authors, that is, authors of works that compile and rewrite materials scattered in a number of works; adapters of works by others who make changes to accommodate them to conditions in Chile, and mere translators. Article 9 of the law makes them all equal.

But who is to do the job of rating and of setting the royalties to which the authors are entitled? We believe this should be done by experts, and that it might be given to a commission from the respective university school with the qualification that two instructors in the particular area should sit on the commission judging textbooks.

The third issue we would like to air in the press is the duration of the copyright on the sale of a book. The provision of the 1834 law which gives the author copyright for life, curtailed to five years for his heirs and with the government empowered to extend it to as many as ten, seems to us to be ill-considered. In this way, an author in his sixties who turned out an original work, perhaps embodying the studies and observations made over a long lifetime, would be entitled to a copyright for himself and his heirs that would seldom exceed twenty years.

An author who published a mere translation when he was 20 or 30 years old, would enjoy a copyright for himself and his heirs that could last for half a century or longer. Is this not inequitable, outrageously inequitable? There is a very simple, obvious way to avoid this. Combine the privilege of heirs with that of the author. For example, an original writer might be given a copyright for sixty years; a mere translator, thirty, and the heirs would be entitled to benefit from it for the number of years the person they represent did not. Sixty and thirty might be the top and bottom figures on the scale. The panel of judges, following the four categories we indicated earlier, would have the authority to set the intermediate figures.

Depending on the extent to which a literary work is more than a simple translation and approaches a genuinely original work, the number of years of the copyright would be brought closer to the maximum. Finally, authors refusing to subject literary productions to the judgment of the panel would still retain exclusive rights for a 30-year interval.

Article 15 of the 1834 law, which punishes infringement of literary copyrights, seems not explicit enough. It stipulates that all infringements on someone else's property shall be punished. What kind of property? Real property, probably. In other words, punishment for lawbreakers who trespass on literary property would be the same as the legislation now in force imposes for theft. But this is still too vague. In our opinion, the law should make provision for the payment of indemnity to the injured party and for public vindication. Rules and regulations should be passed for the assessment of damages.

The subject we have dealt with in these two articles deserves examination and reflection with a view to providing a needed stimulus for literary works here in Chile, by proposing how best to bring this about and set simple, easily implemented standards. We encourage our colleagues to make their views known.

BIBLIOGRAPHIC SOURCES ON
ANDRÉS BELLO AND
EDITIONS OF HIS COMPLETE WORKS

A. BIBLIOGRAPHIC SOURCES

A bibliography of Andrés Bello by Agustín Millares Carlo, the foremost Hispanic bibliographer of our time, was published in Madrid in 1978. Entitled Bibliografía de Andrés Bello, the 239-page volume was put out by the Spanish University Foundation. This was the third edition of a monograph that first appeared in the journal Historia de América, nos. 67-69, January-December 1969 (Mexico, D.F., 1976), and a subsequent 130-page reprint dated 1976. A second enlarged edition was published by the Editorial Universitaria de Maracaibo, followed by the considerable expanded 1978 edition of the Spanish University Foundation. The book is divided into two parts:

a) A bibliography of Bello's writings

b) A bibliography of the life and work of Bello and other related aspects.

Section b) covers materials published prior to the date of completion of Millares Carlo's monograph and may be consulted directly. Our purpose is to review the evolution and development of bibliographic studies on Bello's writings.

Bibliographic research on Bello's work began in 1881, the one hundreth anniversary of his birth. His prize Chilean students, the Amunátegui brothers, conducted the initial work on Bello's writings, as a necessary prelude to an edition of his complete works. Miguel Luis Amunátegui Aldunate, particularly, together with his brother, Gregorio Víctor, relied on their study of the writings published during Bello's lifetime in drafting the authoritative prologues to several volumes of the Chilean edition and in writing a life of Bello (Vida de don Andrés Bello, 1882), which is still the best documented and most complete biography available.

Luis Montt's study, "Notas bibliográficas sobre las obras de don Andrés Bello," came out in the same year in the Revista de Chile (Santiago, September 1881), II, pp. 217-223.

Bibliographic research on Bello also began in 1881 in Caracas, with Arístides Rojas' "Orígenes de la literatura venezolana. Bibliografía de Andrés Bello," published in La Opinión Nacional, November 28, 1881, and in Colombia with a study of Miguel Antonio Caro, "Apuntes bibliográficos relativos a don Andrés Bello," in the Repertorio Colombiano. A la memoria de Andrés Bello en su centenario, Bogotá, 1881, pp. 90-125.

In 1893, the Conde de la Viñaza (Cipriano Muñoz y Manzano), published his monumental Biblioteca histórica de la filología española, which mentions Bello's studies of the Spanish language several times, some rather extensively.

The first organic bibliographic study was done by Emilio Vaïse, "Bibliografía de D. Andrés Bello y de sus descendientes (1781-1916)," in the Revista de Bibliografía Chilena y Extranjera, Santiago, nos. 8 and 9, August-September 1917. This was augmented by Guillermo Feliú Cruz in Estudios sobre Andrés Bello, Santiago, 1966, pp. 255-277.

In 1928, the Revista Chilena, Santiago, XII, January-February 1928, carried a bibliography on international law and diplomatic history to the time of Andrés Bello's death, entitled "Bibliografía chilena sobre derecho internacional e historia diplomática hasta la muerte de don Andrés Bello."

Only bibliographies dealing specifically with Bello are covered herein, to the exclusion of general studies which may make mention of his work, unless a significant part of them is devoted to Bello or represents a contribution by a particular entity.

Eugenio Orrego y Vicuña inserted un "Anexo bibliográfico de Bello" (pp. 275-284) in his study entitled Andrés Bello, which originally appeared in Anales de la Universidad de Chile, Santiago, XCIII, 1935, later printed in a bound volume in several editions. In 1940, two major contributions on Bello's work in philology appeared: Rodolfo Oroz, "Bibliografía filológica chilena (analítico-crítica)," in the Boletín de la Academia Chilena correspondiente a la Academia Española, Santiago, VII (cuad. 25 y 26), 1940, pp. 61-168, and Guillermo Rojas Carrasco, Filología chilena. Guía bibliográfica y crítica, Santiago, 1940, 328 pp.

In 1943, my first bibliographic registry, "Contribución al estudio de la bibliografía caraqueña de Andrés Bello," was published in the Boletín de la Academia Venezolana correspondiente de la Real Española, Caracas, no. 40, July-September 1943, later edited in a 53-page opuscule. In 1947, I inserted a monograph, "Bibliografía de estudios sobre Andrés Bello," in Cultura Universitaria, no. 4, Caracas, November-December 1947, pp. 209-230. In 1952, a "Catálogo de la exposición bibliográfica de Andrés Bello," was published in the Primer libro de la semana de Bello en Caracas, 1952, pp. 329-352.

In the Venezuelan edition of the Obras completas de Bello, each of his writings (books, pamphlets, articles, poems), has a bibliography which has been prepared by me since the first volume came out in 1951. These notes as a whole constitute a bibliographic analysis of Bello's works, with extensive coverage of studies on his writings.

In 1954, Rafael Torres Quintero published the "Bibliografía de Rufino J. Cuervo," in vol. II of Cuervo's Works, Bogota, 1954, pp. 1741-1817, which refers extensively to the editions of Bello's Gramática and the comments made thereon by the Colombian philologist. In 1956, Martín Perea Romero put out the first issue (February) of a multigraphed Catálogo analítico de la hemeroteca de la Biblioteca Nacional, with a bibliography of works on Andrés Bello.

In 1965, several bibliographic monographs appeared in observance of the one-hundredth anniversary of Bello's death. In Chile, Manuel Cifuentes prepared a catalogue of a Bello exhibit displaying bibliographic and iconographic materials and personal objects, held in the National Library, which was published in Mapocho, no. 667, pp. 355-377.

Alamiro de Avila Martel published a 44-page Colección de manuscritos. I. Papeles de don Andrés Bello, listing the papers of Bello that figure in the manuscript holdings of the Central Library of the University of Chile. The study was printed in the series "Catálogos de la Biblioteca Central de la Universidad de Chile."

In Colombia, the Instituto Caro y Cuervo published a work entitled Exposición bibliográfica. Homenaje a don Andrés Bello en el centenario de su muerte, Bogota, 1965, 35 pp. In Argentina, Horacio Jorge Becco published his "Contribución a la bibliografía de Andrés Bello," in Cuadernos del Idioma, Buenos Aires, I, no. 3, 1965, pp. 149-166. In Caracas, the National Centennial Commission edited a 27-page catalogue of the exhibit held in the Bolívar Museum, Caracas, entitled Sala Andrés Bello. Relación de objetos, manuscritos y ediciones. A "Bibliografía de Andrés Bello," was published by me in the Revista Nacional de Cultura, Caracas, no. 172, 1965, pp. 152-159; reproduced in Mapocho, Santiago, vol. 12, no. 3, 1965, pp. 332-354, under the title "Bibliografía sumaria de Andrés Bello."

In 1968, Martín Pérez Romero edited a multigraphed bibliography entitled Andrés Bello, 108 pp. In 1969, Angel Raúl Villasana began publishing his monumental Ensayo de un repertorio bibliográfico venezolano (1808-1950), in several volumes. A bibliography of Bello's work is found in vol. I, pp. 314-333.

In 1978, Horacio Jorge Becco published his excellent Fuentes para el estudio de la literatura venezolana, prologued by Pedro Grases, Ediciones Centauro, 2 vols., containing abundant updated data on Andrés Bello. In the same year, the House of Bello published my 61-page Libros de Bello editados en Caracas en el siglo XIX.

It is evident from this listing of bibliographic repertories on the works of Andrés Bello, or on his life and publications, that this work now constitutes a tradition in American cultural life.

B. EDITIONS OF COMPLETE WORKS OF ANDRES BELLO

The need to compile and publish all the writings of Andrés Bello was regarded in Chile as a tribute due to the memory of the humanist who published the greater part of his work during the years he lived there. The Council of the University of Chile adopted a resolution to this effect on the day following the death of the man who had been the President of the University from the moment it was reorganized in 1843. In this connection, posterity is indebted to Diego Barros Arana, Miguel Luis and Gregorio Víctor Amunátegui Aldunate, and to the latter's son, Miguel Luis Amunátegui Reyes.

In 1881, the year of the one-hundredth anniversary of the birth of Bello, the first two volumes were published. By 1893, the remaining volumes, totalling fifteen in all, were printed, as follows:

I. Filosofía del entendimiento. Introducción de Juan Escobar Palma. 1881, xvii, 514 pp.

II. Poema del Cid. Introducción de Baldomero Pizarro. 1881, xxvi, 588 pp.

III. Poesías. Introducción de Miguel Luis Amunátegui Aldunate. 1883, lxxxiv, 570 pp.

IV. Gramática de la lengua castellana. Introducción de Francisco Vargas Fontecilla. 1883, xli, 494 pp.

V. Opúsculos gramaticales. Introducción de Miguel Luis Amunátegui Aldunate. 1884, lxvii, 507 pp.

VI. Opúsculos literarios y críticos. I. Introducción de Miguel Luis Amunátegui Aldunate. 1883, cxlii, 480 pp.

VII. Opúsculos literarios y críticos. II. Introducción de Miguel Luis Amunátegui Aldunate. 1884, cvii, 476 pp.

VIII. Opúsculos literarios y críticos. III. Introducción de Miguel Luis Amunátegui Aldunate. 1885, cviii, 482 pp.

IX. Opúsculos jurídicos. Introducción de Miguel Luis Amunátegui Aldunate. 1885, cxxiii, 508 pp.

X. Derecho internacional. Introducción de Miguel Luis Amunátegui Aldunate. 1886, xxxvi, 527 pp.

XI. Proyectos de Código Civil. Introducción de Miguel Luis Amunátegui Aldunate. 1887, xiii, 622 pp.

XII. Proyecto de Código Civil (1853). Introducción de Miguel Luis Amunátegui Reyes. 1888, xviii, 640 pp.

XIII. Proyecto inédito de Código Civil. Introducción de Miguel Luis Amunátegui Reyes. 1890, xliii, 630 pp.

XIV. Opúsculos científicos. Introducción de Miguel Luis Amunátegui Reyes. 1893, xlviii, 455 pp.

XV. Miscelánea. Introducción de Miguel Luis Amunátegui Reyes. 1893, xlviii, 455 pp.

By 1881, the Colombian humanist Miguel Antonio Caro, a great connoisseur and admirer of Bello's work, was endeavoring to have all his works edited in the Collection of Castilian Writers, published in Madrid by Mariano Catalina. Caro was seconded in this undertaking by Marcelino Menéndez Pelayo and Rufino José Cuervo. Seven volumes appeared, as follows:

Poesías. Precedidas de un estudio biográfico y crítico, escrito por don Miguel Antonio Caro. Madrid, Editorial Hernando. Impr. de D. A. Pérez Dubrull, 1882, lx, 330 pp., 2 retratos grabados por Bartolomé Maura.

Principios de derecho internacional. Nueva edición ilustrada con notas por don Carlos Martínez Silva. Madrid, Impr. de A. Pérez Dubrull, 1883, 2 vols. I: xxxiii, 357 pp. (Estado de paz); II: 392 pp. (Estado de guerra).

Opúsculos gramaticales. Con una introducción de Marco Fidel Suárez. Madrid, Imprenta y Fundación de M. Tello, 1890-1891, 2 vols. I: 385 pp. (Ortología, Arte métrica. Apéndices); II: 400 pp. (Análisis ideológica, Compendio de gramática castellana, Opúsculos gramaticales).

Gramática de la lengua castellana. Madrid, Editorial Hernando (Tipogr. Sucesores de Rivadeneyra y Revista de Archivos), 1903-1905, 2 vols.

Under the auspices of the University of Chile, a new edition of the Obras completas of Bello was undertaken in 1930, a simple re-edition of the first Santiago collection of 1881-1893. The only change made was in the numbering of the volumes, nine of which were published by the Editorial Nascimento, as follows:

   I. Poesías. 1930. 692 pp. Texto, pp. 1-626. Estudio de Miguel Luis Amunátegui Aldunate, pp. 627-692.

  II. Gramática de la lengua castellana. 1931. 492 pp.

 III. Proyecto de Código Civil. Vol. I. 1932. 608 pp. Introducción por Miguel Luis Amunátegui Aldunate, pp. 7-15.

  IV. Proyecto de Código Civil. Vol. II. 1932. 632 pp. Prólogo de Miguel Luis Amunátegui Reyes, pp. 7-18.

   V. Proyecto de Código Civil. Vol. III (Last of the Civil Code Project). 1932. 630 pp.

  VI. Derecho internacional. 1932. 581 pp. Introducción de Miguel Luis Amunátegui Aldunate, pp. 7-34.

 VII. Opúsculos jurídicos. 1932. 548 pp. Introducción de Miguel Luis Amunátegui Aldunate, pp. 7-106.

VIII. Opúsculos gramaticales. 1933. 516 pp. Introducción de Miguel Luis Amunátegui Aldunate, pp. 7-66.

  IX. Opúsculos literarios. Vol. I. 1935. 540 pp. Introducción de Miguel Luis Amunátegui Aldunate, pp. 7-122.

THE VENEZUELAN EDITION

The Venezuelan edition of the Obras completas of Andrés Bello had been a longstanding project of Venezuela's intellectuals and a common national goal. In 1943, the Patronato Pro Estudios Andrés Bello, established through private initiative in the Instituto Pedagógico in Caracas, announced the publication of all of Bello's writings as an ultimate objective. The idea became a matter of official concern by means of a resolution of the National Assembly, adopted by acclamation at the proposal of its president, Dr. Andrés Eloy Blanco, at a session held on October 27, 1947. On February 27, 1948, Rómulo Gallegos, President of Venezuela, issued a decree ordering a revised edition of Bello's Obras completas, and the creation of a Special Commission to oversee its preparation and publication.

An Editorial Commission was accordingly appointed, composed of Julio Planchart, as its director; Augusto Mijares, Rafael Caldera, and Pedro Grases, secretary. In late 1948, Julio Planchart, who regarded direction of this undertaking as the final and most cherished labor of his life, died. His death, deeply mourned by his colleagues, represented the loss of a man who had approached the problems involved in an all-important edition with a wealth of insight and sound judgment. Rafael Caldera then became director of the Commission, and Enrique Planchart (who died in 1953), replaced him as a Commission member.

When the task of preparing the Obras completas of Andrés Bello began, it was impossible to foresee all the issues that would have to be faced in order to resolve the complex problems that arose as we became more involved in the work. Our initial plan, developed on the basis of what was originally known, soon had to be amended. As we delved deeper into Bello's life and writings, it became evident that considerable changes would have to be made in the earlier editions. The Chilean collection, despite its well-deserved merit which we were the first to acclaim, required careful, attentive treatment. Seventy years had transpired since its publication. The knowledge of Bello acquired since then could not, nor should it have been ignored, and the texts themselves had to be approached using the technical standards developed since the time of that edition.

This meant we had to settle a prior issue of the utmost importance: Whether simply to re-edit the texts from the Chilean collection, better organized, purged of what was repetitious and augmented by what had not been included previously, or whether, given the importance of Bello's work as a part of American bibliography, to undertake a thorough investigation in order to resolve insofar as possible all the problems involved in a new edition.

It was our understanding that the task entrusted to us by the government of Venezuela committed us to the larger of the two efforts. We then set out to exhaust all avenues of investigation so as to publish, as far as humanly possible, a work worthy of the lofty national purposes represented therein. Thus, from the beginning, the Editorial Commission became a research center with a network of collaborators in Venezuela, Chile, England, Colombia, Peru, Ecuador, Spain, the United States, France, Argentina, Mexico, Italy, Canada, Cuba, Brazil, and elsewhere.

The following volumes have been published or are in process of preparation:

I. Poesías. Introducción general y "Advertencia editorial" de la Comisión Editora. Prólogo de Fernando Paz Castillo, "Introducción a la poesía de Bello." Caracas, 1952, cxxxix, 757 pp.

II. Borradores de poesía. Prólogo por Pedro P. Barnola, "La poesía de Bello en sus borradores," y "Advertencia editorial," por la Comisión Editora. Caracas, 1962, cviii, 639 pp.

III. Filosofía. Filosofía del entendimiento y otros escritos filosóficos. Prólogo de Juan David García Bacca, "Introducción general a las obras filosóficas de Andrés Bello." Caracas, 1951, lxxxi, 710 pp.

IV. Gramática. Gramática de la lengua castellana destinada al uso de los americanos. Prólogo de Amado Alonso, "Introducción a los estudios gramaticales de Andrés Bello," y "Ediciones principales de la Gramática de Andrés Bello," por la Comisión Editora. Caracas, 1951, xciii, 545 pp.

V. Estudios gramaticales. Prólogo por Angel Rosenblat, "Las ideas ortográficas de Bello." Caracas, 1951, lxxxvii, 459 pp.

VI. Estudios filológicos I. Principios de la ortología y métrica de la lengua castellana y otros escritos. Prólogo de Samuel Gili Gaya, "Introducción a los estudios ortológicos y métricos de Bello" y "Advertencia editorial" de la Comisión Editora. Caracas, 1955, cxii, 601 pp.

VII. Estudios filológicos II. Poema del Cid y otros escritos. Prólogo de Pedro Grases (In press).

VIII. Gramática latina y escritos complementarios. Prólogo y notas de Aurelio Espinosa Pólit, S.J., "Bello latinista." Caracas, 1958, ic, 656 pp.

IX. Temas de crítica literaria. Prólogo de Arturo Uslar Pietri, "Los temas del pensamiento crítico de Bello" y "Advertencia editorial" de la Comisión Editora. Caracas, 1956, lv, 784 pp.

X. Derecho internacional I. Principios de derecho internacional y escritos complementarios. Prólogo de Eduardo Plaza A. Caracas, 1954, lxvi, 689 pp.

XI. Derecho internacional. II. Temas de política internacional. "Advertencia editorial" de la Comisión Editora. Caracas, 1959, xiii, 666 pp.

XII-XIII. Código Civil de la República de Chile. Texto concorda-
do con los distintos proyectos de Bello. "Introducción
y notas de Pedro Lira Urquieta" y "Advertencia editorial" de la Comisión Editora. Caracas, 1954, I, lxx,
619 pp.; II, 1148 pp.

XIV. Derecho romano. "Introducción" por Hessel E. Yntema.
"Advertencia editorial" de la Comisión Editora. Caracas, 1959, Lxv, 510 pp.

XV. Temas jurídicos y sociales. Prólogo de Rafael Caldera. (In press).

XVI. Textos y mensajes de gobierno. Prólogo de Guillermo
Feliú Cruz, "Andrés Bello y la administración pública
de Chile" y "Advertencia editorial" de la Comisión
Editora. Caracas, 1964, xciv, 699 pp.

XVII. Labor en el Senado de Chile (Discursos y escritos).
Recopilación, prólogo y notas de Ricardo Donoso y "Advertencia editorial" de la Comisión Editora. Caracas,
1958, cxxx, 989 pp.

XVIII. Temas de educación. (In press)

XIX. Temas de historia y geografía. Prólogo de Mariano Picón Salas, "Bello y la Historia" y "Advertencia editorial" de la Comisión Editora. Caracas, 1957, lxiv, 572
pp.

XX. Cosmografía y otros escritos de divulgación científi-
ca. Prólogo y notas de F. J. Duarte. Caracas, 1957,
lii, 737 pp.

XXI-XXII. Derecho internacional (III y IV). Documentos de la
cancillería chilena. Prólogo de Jorge Gamboa Correa,
"Andrés Bello en la Cancillería de Chile." Caracas,
1969, I, cccxi, 264 pp.; II, 534 pp.

XXIII-XXIV. Epistolario (In preparation).